BRITISH ECONOMIC AND SOCIAL POLICY

LLOYD GEORGE TO MARGARET THATCHER

BRITISH ECONOMIC AND SOCIAL POLICY

LLOYD GEORGE TO MARGARET THATCHER

G C PEDEN

University of Bristol

Philip Allan

First published 1985 by

PHILIP ALLAN PUBLISHERS LIMITED
MARKET PLACE
DEDDINGTON
OXFORD OX5 4SE

British Library Cataloguing in Publication Data
Peden, G.C.
British economic and social policy: Lloyd
George to Margaret Thatcher.
1. Great Britain – Economic policy – 1918–1945
2. Great Britain – Economic policy – 1945–
I. Title
330.941′082 HC256

ISBN 0-86003-801-7
ISBN 0-86003-901-3 Pbk

Typeset by MHL Typesetting Ltd, Coventry
Printed and bound in Great Britain by The Camelot Press, Southampton

Contents

List of Figures and Tables

Acknowledgements

I am grateful to John Beath, Susan Howson, Russell Jones, Rodney Lowe, Andrew McDonald, Roger Middleton, Roy Parker, Neil Rollings, Pat Thane and Tom Wilson for the trouble they have taken to read parts of the text and to comment upon them; to the Controller HM Stationery Office, for permission to reproduce copyright material held in the Public Record Office, London; and to Rosemary Graham and Anne Griffiths for the cheerfulness and skill with which they produced the typescript from my handwriting.

Preface

Studies of economic policy and social policy tend to be carried out in isolation from each other, reflecting the disciplinary boundaries of Economics on the one hand, and of Sociology and Social Administration on the other. This book's main claim to originality is that it is an attempt to provide an economic history of the interaction between economic and social policies in the twentieth century. The balance of the book has been determined in part by the fact that other authors have already surveyed the evolution of the 'welfare state' down to the 1940s, and there seemed no point in duplicating the work of Fraser (1984) or Thane (1982).[1] What seemed to be required was a book which placed the development of social policy in the context of economic and financial policy, and which then discussed how the 'welfare state' (including the commitment to 'full employment') had fared since the 1940s. The focus is on the policies of central government, and if little is said about local authorities or private charity, this is not because these subjects are unimportant but because each would require a book of comparable length.

Social scientists are generally expected to have an explanatory model or theory. What is offered here is really a view of human

1. References are given in parentheses in the text, using the author–date system. Full bibliographical details of the works cited are given at the end of each chapter. Parliamentary papers are cited by their Command Paper number, and are listed as documents before each alphabetical list of authors.

nature. People normally feel concerned when they are brought face-to-face with other people's poverty, but concern rarely takes the form of a voluntary reduction in personal consumption on a scale which would make possible a transfer of purchasing power, or the provision of services, to the poor on a scale which would result in greater equality of living standards. Charity is usually financed out of spare cash. Moreover, while people are often in favour of public expenditure being used for particular purposes, for example to raise social security, to improve health services, or to subsidise a particular industry, the same people are usually much less in favour of paying taxes to meet the cost of a general rise in public expenditure. Naturally one hopes that other people will bear the burden of increased taxation or that other forms of expenditure will be cut so as to accommodate one's favoured proposal within the existing level of public expenditure. Alternatively, one may try to achieve sufficient economic growth to enable the community to enjoy the fruits of increased public expenditure while maintaining, or increasing, existing levels of personal consumption. Alas, that 'best of all possible worlds' has not always been achieved and, even when it has, the sum total of proposals for public expenditure has always been greater than what the community could be expected to finance. Economics is the study of the distribution of scarce resources, and while there have often been some unemployed resources to be brought into play, eventually, both in economic and social policy, choices have had to be made.

References

Fraser, D. (1984) *The Evolution of the British Welfare State,* Macmillan.
Thane, P. (1982) *The Foundations of the Welfare State*, Longman.

G C Peden
University of Bristol

Abbreviations

BPP	British Parliamentary Papers
CSO	Central Statistical Office
EEC	European Common Market
GATT	General Agreement on Tariffs and Trade
GDP	Gross domestic product
IMF	International Monetary Fund
LRC	Labour Representation Committee
MLR	Minimum lending rate
MTFS	Medium-term financial strategy
NEDC	National Economic Development Council
NHS	National Health Service
OECD	Organisation for Economic Cooperation and Development
OPEC	Organisation of Petroleum Exporting Countries
PAC	Public Assistance Committee
PESC	Public Expenditure Survey Committee
TUC	Trades Union Congress
UAB	Unemployment Assistance Board

1

The Victorian Legacy

In January 1901, when the new century was just 22 days old, Queen Victoria died; later that year Lord Salisbury, the last prime minister to sit in the House of Lords, resigned. These two events marked the passing of an era. Yet the student of economic and social policy is struck by the extent to which some ideas and institutions of the Victorian age persisted into the twentieth century. That there should be continuity is not surprising. Almost all the leading figures in politics and in economic and social thought in the first half of the twentieth century had been born during Victoria's reign, and most of them, consciously or not, carried considerable intellectual baggage from the nineteenth century into the twentieth.

On the other hand, these ideas were subject to strong modifying influences. Some of the influences came as a result of long-term trends in the economy and society – for example, the reduction in the birth-rate down to 1941 and greater longevity changed the age structure of the population so that the ratio of aged dependants to working population increased, with the result that Victorian ideals of 'self-help' or family support became harder to sustain. Other modifying influences came from the experience of state controls over the economy and society in two world wars, or from the experience of heavy unemployment between the wars. By mid-century new ideas about 'Keynesian' economics and the role of a 'welfare state' had acquired the status of orthodoxy once accorded to Victorian economic and social ideas. Yet the searing experience of high inflation in the 1970s challenged the new orthodoxies in turn, and by 1979 the Prime Minister, Margaret Thatcher, could speak of Victorian virtues with approbation. This continuity and change suggests that an understanding of economic and social policy in the twentieth century requires some knowledge of the relevant values, attitudes and beliefs inherited from the nineteenth century.

Economic and Social Ideas

The central article of faith in orthodox Victorian political economy was a belief in market forces as the best method of allocating goods and services, and as the best means of matching labour and jobs. The idea that individuals, who were pursuing their own interests, would be guided by competition to act in the economic interests of society, 'as though by an invisible hand', had first been given authoritative expression by Adam Smith in his book *The Wealth of Nations* (1776). Smith had taken governments as he found them in the eighteenth century – venal, and inclined to grant economic privileges, such as tariff protection or trading monopolies, for the benefit of particular interests rather than for the benefit of the community as a whole. He wrote at a time when industry was made up of many small businesses and when the economist's ideal of a market in which there was perfect competition did not seem, at first sight, to be too remote from reality. In fact Smith believed that men of the same trade rarely met, even on social occasions, without hatching some scheme to fix prices or otherwise defraud the public. There was, and is, a conflict of interests between producers (whether masters or men) and consumers, and he saw the market mechanism as the most impartial means of resolving that conflict. Competition could be stimulated by free trade between nations, for then domestic prices could not be fixed above the price of imports. Smith's economic philosophy was developed by the great nineteenth-century economists – Malthus, Ricardo and Marshall – and was also popularised, and simplified, by lesser writers. The general tendency, especially of the latter, was to play down the exceptions which Smith had made to the free market (such as his support for protection for British shipping, on the grounds that merchant seamen and ships would be needed in war). Again there was a tendency to apply market economics to social relationships in a way which Smith had not done. (Indeed, Smith had favoured the use of public funds to support education and the arts as a means of offsetting the harmful effects on human personality of tedious, repetitive jobs in industry.)

The other seminal eighteenth-century influence on nineteenth-century thought was the work of Jeremy Bentham. Bentham was no more impressed than Smith had been by the character of people in power, and, in working out his ideas on the proper agenda for government, he assumed that state intervention was to be regarded as a necessary evil which would be acceptable only when there was no other way to secure the greatest happiness of the greatest number of people. Such a philosophy could lead to acceptance of more state intervention, as social problems, such as disposal of sewage or prevention of disease, were exacerbated by urbanisation. However, the dominant Victorian opinion was that central government action was a last resort and that self-help by individuals or local communities was to be preferred. The principle that the state should adopt a *laissez-faire* attitude to most economic and social problems remained central to Victorian political thought. As John Stuart Mill wrote in his *Principles of Political Economy* (1848), 'letting alone should be the general practice, every departure from it unless required by some great good is a certain evil'.

The belief that sturdy independence improved a man's character was given its best-known expression by Samuel Smiles, whose book *Self-Help* (1859) sold 55,000 copies in four years. Smiles had raised himself from humble origins by abstinence and hard work, and he saw no reason why others should not do likewise. For men of this mould, charity to the able-bodied poor was destructive to the recipient's character. This attitude was given a pseudo-scientific twist by some writers who borrowed ideas from Charles Darwin's work on evolution. In his *On the Origin of Species*, which also appeared in 1859, Darwin portrayed the natural world as one of ceaseless struggle which ensured, by natural selection, the survival of the fittest. It was possible, by analogy, to draw the conclusion that efforts to protect the weak at the expense of the strong would retard the natural evolution of society. Social Darwinism is now most commonly associated with Herbert Spencer, whose *Man Versus the State* (1884) certainly made use of biological analogies and accepted that suffering was a necessary aspect of progress. Spencer also equated collectivism with socialism, and socialism with 'slavery', in the sense that society became the owner of the individual.

Social and economic ideas were closely intertwined in the Victorian mind, and these ideas were passed on to the twentieth century as a philosophy which pervaded all respected studies of man in society.

One man acting as a bridge between the centuries was G.M. Trevelyan, who was born in 1876 and who was Regius Professor of Modern History at Cambridge from 1927 to 1940. His book *British History in the Nineteenth Century and After* first appeared in 1922 and was still being printed as a paperback in the 1960s. In it, Trevelyan gave a classic defence of the Poor Law Amendment Act of 1834. Before that date magistrates in England and Wales had had the power to supplement inadequate wages out of local rates – a form of relief which Trevelyan described as destructive of self-respect and self-help, virtues which could be restored to what he called the 'cringing poor' only by the 'intellectually honest' if 'harsh' reform of 1834 (Trevelyan 1965, pp. 248–9). The Act of 1834 set up workhouses in England and Wales, to be administered by locally-elected guardians, who would be supervised by a central authority (from 1871 the Local Government Board). All applicants for poor relief had to be prepared to enter the workhouse, where a rigorous regime and hard labour (if they were able-bodied) would ensure that the poor would prefer to find work or family support outside. This was the principle of 'less eligibility'. In practice poor relief was still often given to people outside the workhouse, if only because the building itself might be too small to contain all the paupers in the area. Moreover, conditions in the workhouse itself tended to improve in line with social conditions generally, although its reputation and social disgrace remained (Crowther 1981; Rose 1972).

Victorian attitudes to the able-bodied poor were based on a belief that any man who wanted a job could find one if he looked hard enough and was prepared to accept a cut in wages. Despite the experience of booms and slumps throughout the nineteenth century, economists, following Ricardo, argued that the economy would always tend towards full employment. The community's income from production (wages and profits) would always be spent on consumption or invested. There might be an over-supply of a particular product, because of miscalculation or because of a change in taste, but there would be no general glut of goods, so that, by implication, there could be no general unemployment. The price mechanism (including flexible wages for labour) would always direct capital and labour to where there was demand. It was only as a result of prolonged, high unemployment in the interwar period that John Maynard Keynes was to grasp that the market mechanism might not lead to full employment; that all savings might not be invested, so that the community's income from production might not create effective demand for further production. Keynes was also to take account of the changed behaviour of wage earners by the later 1920s, when it became apparent that labour had become more unionised and better able to resist wage cuts than in the nineteenth century. His conclusion was that only state investment in public works could ensure that all savings would be invested and that there would be no general lack of demand for labour at existing wage levels (Stewart 1972, chs. 2–5).

Victorian faith in the market economy was based on moral philosophy as well as on general abstract assumptions and on the particular conditions of the Victorian labour market. For example, Alfred Marshall, whose *Principles of Economics* (1890) provided much of the foundations for the teaching of the subject in the early twentieth century, claimed that decentralised free enterprise encouraged rational forethought, initiative, industry and thrift, besides producing an optimum allocation of resources. On the other hand, socialism, in his view, would not be conducive to 'firmness of character'.

An Age of *Laissez-Faire*?

There has been a good deal of controversy among economic and social historians as to whether the nineteenth century was, or included, an age of *laissez-faire* (Taylor 1972). *Laissez-faire* is an example of how historians try to explain attitudes and policies by bringing them together under some general concept. An appropriate concept can show that apparently unrelated events or statements can share common origins and themes. In the case of *laissez-faire* the concept brings together various strands of opinion hostile to state intervention and draws attention to their common features. The concept thus links the ideas of Smith, Bentham, Mill, Spencer and Marshall with the attitudes of politicians, taxpayers and ratepayers and the actual course of policy. It is possible, by listing a long series of nineteenth-century Acts of Parliament dealing with child or female labour in factories, or public health in congested or ill-planned cities, or elementary education for children whose parents could not afford to pay for it, to suggest either that the Victorian period was not an age of *laissez-faire*, or that it had ceased to be so well before the end of the century. Certainly from about 1870 one finds economists such as William Jevons and Marshall more and more inclined to stress the limits to *laissez-faire* and to stress the social benefits of state regulation on matters such as public health or housing, or state provision of education (Hutchison 1978, ch. 4). However, the fact that politicians and economists were recognising a widening range of exceptions to the principle of *laissez-faire* is not proof that the principle was not important. Although the list of social and economic legislation by the end of the century was a long one, the market economy was not seriously compromised. In particular, factory legislation was designed to prevent the exploitation of women and children, who were not expected to be fully capable of self-help, and was not intended by Parliament to interfere with agreements freely arrived at by employers and adult male workers.

Arguments about the importance of *laissez-faire* attitudes by the end of the nineteenth century should also take account of the importance of what was not done by the state. Free trade remained central to Victorian political economy, and although calls for protection became insistent from some quarters of industry from the Edwardian age onwards, there was no general tariff until 1932. The goal of economic policy was, in fact, for government to have a neutral effect on the economy. There were to be no American-style politics, whereby legislators and businessmen traded in tariffs and other political favours. Public expenditure rose but remained at about 9 per cent of gross national product between 1870 and 1890, with social services accounting for only 1.9 per cent in the latter year (Taylor 1972, p. 62). Fiscal policy continued to be based on the assumption that central government expenditure should normally be paid for out of revenue and that taxation should be levied purely for revenue and not for redistribution.

The state had an ultimate responsibility to maintain a sound currency, but the means by which the currency was regulated was the gold standard, managed by the Bank of England, which had the status of a private company. The governor of the Bank would consult with the Treasury from time to time, as was inevitable considering that the government was the main customer of the Bank. Nevertheless, down to 1914, decisions on Bank Rate, which was the basis of the structure of interest rates in the country, were taken by the governor on technical, not political, grounds. The Bank's primary duty was to maintain the value of sterling against gold, and therefore against all other currencies whose value was also fixed in terms of gold. It was possible to keep the monetary system out of politics because the gold standard worked fairly painlessly for Britain before 1914. Demand for British exports, including financial and shipping services, was generally buoyant, and Britain had a balance of payments surplus every year. In these circumstances, no large-scale adjustments of prices and wages were required. Matters were to be different in the 1920s, however (Tomlinson 1981, ch. 2).

In general it may be said that the goals of pre-1914 fiscal and monetary policy were to provide a stable environment in which capitalism could flourish. At the same time competition and efficiency were encouraged by allowing foreign goods to enter the country free of protective tariffs. Where there were natural monopolies, such as the railways, the state would regulate private enterprise by determining rates and standards of service, but such regulation was exceptional.

The State and Labour

Industrial relations were another area in which, compared with the post-1914 period, Victorian and Edwardian governments were comparatively inactive. For most of the nineteenth century, strikes were localised affairs, affecting only one firm or a small number of firms at a time. However, as the scale of firms grew, and as trade unions and employers' organisations began to embrace more and more firms, the consequences of strikes or lockouts for the rest of the community grew more serious. Concern about the inability of free collective bargaining to ensure stable industrial relations unaided led to the Conciliation Act of 1896. Under this, the Board of Trade was empowered to 'inquire' into the causes and circumstances of any industrial stoppage, and to appoint a conciliator or arbitrator at the request of the parties to the dispute. Although the arbitration procedure was purely voluntary, the Board of Trade's Labour Department did have some success in moderating industrial unrest. Significantly, the Board of Trade's *laissez-faire* principles were sufficiently strong for it to resist proposals for compulsory arbitration, on the grounds that such arbitration would distort the labour market and thereby the cost structure of British industry, rendering it vulnerable to foreign competition (Davidson 1979).

Whatever the merits of the market economy from the point of view of economic efficiency, governments could not ignore the social problems arising from unemployment caused by the trade cycle. The pre-1914 statistics for unemployment are highly imperfect, being based on figures collected by trade unions of unemployment among their members. Only a minority of the working population belonged to a trade union, and many members of the working classes depended upon casual, day-to-day employment, a feature of the labour market which led to widespread under-employment rather than general unemployment. Adjusted figures by Feinstein (1972, T125) suggest that the percentage of the working population unemployed varied from as low as 0.9 in 1872, 2.3 in 1882 and 2.1 in 1889–90, to as high as 10.7 in 1879, 10.2 in 1886 and 7.5 in 1893. After the mid-1870s booms were rarely sustained, but then neither were depressions, so that, while the word 'unemployment' entered the English language in the 1880s, the belief that the economy had a natural tendency to full employment remained unshaken. Even so, there was a problem of what to do about the unemployed while the economy was righting itself. The 'less eligibility' of the Poor Law was designed to force workers into the labour market, but what if private enterprise did not absorb all the labour on offer? To have recourse to the Poor Law involved social stigma, and perhaps exposure to petty tyranny, and many members of the working classes preferred to maintain their respectability by drawing upon savings or by borrowing from pawnbrokers.

The Local Government Board wished to encourage this attitude, believing, perceptively enough, that if ever the working classes became accustomed to poor relief, it was probable that they would resort to it on the slightest occasion. Consequently, in 1886, when unemployment was high, the President of the Local Government Board, Joseph Chamberlain, took action to keep 'respectable' workers away from the workhouses. He issued a circular to boards of guardians, recommending them to encourage local authorities to start public works, such as paving streets, or extending sewage works, to provide temporary, unskilled work, at wages which would encourage men to return to their normal occupations as soon as possible (Fraser 1984, pp. 274–6). Local authorities would be able to raise loans, as they did for other purposes, once schemes had been approved by the Local Government Board. While the Chamberlain circular can be seen as a measure to offset the social effects of the trade cycle, there was no conscious Keynesian theory of counter-cyclical demand management behind it. Rather, unemployment was seen by government as a social problem, with the main purpose of policy being to keep 'respectable' members of the working classes free of the 'contagion' of the attitudes of habitual paupers. Indeed, it was laid down that men engaged on public works were not to be regarded as paupers. In the event, although the Chamberlain Circular was issued five times between 1886 and 1893, the policy was almost completely unsuccessful; many local authorities retained permanent staffs to carry out construction work and were unwilling to take on extra hands, especially since the Local Government Board was slow to approve loans, while the better class of unemployed workmen tended to shun work which attracted large numbers of chronically under-employed casual workers (Harris 1972, chs. 1–3; Tomlinson 1981, ch. 1).

Nevertheless, it is clear that a policy of keeping 'respectable' workers away from the Poor Law was a conscious attempt to maintain these workers' attitudes toward public relief. This brings one to the concept of 'social control'. Marxist historians have long puzzled over the persistence of capitalism and the slow development of the Labour movement in Britain. For some social historians, the answer lies in the nature of the British working class as it emerged from nineteenth-century industrialisation; in particular, attention is drawn to the division between skilled artisans and unskilled workers, and to the willingness of trade unions to operate within the capitalist system, seeking higher wages for their members rather than socialism for the working class as a whole (Hobsbawm 1964). For other social historians, the key to the success of the British ruling class in maintaining its position has been a series of policies and tactics which, although apparently unconnected, are best understood if seen as different forms of social control. Examples which have been given include education, the media and even organised sport, all of which have been means by which the ruling class could consciously impose values, attitudes and beliefs which would maintain the class structure of an industrial society. Indeed, the term 'social control' has been employed so variously that there is some doubt whether the concept has been sufficiently closely defined to be useful (Thompson 1981). Taken to its logical extreme, the concept might be applied to all social policy, in so far as social policy has made the working class contented with their lot while capitalism has remained untouched, or even strengthened (Davidson 1985, pp. 11–22; Higgins 1980).

While the concept of social control alerts one to the fact that welfare services are not solely for the benefit of the recipients, it should not be allowed to obscure the fact that many welfare services are desired by the recipients. It is true that prior to 1914, organised working-class opinion seems to have been sceptical about state social welfare, especially policies which might undermine self-help institutions, such as trade unions and friendly societies, by deflecting working-class earnings into state schemes. On the other hand, there is no reason to suppose that poor people were anything but grateful for any amelioration of their hard lives – for example, old people welcomed state pensions in 1908 (Thane 1984). Moreover, politicians seem to have assumed that welfare policies would be popular with the working classes, and what politicians believed was what mattered from the point of view of formulation of policy. The extension of the franchise to some members of the working classes in 1867 and 1884, and the emergence of a stronger trade-union movement in the 1880s and 1890s, opened up the possibility of a radicalisation of British politics. In 1900 trade-union leaders and socialist groups came together to set up the Labour Representation Committee, the precursor of the Labour Party, and although only two of its candidates were successful in the general election of that year, Lloyd George felt concerned enough to warn fellow Liberals in 1904:

> We have a great Labour Party sprung up. Unless we can prove, as I think we can, that there is no necessity for a separate party to press forward the legitimate claims of labour, you will find the same thing will happen in England as has happened in Belgium and Germany – that the Liberal Party will be practically wiped out, and that, in its place, you will get a more extreme and revolutionary party, which will sail under the colours of socialism or Independent Labour. (Wrigley 1976, p. 26)

The Labour Party did not adopt an explicitly socialist constitution until 1918, but even before 1914 the threat from the left was a spur to Liberals to carry out social reforms.

Concern in government circles about working-class welfare need not, however, have anything to do with socialism. When the Boer War broke out in 1899, thousands of young Britons volunteered to fight in South Africa, but a disturbingly high proportion had to be rejected by the army because of poor health or physique. Concern about the dietary and other health-related needs of the working classes thus came to be shared by some members of the War Office no less than by socialists, although for rather different reasons. Subsequently the Report of the Interdepartmental Committee on

Physical Deterioration in 1904 recommended that school meals and medical inspection should be provided in state schools. This was followed in 1906 by the Education (Provision of Meals) Act, which permitted local authorities to provide necessitous children with subsidised meals, without their parents being considered to be paupers; and by the Education (Administrative Provisions) Act of 1907, which required school children to be medically inspected. It would be wrong, however, to ascribe these Acts solely to the influence of the Boer War. The Act of 1906 was based on a bill introduced by a Labour backbencher, and public opinion had been prepared by recent social surveys which had shown that poverty was more widespread than hitherto realised.

The concept of the 'poverty line' first appeared in Charles Booth's massive *The Life and Labour of the People of London* (1889–1903), and was further refined in Seebohm Rowntree's survey of York, *Poverty: A Study of Town Life* (1901). Booth defined poverty as 'having no surplus', that is, having enough to live off most of the time but being unable to meet contingencies such as sickness or interruption of earnings. Rowntree drew his poverty line at an income just sufficient to buy what was absolutely necessary for the maintenance of physical efficiency – which meant, for example, a diet which was less varied than that received by paupers in a workhouse. Excluding rent, Rowntree allowed only 17s. 6d. for a family of two adults and three children, or £28.87 at 1983 prices. The reason for choosing so stark a poverty line was that there should be no doubt that what was being measured was indeed poverty. A household survey showed that 10 per cent of the population of York lived below the poverty line, a condition which Rowntree called 'primary poverty'. Another 18 per cent had incomes which raised them above Rowntree's poverty line, but these people did not spend their money in ways most consistent with health, and consequently lived in 'obvious want and squalor', a condition which Rowntree called 'secondary poverty'. Rowntree's total of 28 per cent of people in primary or secondary poverty was close to Booth's more impressionistic estimate of 30 per cent as the proportion of Londoners in poverty. One inheritance from the nineteenth century was thus a perceived need to tackle poverty, perhaps through encouragement of abstinence (expenditure on alcohol was a major factor in secondary poverty) but also by tackling the problem of low and irregular wages. Rowntree estimated that 75 per cent of poverty in York in

1899 (the year of his survey) was the result of either low wages or incomes which were insufficient because of the number of children in a family.

Concern about the fitness of recruits, or the population at large, was an aspect of a general concern about what was called 'national efficiency'. National efficiency could be concerned with Britain's ability to compete in international trade as well as on the battlefield. Already in the 1880s there was concern in the Board of Trade about Germany's superiority in technical industries, and it was not necessary to believe in social justice to believe that the British working man should be provided with an education equal to that of his German counterpart. The Royal Commission on Technical Instruction reported in 1884 that 'our industrial empire is vigorously attacked all over the world. We find that our most formidable assailants are the best educated peoples' (Lawson and Silver 1973, p. 346). It was following reports such as this that Parliament passed the Technical Instruction Acts, which in 1889 empowered local authorities to support technical instruction out of rates and which in 1890 set aside some surplus government funds for the purpose. Although national efficiency had become a term much used in political debate by the Edwardian period, and clearly played a part in the passage of legislation on school meals and medical inspection (Searle 1971), one should not exaggerate the importance of concern about national efficiency. *Laissez-faire* attitudes inhibited governments from providing finance or from undermining self-help. Following the Education (Provision of Meals) Act, only a minority of local authorities chose to provide free meals, and as late as 1939–40 the evacuation of children from inner-city areas was to reveal shockingly poor standards of health and physique.

Twentieth-Century Challenges

It was inevitable that new economic and social challenges should alter the scope of politics, even if there had been no organised labour movement to demand change. Britain's economic position was changing. The industrial supremacy which it had achieved as the world's first industrial nation was already being challenged by new industrial nations, notably Germany and the United States (Hobsbawm 1969, ch. 9). Indeed, British economic policy in the twentieth century was to be at least as much concerned with Britain's decline relative to other powers, and the need to maintain international competitiveness, as with unemployment. The problem for government was that the most important decisions regarding the adoption of new techniques, which would raise the productivity of labour and capital, were taken by managers and trade unionists, not by politicians or civil servants. Those responsible for policy had to face the question of whether progress in industry, and international competitiveness, could be better promoted by assisting industry with tariffs and, later, subsidies, or by exposing it to the invigorating influence of international competition. Ultimately the wealth of the community could be increased only through greater productivity of labour and capital, and economic stagnation would mean that there would be no increased surplus with which to finance social or other policies.

Paradoxically, economic progress increased the demand for social services. Poverty had been defined by Rowntree in 1899 as a weekly income equivalent to £28.87 at 1983 prices, for a family of two adults and three children, after payment of rent. When in the 1930s Rowntree came to repeat his earlier study of poverty in York, he revised his poverty line to allow for a better diet and for expenditure on some non-essentials, such as newspapers and a wireless. The last item was, of course, something which no-one could have bought in 1899. In Rowntree's *Poverty and Progress* (1941) the poverty line for 1936 was equivalent to an income of £42.75 at 1983 prices, again for a family of two adults and three children after payment of rent. By 1973 long-term supplementary benefit, on the same basis, was equivalent to £72.0 at 1983 prices. Yet this income represented only 49.4 per cent of average male manual earnings in 1973, whereas Rowntree's poverty lines in 1899 and 1936 had represented respectively 61 per cent and 67 per cent. It is important in studying policy over the twentieth century to remember that living standards were constantly rising and that as general living standards rose, people expected more of state benefits than mere subsistence.

There were to be other challenges to policy makers. For example, high Edwardian birth-rates contributed to the problem of unemployment in the interwar period, as young people flocked on to the labour market (an experience repeated in the 1980s after the 'baby boom' of the 1960s). The decline in the birth-rate down to 1941 helped to reduce poverty by reducing the size of families to be supported from low wages, but greater longevity increased the number of elderly dependants. In 1901 34 per cent of the population was under 14 years of age; by 1951 this proportion had dropped to 24 per cent. On the other hand, in 1901 only 4 per cent of the population was aged 65 years and over, whereas by 1951 the proportion was 9 per cent and in 1981 it was 15 per cent.

However, policy makers were anxious not to undermine self-help or voluntary organisations. These had proliferated in the Victorian period in the form of friendly societies, philanthropic organisations and charitable trusts. William Beveridge, often seen as the father of the welfare state, wrote a book, *Voluntary Action* (1948), which stressed the importance of voluntary service in the welfare state, and few today would disagree with him that state services alone are never likely to be able to cope with the complexity of the human condition. The problem of how the state can provide support in social and economic affairs without undermining individuals' initiative or sense of responsibility has, perhaps, been the greatest challenge of the twentieth century.

References

Crowther, M.A. (1981) *The Workhouse System 1834–1929*, Batsford.

Davidson, R. (1979) 'Social conflict and social administration: The Conciliation Act in British industrial relations', in T.C. Smout (ed.), *The Search for Wealth and Stability*, Macmillan.

Davidson, R. (1985) *Whitehall and the Labour Problem in Late-Victorian and Edwardian Britain: A Study in Official Statistics and Social Control*, Croom Helm.

Feinstein, C. (1972) *National Income, Expenditure and Output of the United Kingdom*, Cambridge University Press.

Fraser, D. (1984) *The Evolution of the British Welfare State*, Macmillan.

Harris, J. (1972) *Unemployment and Politics: A Study in English Social Policy 1886–1914*, Oxford University Press.

Higgins, J. (1980) 'Social control theories of social policy', *Journal of Social Policy*, vol. 9, pp. 1–23.

Hobsbawm, E.J. (1964) 'Trends in the British Labour Movement since 1850', in his, *Labouring Men. Studies in the History of Labour*, Weidenfeld and Nicolson.

Hobsbawm, E.J. (1969) *Industry and Empire*, Penguin Books.

Hutchison, T.W. (1978) *On Revolutions and Progress in Economic Knowledge*, Cambridge University Press.

Lawson, J., and Silver, H. (1973) *A Social History of Education in England*, Methuen.

Rose, M. (1972) *The Relief of Poverty 1834–1914*, Macmillan.
Searle, G.R. (1971) *The Quest for National Efficiency*, Basil Blackwell.
Stewart, M. (1972) *Keynes and After*, Penguin Books.
Taylor, A.J. (1972) *Laissez-Faire and State Intervention in Nineteenth-Century Britain*, Macmillan.
Thane, P. (1984) 'The working class and state "welfare" in Britain, 1880–1914', *Historical Journal*, vol. 27, pp. 877–900.
Thompson, F.M.L. (1981) 'Social control in Victorian Britain', *Economic History Review*, 2nd series, vol. 34, pp. 189–208.
Tomlinson, J. (1981) *Problems of British Economic Policy 1870–1945*, Methuen.
Trevelyan, G.M. (1965) *British History in the Nineteenth Century and After*, Pelican.
Wrigley, C. (1976) *David Lloyd George and the British Labour Movement*, Harvester Press.

2

The Liberal Reforms and the People's Budget

The period when the Liberal Party was in power from 1905 to 1915 saw a remarkable series of social reforms which, without their authors' fully intending it, laid the foundations of the modern British welfare state. The Education Acts of 1906 and 1907, permitting local authorities to provide subsidised school meals and requiring them to provide medical inspection for schoolchildren, have already been mentioned, and from 1914 Exchequer grants of half the cost of school meals were made available. These measures to help the young were supplemented in 1908 by a Children's Act which dealt with the problems of parental neglect and of juvenile offenders and which, by codifying earlier legislation, established clearly both children's rights and community responsibilities. Also in 1908 long-debated state old age pensions were granted on a non-contributory, means-tested basis. These measures to help the young and old were followed in 1909 by measures to help wage earners. Trade boards were established to regulate wages in low-paid industries, and a national system of labour exchanges was set up. The year 1909 also saw a step towards more active state participation in the economy with the creation of a Development Fund (derived from general taxation) to promote rural employment and fisheries, and a Road Fund (derived from new taxes on road users) to pay for new roads.

The most important element in Liberal policy towards wage earners was the National Insurance Act of 1911. This provided for state-supervised contributory insurance schemes against ill-health for wage earners, and against unemployment for some trades subject to fluctuations in the trade cycle. The 1911 Act set a pattern for the future welfare state by setting up insurance funds to which employees, employers and taxpayers contributed. Unlike the post-1945 welfare state, however, the Liberal national insurance schemes were not universal in their application. Nevertheless, Lloyd George, the politician most closely associated with the 1911 Act, intended it to be the beginning of a campaign against poverty, and sought to secure new sources of taxation so that social policy could be extended.

Trade Unions and the Rise of Labour

Although the Liberal governments of Sir Henry Campbell-Bannerman (1905–08) and Herbert Asquith (1908–15) are best remembered for social reform, it was not the issue of social reform which brought the Liberals to power. Campbell-Bannerman became Prime Minister in 1905 because the Conservative Prime Minister, Arthur Balfour, could no longer keep his party, which had a parliamentary majority, united on the issue of free trade or protection. The subsequent election of 1906 was fought largely on that issue, with the Liberals standing unequivocally for free trade, while the majority of Conservative candidates advocated protection or, as they called it, 'tariff reform' (Cain 1979). The issue of 'Rome on the rates' also spurred on the Nonconformists in the Liberal Party, for Balfour had pushed through an Education Act in 1902 providing for local authority funds to be made available to denominational schools (most of which were Anglican or Roman Catholic). Nonconformists wished to be freed from having to subsidise what they considered to be sectarian education.

It would be an exaggeration to say that social policy issues played no part in the 1906 election. About two-thirds of Liberal candidates were pledged to social reforms other than traditional Nonconformist concern with temperance. The proposed reforms included old age pensions, poor law reform and public works to combat unemployment (Russell 1974, pp. 65–6, 71–3). On the other hand, the party as a whole offered no definite programme of social reform, and both Campbell-Bannerman and his Chancellor of the

Exchequer, Asquith, were more concerned to balance the budget than to spend money on social policy.

A fourth great issue in the election, although not one so sharply dividing the Liberals and Conservatives, was trade-union reform. The Conservative Government had fallen foul of the trade unions over the Taff Vale judgment. This decision by the law courts, arising from a minor railway strike in South Wales in 1900, had had the effect of allowing employers to sue trade unions for damage caused by union officials. As recently as 1891 a Royal Commission on Trade Disputes had assumed that trade unions, as unincorporated associations, were immune from civil actions, but now trade-union leaders had good reason to suppose that their funds might be in danger. The Conservative Government did nothing about the Taff Vale judgment, except appoint a Royal Commission on Trade Disputes and Trade Combinations in 1903 without any trade-union representatives. The trade unions boycotted the Commission and contributed handsomely to the funds of the Labour Representation Committee (LRC), whose income in the election year of 1905/6 was £12,000, compared with £243 in the previous election year, 1900/1. As a result, the LRC was able to field more candidates, 29 of whom were elected in 1906, compared with two in 1900. This electoral success was largely due to a pact with the Liberals whereby 24 of the LRC candidates were to have a straight run against the Conservatives.

The political pressures to do something about the Taff Vale judgment were greater than the LRC's strength in Parliament would suggest. Despite the restricted franchise, most MPs could not afford to alienate working-class voters. There was, however, some debate among trade-union leaders as to what should be done. Some saw the Taff Vale judgment as a helpful development in that the risks to funds of unauthorised action could be used to impose discipline on members. In the end, however, most union leaders preferred legislation which would safeguard their funds. The Royal Commission set up by the Conservatives concluded that Parliament in its earlier trade-union legislation could not have intended unions to bear no responsibility for the actions of their agents, and most members of the Liberal Government were willing to grant no more than partial immunity to union funds. Nevertheless, when the LRC introduced a bill, drafted by the TUC Parliamentary Committee, providing for complete immunity against civil actions, Campbell-Bannerman accepted it. The Conservative Leader in the House of Lords, Lord

Lansdowne, expected the Bill to embitter industrial relations, and said privately that he regarded it as 'conferring excessive privileges upon one class and on one class only' (a curious complaint from a peer). Nevertheless, he felt it useless for political reasons to oppose the Bill, which duly became the Trades Disputes Act in 1906 (Macdonald 1960, ch. 5). Trade unions had achieved a privileged position, a development which was to provide an effective countervailing power to future increases in the power of the state over the economy. Meanwhile employers' associations had been developing in parallel with trade unions, with much less fuss in the courts or Parliament – indeed, the Permanent Secretary of the Board of Trade publicly recommended in 1900 that employers should combine to provide an effective countervailing power to trade unions (Davidson 1974, pp. 5f).

Social Reform or Social Control?

It would be possible to argue, given the Liberal leadership's limited enthusiasm for social reform before 1908 and given developments in the Labour movement, that the Liberal reforms after 1908 can best be understood through the concept of social control. In this view, the Liberals, the party of economic *laissez-faire*, adopted social reform as a means of pre-empting the Labour Party's claim to working-class votes (while at the same time showing trade-union leaders that all they required in labour legislation could be achieved through co-operation with the Liberals). There is evidence to support this view, but one must take care that the insights provided by using the concept of social control do not lead one to suppose that one has arrived at a complete explanation of events. Edwardian politics were shaped by the division between free trade and protection as well as by the division between capital and labour. The immediate electoral challenge to both Liberals and Labour came from the Conservatives. There was a recession from late 1907, with unemployment more than doubling from 3.7 per cent in that year to 7.8 per cent in 1908 and 7.7 per cent in 1909 (Feinstein 1972, Table 57), giving Conservative tariff reformers the opportunity to claim that tariffs would protect jobs. The Liberals had a bad run of by-election results in 1907 and 1908, but there were Conservative as well as Labour victories, so that the Liberals had the delicate task of winning the working-class vote without losing their traditional middle-class support to the Conservatives. The concept of social control, by implying a dualistic relationship between ruling class and working class, can over-simplify the actual workings of the political system. Moreover, as the best historian of the period pointed out long ago, those responsible for social policy were as much concerned with the survival of the British Empire in a competitive international environment as they were with the rise of Labour (Halévy 1961). At the very least one must bear 'national efficiency' in mind, as well as social control, if one believes that the Liberal reforms were a means to security for a ruling class.

There is also the possibility, which the more cynical social control theorist might overlook, that the Liberal reforms, or some aspects of them, were at least in part a response to changes in public opinion. Old age pensions are a case in point. Down to the 1890s the balance of organised working-class opinion, as represented by trade unions and friendly societies, had been against state pensions on the grounds that they would undermine the labour movement and reduce the functions of the friendly societies. But by the turn of the century the balance of opinion had changed, with almost all sections of the labour movement, and some friendly societies, being in favour of state pensions, and the debate had shifted to whether they should be contributory or non-contributory (Thane 1978). A Treasury Committee had been set up to examine the cost of different schemes as early as 1896, and in April 1907 the Liberal Cabinet had decided upon the creation of a fund for the provision of non-contributory pensions – a fact which has been taken to imply that by-election defeats later that year played no serious part in Liberal calculations (Hay 1975, p. 46). On the other hand, an important change was made to the Liberal Bill during its passage through Parliament, and it seems likely that this change was a result of Liberal by-election defeats. Lloyd George, as Chancellor of the Exchequer, was responsible for the passage of the Bill, and he spoke of the need to do something that appealed to the people, to 'help stop this electoral rot'. Lloyd George had been associated with old age pensions since 1899, when he had been a member of a Commons Select Committee which had recommended non-contributory pensions paid for out of taxation. Asquith, his predecessor as chancellor, had indeed promised to introduce non-contributory pensions in 1906, but the scheme prepared under his direction was far from generous: 5s a week for people over 70 with, as an economy measure, only 7s 6d for married couples. It was Lloyd George, in 1908, who deferred to backbench opposition to this clause, and removed the discrimination against married couples (Fraser 1984, p. 153). On the other hand, Treasury officials had won one victory for economy; by insisting on a limit of £7 million a year to be spent on pensions they had forced a raising of the pensionable age from 65 to 70 before the scheme was put before Parliament (Thane 1978).

Even limited old age pensions had a strong electoral appeal. Most working-class incomes were too low to allow for adequate provision for old age through private pensions or savings. As a result, care for the old was a heavy burden on working-class family incomes, with acceptance by the old of pauper status being the only alternative. Five shillings a week was an inadequate pension in many areas of Britain (Rowntree had estimated in 1899 that a married couple needed 6s a week for food alone), but many old people had sources of support other than their pension, and an income of £21 a year was allowed before deductions were made from the state pension. The fact that pensions were income-related meant that they had to be means-tested, and this raised a problem for Lloyd George, since the most obvious people to carry out the means testing were the Poor Law officials, yet one of the reasons pensions were popular was that they would remove the stigma which came with recourse to the Poor Law. Lloyd George got over this difficulty by using officials of the Customs and Excise to do the means testing, while the pensions were paid through the Post Office. The former expedient, in particular, emphasises the limited bureaucratic resources of central government at the beginning of the century.

The year 1908 also saw the beginning of an Act limiting underground work in coal mines to eight hours a day. This legislation seems to have been an unsuccessful attempt by the Liberals to hold their traditional support among the miners at a time when the Miners' Federation and its 14 'Lib–Lab' MPs were transferring their party affiliation from the Liberals to Labour. Indeed 1908, the year Asquith had succeeded Campbell-Bannerman, saw the Liberals' fortunes at a low ebb. The Conservative majority in the House of Lords had frustrated Liberal attempts to reform Balfour's Education Act (to the fury of Nonconformists), and other causes dear to Liberal hearts, such as temperance and Welsh disestablishment, also seemed likely to be similarly frustrated. As winter drew on, unemployment increased and with it discontent among the working classes. These combined circumstances provide the background to a remarkable letter to Asquith from his President of the Board of Trade, Winston Churchill (Churchill 1969, pp. 862–4).

Writing at the end of 1908, Churchill suggested a political strategy based on what he called, significantly, 'Social Organisation'. His references to Germany suggest a concern for 'national efficiency' as well as for party politics:

> Germany, with a far harder climate and far less accumulated wealth, has managed to establish tolerable basic conditions for her people. She is organised not only for war but for peace. We are organised for nothing except party politics . . . Oddly enough the very class of legislation which is required is just the kind the House of Lords will not dare to oppose. The expenditure of less than ten millions a year not upon relief, but upon [administrative] machinery, and thrift-stimuli, would make England a different country for the poor.

He also believed that such a policy would win 'solid support' for the Liberal Government. The measures he proposed were:

(1) Labour exchanges and unemployment insurance
(2) National health insurance
(3) 'Special expansive state industries', such as afforestation and roads
(4) A modernised Poor Law
(5) Amalgamation of, and state control over, private railway companies
(6) Education compulsory until seventeen

Nothing came of the last three on the list, but the first three, which Churchill described as 'a big slice of Bismarckianism', were central to Liberal social policy thereafter. The reference to 'Bismarckianism' was to the compulsory sickness and accident insurance and old age pensions introduced by the German Chancellor, Bismarck, in the 1880s. Bismarck, who drew his political support from big landowners and industrialists, had failed to curb the expansion of the German Social Democratic Party by persecution, and his welfare legislation had been an attempt to 'kill socialism with kindness'. The Social Democratic Party, in fact, continued to grow, but it is arguable that social insurance managed by the state had given workers reason to look to the state for help rather than to their own resources. As suggested above, it is also arguable that similar 'social control' motives were present in Liberal thinking.

Churchill was only one, and not the senior, of the Liberal ministers to press for national insurance. The main driving force was Lloyd George, who had proclaimed the virtues of contributory national insurance after a visit to Germany in 1908. For a chancellor of the Exchequer the attractions of a contributory scheme were considerable; non-contributory pensions had to be paid for by raising taxation, whereas the German scheme was paid for by compulsory contributions by employers and employees. (The latter, forced savings, were Churchill's 'thrift-stimuli'.) The importance of the German example for Lloyd George should not be exaggerated, however; his official advisers were largely ignorant of the workings of German national insurance, and Lloyd George used the German model mainly to make comparisons which, he claimed (not always accurately), showed that his scheme would be better (Hennock 1980). In any case, German national insurance covered only sickness and disability, whereas the British scheme Lloyd George was to introduce had an element of insurance against unemployment.

Although Lloyd George outlined his plans for national insurance in 1909, the scheme was too vast, and needed too much preparation (given the lack of official machinery to manage it), to be implemented at once. Meanwhile there was other social legislation which indicated the drift of Liberal thought away from *laissez-faire*. For some time the TUC had been canvassing the idea of legal minimum wages in industries. The Liberals' response was the Trade Boards Act of 1909. This measure, introduced by Churchill, set up boards, consisting of equal numbers of employers, workers and neutral members, with a neutral chairman, to fix minimum rates for timework, and which might fix rates for piecework, in certain trades. The law was confined to the so-called 'sweated trades' such as needlework, where employees, often women or immigrants, were scattered in small workshops and could not combine effectively in unions. Churchill's justification of this measure implied that the market economy might not always be conducive to national efficiency:

> It was formerly suggested that the workings of supply and demand would naturally regulate [he said] ... But where you have what we call sweated trades, you have no organisation, no parity of bargaining, the good employer is undercut by the worst ... Where these conditions prevail, you have not a condition of progress, but a condition of progressive degeneration. (Churchill 1967, pp. 298–9)

The other legislation introduced by Churchill in 1909 also implied that the workings of supply and demand, unaided by state action, did not lead to the most efficient use of labour. In 1905 the Conservative Government had appointed a Royal Commission to study the effectiveness of the Poor Law, and in the meantime there had been a number of local experiments with labour exchanges. Labour exchanges were already in existence abroad, notably in Germany, to provide information on vacancies and to register men seeking work, making the labour market more efficient. By 1909 the Royal Commission had reported that the British experiments had proved their worth. Churchill's Labour Exchanges Act set up a network of exchanges, under the control of the Board of Trade, throughout the country, and in doing so he had support from articulate groups of businessmen. Birmingham Chamber of Commerce, for example, had advocated such a system since 1905 (Hay 1977).

The People's Budget

Churchill's legislation in 1909 did not arouse much controversy. Lloyd George's Budget of that year, on the other hand, provoked such opposition that there was a constitutional crisis over the powers of the House of Lords. As Churchill had predicted at the end of 1908, the House of Lords dared not oppose reforms which might appeal to the working classes, but the Conservative majority in the Lords was prepared to stand and fight Lloyd George's proposals on how taxation should be raised to pay for the necessary government expenditure. *Central* government expenditure was necessary because the financial structure of the local authorities, which had administered most nineteenth-century welfare services, could not cope equitably with any major expansion in welfare expenditure. Already there were serious inequalities between inner city areas, with social deprivation and poor ratepayers on the one hand, and suburban areas with limited social needs but comparatively wealthy ratepayers on the other. There were central government grants for various purposes, and these could be used to mitigate differences between local authorities, but Treasury officials, with a shrewd understanding of human nature, reckoned that local authorities would spend central government funds more freely than their own ratepayers' money, so that most central government grants were conditional on some proportion of expenditure being met out of rates. Short of a major reconstruction of local government finance (something more likely to arouse more political opposition than popularity), new social policy expenditure had to be directed from Whitehall if there was to be effective Treasury control.

The rules of public finance inherited from the nineteenth century required the chancellor of the Exchequer to balance all normal current expenditure in his budget with revenue and, therefore, policy had to be kept within the limits of what could be raised from taxation. As it happened, the Liberals had committed themselves to greater financial rectitude than their Conservative predecessors. Asquith, in his 1906 Budget, had denounced the practice of passing special Defence Loans Acts, a practice which had been used since the 1880s to permit governments to borrow to pay for long-term projects even in peace. Asquith argued that this expenditure, unmatched by taxation, encouraged 'crude, precipitate and wasteful experiments' by defence departments, and he therefore stopped the practice as soon as he could. The Liberals felt able to renounce the use of Defence Loans Acts since part of the Liberal election programme was to reduce defence expenditure, which was still above pre-Boer War levels. In fact, although naval expenditure was reduced in 1906/7 and 1907/8 and army expenditure in 1906/7, 1907/8 and 1908/9, further reductions were impossible since a European arms race had developed, a particular feature of which was the naval rivalry between Germany and Britain. Consequently, Lloyd George was faced with mounting demands from the Admiralty and War Office (and the Conservatives and certain sections of the press) for increased defence expenditure just at the time he was contemplating increased social expenditure.

In framing his Budget for 1909/10, Lloyd George had to reckon on an additional £4 million for the armed services and an additional £6 million for old age pensions. The latter had proved more expensive than estimated in 1908 since, although steps had been taken to reduce the number of applicants by excluding 'lunatics, paupers, criminals, loafers and wastrels', far more old people applied for pensions than expected. This was particularly so in Ireland, where in many districts there was no documentary proof of age. The 1911 census was to show a remarkable 84 per cent increase over the 1901 figure for the population claiming to be aged between 70 and 80 years. While expenditure was expected to increase in 1909/10, revenue on the existing basis of taxation was expected to fall by £3 million on account of depressed trade. Clearly something would have to be done to increase the revenue, and as early as June 1908 Lloyd George shocked Parliament with the warning:

> I have no nest eggs. I have got to rob somebody's hen roost next year. I am on the look-out which will be the easiest to get and where I shall be least punished, and where I shall get the most eggs, and not only that, but where they can be most easily spared . . .
> (Murray 1980, p. 86)

British politics were to be dominated for over two years by the question, 'from whom were Lloyd George's eggs to come?'

For most Conservatives, the answer to the revenue problem was an end to free trade. In their view, tariffs would not only help British industry (and therefore the revenue) by reducing imports of foreign manufactures, but would also provide revenue in themselves, making increases in direct taxation on incomes unnecessary. 'Tariff reform' had an obvious appeal to those who might otherwise be called upon to pay extra income tax, which then fell exclusively on the middle and upper classes, and there was much talk of the need to 'broaden the basis of taxation'. Tariffs would mean that all who consumed imported food and goods would contribute to the Exchequer, although not in proportion to their income. Lloyd George in his 1909 Budget Speech agreed that 'all classes of the community in this financial emergency should be called upon to contribute' but, looking at the existing balance between direct and indirect taxation, he concluded that workers were paying more in proportion to their incomes than those who were better off. He therefore proposed to alter the balance, chiefly by raising income tax from 1s to 1s 2d in the pound, and by levying a new tax, called supertax, of 6d in the pound, to be paid additional to income tax by all those with an income of over £5,000 a year. What really roused the fury of the landed classes (and therefore the Conservatives and the House of Lords), however, were Lloyd George's proposals for the valuation of land, with a view to future taxation on profits from increases in land values. Such taxation would be necessary, he claimed, to meet what he called the 'growing demands of the social programme', and he described his Budget as a 'war budget' for waging 'implacable warfare against poverty and squalidness'. His friends hailed it as 'the People's Budget'; his enemies saw it as being a war budget against property and denounced it as socialistic (Mallet

1913, pp. 303–7). There were those in both Houses of Parliament who feared that democracy would simply become a means of soaking the rich to buy the votes of the poor, and in consequence Lloyd George was attacked bitterly by Conservatives.

In fact, scholarly research (Murray 1980) has shown that the People's Budget was a carefully worked out strategy of meeting the growing cost of social reform (and defence expenditure) in ways which would enable the Liberal Party to retain most of its middle-class support while rallying working-class voters. This strategy, which was continued down to 1914, was to ensure that the increased direct taxation did not fall on the main body of middle-class salary earners, who might have been attracted to tariff reform had it done so. Instead, supertax and land values taxes would fall on those who would support the Conservative Party anyway,[1] as would major increases in licence duties (these last also appealed to the Liberals' temperance lobby). Although this strategy commanded wide support in the Liberal Party, the People's Budget was very much Lloyd George's personal handiwork, and he had to work hard to persuade Cabinet colleagues and Treasury officials that his proposals were practical politics. In the event, Lloyd George provoked the Conservatives to use their majority in the House of Lords to throw out the Budget. The Liberals, and their Labour allies, fought two elections in 1910 on the issues of the People's Budget and the need to curb the Lords' veto. The elections, both of which had similar results, cost the Liberals their absolute majority in the House of Commons, forcing them to look to the support of the Irish Nationalist and Labour parties in order to push through further social legislation. On the other hand, the threat of the creation by the King of enough Liberal peers to create a Liberal majority in the Lords was enough to ensure the passage of the Parliament Act of 1911, which eliminated the Lords' veto over money bills, and reduced the Lords' veto over other bills to a power to delay for two years. Lloyd George's strategy thus cleared the way for further social reform, the People's Budget being finally passed in 1910.

1. Significantly, Lloyd George abandoned his land values taxation, the key element in his People's Budget strategy, when he was leader of a Conservative-dominated coalition in 1918–22.

The Birth of National Insurance

From the point of view of the future shape of the welfare state, Lloyd George's most significant decision in 1908–09 was to adopt the principle of compulsory and contributory national insurance. Contributions to an insurance fund meant that payments made to the insured during interruption of earnings were made as of right, so that no stigma was attached, in contrast to relief through the Poor Law. On the other hand, the Poor Law was maintained through the rates, which meant that the poor contributed little, whereas insurance contributions were flat rate, that is not proportional to income. As it emerged in the National Insurance Act of 1911, the Liberal scheme covered parts, but by no means all, of the population against sickness and unemployment. Part I of the Act dealt with health insurance and covered most wage earners, but the salaried middle classes were expected to be able to take out private insurance. Employees covered by national health insurance were to contribute 4d. a week; their employers would contribute 3d. a week and the state 2d. a week. Lloyd George claimed that wage earners would thus get 9d. for 4d. Not all workers could easily afford 4d., however; for example, in Dundee (Churchill's constituency) jute weavers struck for an extra 6d. a week in 1912, only to find that most of their hard-won increase went in health insurance contributions when the Act went into force that year. Workers in some other trades also had to pay a further 2½d. a week under Part 2 of the Act which covered unemployment insurance. In their case, employers made a matching contribution and the state paid 1⅔d. The unemployed insurance scheme was avowedly experimental, and limited to trades, such as those associated with construction or shipbuilding, which were particularly subject to fluctuations in the trade cycle, but the scheme was to be extended to other trades if successful.

There was little in common between the two parts of the Act. If an insured worker could not earn because he was sick, he would receive 10s. a week; if an insured worker were unemployed he would receive only 7s. a week, up to a maximum of 15 weeks. What was common to the two schemes was that health insurance was largely, and unemployment insurance was entirely, concerned with interruption of earnings. The Royal Commission on the Poor Laws had recommended state action in 1909 to improve the nation's health so as to remove a major source of poverty, and had stressed the undesirability of continued association of public health services with deterrent aspects of the Poor Law (Cd. 4499, pp. 288–90, 293–302, 889–90). The national health insurance scheme did not deal adequately with these issues. Even insurance against loss of earnings was no guarantee against poverty. While wage earners were covered, their dependants were not, even though poverty might easily hit a family where the mother was unable to attend to her duties or required expensive treatment. There was a maternity allowance of 30s., but the free medical treatment under the scheme was limited to the wage earner. As for prevention of sickness, the Act did nothing to co-ordinate the various health services then offered by the Poor Law and voluntary hospitals, private insurance, and public health authorities. Provision was made for sanatoria for sufferers from infectious diseases, and money was provided for medical research, but a national health service, such as developed after the Second World War, was still a long way off.

Lloyd George's scheme must be judged in the light of what was politically practicable at the time. He regarded health insurance as an emergency measure – he called it an 'ambulance wagon' – which could subsequently be supplemented by other measures, and in 1914 he did make grants to local authorities for nursing and clinical services. He could not simply copy the German model of health insurance, which was run directly by the state, although with provision for workers' participation. In Britain the absence of state provision had allowed self-help to flourish in the form of numerous friendly societies, which were self-governing local 'lodges' affiliated to national 'orders' and which ran 'sick clubs' and offered medical benefits. Although this form of self-help did not reach down to the poorest of the poor, who had no recourse but to the Poor Law, friendly societies' membership was widespread enough for the Government to respect their wish to retain their existence and functions. Lloyd George proposed originally to operate national health insurance through approved, self-governing, friendly societies which would collect contributions and pay out benefits. There were other interested parties, however – the industrial insurance companies and the so-called collecting friendly societies. Both of these were engaged in selling life insurance and had not hitherto dealt in health insurance, but they feared that if the friendly societies proper had a monopoly of the national scheme, then the friendly societies' business would expand and they would take over the life insurance business. Unlike the friendly societies, the industrial insurance companies and the collecting friendly societies were not controlled by those who were insured. The industrial insurance companies were run by directors responsible to shareholders, while the collecting friendly societies were effectively controlled by the collectors who earned commissions by selling policies. Nevertheless, both kinds of commercial insurance organisation, particularly the former, which were generally larger, had the means to influence public opinion. Lloyd George recognised that between them they had thousands of agents and collectors who were trusted in millions of households where they collected weekly premiums of a few pence. When, in 1911, the commercial insurance interests demanded the right to share national health insurance administration with the friendly societies, Lloyd George decided to give way.

The tangled tale of how the commercial insurance interests, and in particular their spokesman Kingsley Wood (who became Minister of Health in the 1930s), negotiated concessions from the Government is worthy of a chapter in itself. The most comprehensive account is by Bentley B. Gilbert (1966b, ch. 6). Indeed, Professor Gilbert's work, although overtaken by more recent research on points of detail, remains the standard work on the 1911 National Insurance Act. What should be pointed out here is that, as is so often the case, it was to the advantage of both the interest groups concerned and the Government to reach agreement. Administration of national health insurance would give the industrial insurance companies the chance to find new customers for life insurance policies. On the other hand, the manpower available to the companies was greater than that available to the self-governing friendly societies, and the companies could reach out to the lower third of the working classes who had not been able, or willing, to join friendly societies. Moreover, the fact that private agencies were to handle the national insurance scheme without any financial guarantee from the state, albeit under state supervision, had a further advantage from the point of view of the Chancellor of the Exchequer: losses resulting from false claims for sickness benefit would be borne by the private agencies, who would thus have every inducement to check malingering (Braithwaite 1957, pp. 93–5).

There was another important interest group with whom Lloyd George had to reach a compromise: the medical profession. For a variety of reasons the British Medical Association wished to see a state medical service, but they wanted one on their own terms. Co-operation from doctors was vital to the success of national health insurance, as the awful example of the doctors' strike in Leipzig in Germany in 1904 had shown (Marshall 1975, p. 62). In Britain, competition between doctors for contract work with the friendly societies had often enabled the societies to force the rates for fees down, and the doctors hoped that a state service could give them a secure and substantial income. Moreover, some voluntary hospital funds were so low that doctors feared that the hospitals would have to accept state control, on the state's terms, in return for public funds. What the British Medical Association wanted was a public medical service to cater for people just above the Poor Law, and for that reason it wished national health insurance to be limited to those with incomes under £100 a year, leaving other workers to be treated as private patients. Lloyd George insisted on a £160 income limit, but offered concessions, increasing capitation fees to a doctor for each patient on his list and transferring control of medical treatment from the friendly societies to insurance companies which would be more representative of the doctors' interest. Even so, the British Medical Association threatened not to take part in the scheme, only to give way when it found in 1912 that too many of its members could not resist Lloyd George's increased capitation fees (Gilbert 1966b, chs. 6–7).

Part 2 of the National Insurance Act aroused far less resistance from interest groups, mainly because trade unions in the industries affected by the Act found the burden of supporting unemployed members in trade depressions a heavy one. Trade unions which were least affected by the trade cycle, and which would be more reluctant to see flat-rate contributions levied by the state on their members, were not invited to join the scheme at this stage. Employers affected by the legislation could be expected to be generally in favour of it, since their labour force would now be maintained by national insurance in periods when they were not required for work. Although unemployment insurance was included in Lloyd George's National Insurance Act, the politician chiefly responsible for designing Part 2 insurance was Churchill during his period as President of the Board of Trade (1908–10). Churchill had been aided by a young civil servant, William Beveridge, who had already made his mark with his book *Unemployment: A Problem of Industry* (1909), and who was to become famous as the author of the Beveridge Report on *Social Insurance and Allied Services* in 1942. Two other people who had some influence on Churchill, but who would have liked to have had much more, were the Fabians Sidney and Beatrice Webb. However, Churchill ignored their ideas for a reformed Poor Law, and went for labour exchanges and unemployment insurance under the control of the Board of Trade. He preferred workers to be protected against trade depressions as a matter of right, through contributory insurance, rather than by means-tested relief. The labour exchanges would test men's willingness to work, and it was hoped that up to 15 weeks of benefit would give willing men time to find work (Gilbert 1966a and 1966b). Such a hope implied continued faith in private enterprise to provide employment for all except in exceptional circumstances. Workers who had not earned, or had exhausted, insurance benefit would have to apply to the Poor Law or hope to find employment on some public works scheme, but, as we shall see, the idea of state employment to counteract the trade cycle was still in its infancy.

The Trend of Liberal Policy

The National Insurance Act of 1911 laid the foundations for state welfare down to the 1940s and, arguably, for longer. Whereas the Majority Report of the Royal Commission on the Poor Laws had been in favour of a reformed Poor Law, the Liberals had embarked on a series of social reforms outside the Poor Law, which was destined to lose more and more of its functions. As Prime Minister of a Coalition Government, Lloyd George was to extend unemployment insurance greatly in 1920. The Poor Law had been comprehensive in scope, and had been run by locally-elected guardians, although subject to supervision by the Local Government Board. Now the trend of social policy was to *ad hoc* agencies, supervised by different central government departments, which could, and did, lead to administrative duplication and muddle. Moreover, there is a case for believing that the private interests responsible for administering health insurance raised administrative costs and prevented subsequent rationalisation and expansion of health services (Gilbert 1970, ch. 6) – although the last charge has been challenged on the grounds that health insurance, like other aspects of social policy, was in any case subject to financial restraint in the interwar period (Whiteside 1983).

Be that as it may, the Liberal reforms were given little chance to prove their worth before war and depression radically changed conditions. In the case of unemployment insurance this was perhaps as well, for the insurance fund might not have been in surplus, as it was in 1912–14, had these years not been part of an economic boom. What one can say is that despite a booming economy and low unemployment after 1910, the Liberal reforms did not eliminate poverty, and the fall in numbers on poor relief between 1911 and 1914 owed more to economic recovery than to welfare legislation. Moreover, low wages and casual, irregular employment served to keep many family incomes below the level which Rowntree believed to be the minimum cost of rent, food and clothing for a working-class family of five (Rose 1972, pp. 50–3). The mass of people lived lives hardly affected by the state, and if state welfare was beginning to fill the ample gaps left by private provision, there was little danger of people being discouraged by state largesse from entering the labour market.

In economic policy the Liberals eschewed tariffs. Nevertheless, the Liberals' commitment to *laissez-faire* economics was less than complete, as the establishment of trade boards showed. Moreover, by creating a Development Fund in 1909 to promote agriculture, rural industries, land reclamation, forestry and fisheries, Lloyd George was taking a step towards state assistance to particular economic interests, a feature of so much of later twentieth-century economic policy. Significantly, the Conservatives, the representatives of the landed interest, did not oppose a bill which would tend to raise rural rents as well as incomes. The Development Act, however, was also a concession to the considerable body of expert opinion in favour of public investment in projects which would assist, but not compete, with private enterprise. The Minority Report of the Royal Commission on the Poor Laws called for public expenditure on afforestation and land reclamation to be concentrated in years when the demand for labour was low, to stabilise employment. Lloyd George, however, admitted that expenditure from the Development and Road Funds would not eliminate fluctuations in employment, and he seems to have been moved by national efficiency arguments about the need to provide 'healthy labour' rather than by economic arguments about countering the trade cycle. In 1914 the Treasury did appoint a committee to inquire into the possibility of eliminating depressions by expenditure on public works, but the inquiry seems to have been the result of parliamentary pressure, and there is no evidence that the Treasury committee ever produced a report. Liberal employment policy before 1914 was, in fact, based overwhelmingly on free market economics. Labour exchanges were intended to improve labour mobility; national insurance was to cover interruptions of earnings. Both measures were intended to change working-class habits by discouraging casual employment and, in the case of the latter, by enforcing thrift. Contributory insurance, as Churchill remarked, would also give workers a 'stake in the country' (Harris 1972, pp. 338–47, 357–60, 364–5).

In conclusion, in so far as Liberal policy was concerned with poverty, the goal was to eliminate destitution without discouraging individualism or competition between people above the poverty line. Again, for all the rhetoric of the People's Budget, the Liberals were far removed from a socialist hostility to private property, their attacks on the landed interest being quite compatible with continued support for industrial capitalism and for the businessmen who contributed to Liberal Party funds. The difference between the Liberals and Conservatives was essentially about how to pay for social policy (and defence policy): whether by direct taxation or by tariffs. But the Liberal conception of a limited degree of state welfare was one which Conservatives could and did share. It had been the Conservative leader, Balfour, who had said that social legislation was not socialist legislation but its most effective antidote (Fraser 1984, p. 139). The antidote of limited national insurance, created by the Liberals, was available for subsequent use by the Conservatives.

References

Document

Cd. 4499 *Report of the Royal Commission on the Poor Laws and Relief of Distress*, British Parliamentary Papers (BPP) 1909, Vol. XXXVII, pp. 1–1260.

Books and Articles

Braithwaite, W. (1957) *Lloyd George's Ambulance Wagon*, Methuen.

Cain, P. (1979) 'Political economy in Edwardian England: the tariff-reform controversy', in A. O'Day (ed.), *The Edwardian Age: Conflict and Stability 1900–1914*, Macmillan.

Churchill, R. (1967) *Winston S. Churchill*, vol. 2, Heinemann.

Churchill, R. (1969) *Winston S. Churchill*, vol. 2 Companion (Part 2), Heinemann.

Davidson, R. (1974) 'War-time labour policy 1914–1916: A Reappraisal', *Scottish Labour History Journal*, vol. 8, pp. 3–20.

Feinstein, C. (1972) *National Income, Expenditure and Output of the United Kingdom*, 1855–1965, Cambridge University Press.

Fraser, D. (1984) *The Evolution of the British Welfare State*, Macmillan.

Gilbert, B.B. (1966a) 'Winston Churchill versus the Webbs: the origins of British unemployment insurance', *American Historical Review*, vol. 71, pp. 846–62.

Gilbert, B.B. (1966b) *The Evolution of National Insurance*, Michael Joseph.

Gilbert, B.B. (1970) *British Social Policy 1914–1939*, Batsford.

Halévy, E. (1961) *History of the English People in the Nineteenth Century*, Vol. 5: *Imperialism and the Rise of Labour*; vol. 6: *The Rule of Democracy, 1905–14*, Ernest Benn. First published in 1932 in French.

Harris, J. (1972) *Unemployment and Politics*, Oxford University Press.

Hay, J.R. (1975) *The Origins of the Liberal Welfare Reforms, 1906–1914*, Macmillan.

Hay, (J.)R. (1977) 'Employers and social policy in Britain: the evolution of welfare legislation, 1905–1914', *Social History*, vol. 2, pp. 435–55.

Hennock, E.P. (1980) 'The origins of British national insurance and the German precedent 1880–1914', in W.J. Mommsen (ed.), *The Emergence of the Welfare State in Britain and Germany*, Croom Helm.

Macdonald, D.F. (1960) *The State and the Trade Unions*, Macmillan.

Mallet, B. (1913) *British Budgets 1887/88–1912/13*, Macmillan.

Marshall, T.H. (1975) *Social Policy in the Twentieth Century*, Hutchinson.

Murray, B.K. (1980) *The People's Budget 1909/10: Lloyd George and Liberal Politics*, Oxford University Press.

Rose, M.E. (1972) *The Relief of Poverty 1834–1914*, Macmillan.

Russell, A.K. (1974) *Liberal Landslide: The General Election of 1906*, David and Charles.

Thane, P. (1978) 'Non-contributory versus insurance pensions 1878–1908', in her *The Origins of British Social Policy*, Croom Helm.

Whiteside, N. (1983) 'Private agencies for public purposes: some new perspectives on policy making in health insurance between the wars', *Journal of Social Policy*, vol. 12, pp. 165–94.

3

War and Postwar, 1914–22

The First World War made unprecedented demands on the economy and on society. The laws of supply and demand, while by no means in suspense, could be relied upon neither to mobilise the nation's resources nor to secure the equitable distribution of goods and services. A system of controls slowly evolved whereby the state directed more and more of the nation's economic activities. Britain's prewar plans had not required total mobilisation of national resources. British strategy was to have been based on naval blockade, with only a small army of about 130,000 men being committed to land warfare. Conscription, finally introduced in 1916, had not figured in prewar plans, and no-one anticipated that the army would be enlarged by over a million volunteers by December 1914. This development has been advanced as one reason why the British army was short of munitions early in the war (French 1982a and b), but there is also evidence that industrial preparations had been inadequate even for 130,000 men (Trebilcock 1975). The shortage of shells early in 1915 caused a political scandal and forced the Liberals into a coalition with the Conservatives. Eventually Asquith was replaced as prime minister by Lloyd George, in December 1916, but with the Conservatives now dominating the Coalition. It was under Lloyd George that the system of controls was developed to its fullest extent. It was also Lloyd George who made promises of postwar social reform so as to make wartime restrictions politically acceptable.

The Growth of Controls

The Government responded to the 'shells scandal' of 1915 by establishing a Ministry of Munitions to which Lloyd George transferred from the Treasury. The War Office had already recruited one or two businessmen to deal with production problems, but Lloyd George recruited far more, believing that businessmen were far more able than career civil servants 'to create and hustle along a gigantic new enterprise'. The emphasis was on production, and strict financial control was not a feature of the Ministry. Political protests against profits made on munitions contracts led to the Ministry fixing prices in relation to costs of production. However, this meant that the greater the manufacturer's costs, the greater were his profits. Control of munitions prices, therefore, entailed control of sub-contractors' prices as well, so that state involvement gradually spread. Manufacturers were helped to produce goods which they had not produced before and were encouraged to adopt mass production methods. Substantial improvements in productivity were made, although this was perhaps at least as much the result of labour shortages as of the Ministry's efforts. Finally, to supplement private manufacture, National Shell Factories were built for, and run by, the state, which thereby became a major direct employer of labour (French 1982b, pp 21–4; Wrigley 1982).

War production required heavy capital investment, and the Government took steps to limit the raising of capital for other purposes. From the beginning of 1915 Treasury approval of new issues was required, and a licensing system was introduced for building work. There was, however, no lack of investment opportunities. As a result of a free trade policy and the international division of labour, Britain had been dependent before 1914 on a number of imports which were vital in war. In particular, Britain relied on German science-based industries to provide about 90 per cent of its dyestuffs and optical instruments. During the war the Government encouraged the development of native chemical and optical industries by providing low-interest loans and technical assistance. The Department of Scientific and Industrial Research was established in 1916 to co-ordinate research by private firms and to set up its own laboratories (MacLeod 1975; Reader 1970, Part IV).

Britain was also dependent upon imports for staple foodstuffs, 70 per cent of its wheat coming from abroad. The fact that 'Britannia ruled the waves' at first seemed to guarantee these supplies, but the threat under the waves became apparent from the autumn of 1916, when Germany began unrestricted submarine warfare. To increase domestic production, the Corn Production Act of 1917 not only guaranteed a minimum price for wheat, oats and potatoes for six years but also gave the Board of Agriculture compulsory powers to direct farmers to use land in the way it directed. The Act came too late to have an impact on food supplies before 1918 and, long before that, shortages of raw materials as well as food had led the Government to take steps to control transport and distribution.

The railways had been placed under state control at the outbreak of war, initially to transport troops. The day-to-day running of the railways was left to the existing managers, but profits were fixed by the Government. The risk of enemy action at sea tended to raise insurance premiums, so the Government provided a war-risks insurance scheme, at lower than market rates, for shipping from 1914 and for cargoes from early 1915. On the other hand, the Government itself contributed to a shipping shortage by requisitioning vessels to transport troops and their supplies. In September 1915 Lloyd George's successor as chancellor, Reginald McKenna, imposed customs duties on certain imported 'luxuries', including motor cars and cinematographic films, to save shipping space and foreign exchange, but the problem could only be overcome by the Government taking direct control of shipping and imports. From November 1915 the Government had powers to requisition ships for commercial cargoes or to withhold licences to import. These powers were not much used until an acute shipping shortage occurred in 1917, but thereafter practically all shipping movements were directed by the Government (Ashworth 1960, ch. 11).

The distribution of food within Britain was at first left to the free market. Wheat prices rose 80 per cent and meat prices 40 per cent in the first twelve months of war. There were complaints from labour, but a Ministry of Food was not set up until December 1916, and in the case of the first Minister, Lord Devonport, Lloyd George's faith in the businessman's ability 'to create and hustle along' was not rewarded. Devonport, the owner of a retail grocery chain, was too concerned to preserve the existing channels of retail trade to be willing to adopt his officials' plans for compulsory rationing. By 1917 food shortages and rising prices were being exploited by militant shop stewards in the munitions industries. Devonport was replaced by Lord Rhondda, a coal-mine owner, who embarked on bulk buying of food abroad, while at home flour mills, milk distribution and livestock markets were placed under direct public control. The marketing of oils, fats, butter and meat was controlled by quasi-autonomous associations of tradesmen set up at the Ministry's instigation. A bread subsidy from the autumn of 1917 helped to reduce the rise of the official index of the working-class cost of living, especially as the index was heavily weighted towards food. Nevertheless, price controls did not prevent shortages and by the winter, food queues were lengthening; in December 1917 *The Times* reported a queue of 3,000 people outside a London shop waiting for margarine. At last the Government agreed to a rationing scheme worked out by an official committee under William Beveridge, and gradually, as administrative difficulties were overcome, rationing was extended to sugar, meat, bacon, jam, butter, margarine and lard. By the end of the war the Ministry of Food was responsible in one way or another for over 85 per cent of the nation's food supplies (Harris 1982).

Some gaps in the Government's control of the economy remained to the end. Prominent among these was the supply of consumer goods other than food and a few standardised types and qualities of clothing and footwear. Rising prices quickly cleared unregulated markets. Rising prices, and consequent working-class discontent, helped to frustrate government attempts to control the supply of the scarcest factor of production of all, labour, and it is to the related topics of inflation and labour unrest that we now turn.

Financial Policy, Inflation and Profits

The enormous increase in the numbers of men in the armed forces quickly eliminated the small increase in unemployment resulting from wartime dislocation of trade. Full employment of the prewar labour force meant that war-related demands on British industry could only be met by diverting labour from production of civilian goods or exports, by increasing productivity, and by recruiting women not previously employed in industry. All three methods were used and down to 1917 the gross domestic product increased, while consumers' real expenditure shrank (Table 3.1). Tax rates were increased, but most of the Government's increased demand was

Table 3.1 The War Economy

Calendar year	Index of gross domestic product at constant factor cost	Index of consumers' expenditure	Central government expenditure as a percentage of gross domestic product
1913	100.0	100.0	7.5
1914	101.0	100.5	13.2
1915	109.1	102.6	38.6
1916	111.5	94.1	44.2
1917	112.5	86.7	45.7
1918	113.2	85.9	44.7
1919	100.9	98.3	27.8
1920	94.8	98.5	17.6
	91.3	94.3	17.4
1921	83.9	88.7	21.0

Source: Feinstein (1972), Tables 4, 7 and 12.
Note: The second line of figures for 1920, and the figures for 1921, exclude Southern Ireland.

financed by borrowing (Table 3.2). Given that the economy was more or less at full employment, and given the slow introduction of physical controls by Government, it is not surprising that increased demand resulted in rising prices. The cost of the war was borne not only by people who paid taxes, but also by people whose incomes did not keep up with rising prices, and average wage earnings lagged behind retail prices until 1918 (Table 3.3).

War offered opportunities for great profits and for more regular work, but the social effects of inflation on people with small savings, pensions or other fixed incomes was severe. One effect of wartime financial policy was to give deficit finance a bad name. No official national income statistics were compiled at the time, but if one takes Feinstein's (1972) estimates of gross domestic product and of the government's revenue and expenditure within the United Kingdom it would appear that central government's share of the gross domestic product (GDP) rose from 7.5 per cent in 1913 to

Table 3.2 Current Account of Central Government (£ Million at Current Prices)

Calendar year	*Internal receipts*	*Internal expenditure*	*Surplus (+) or deficit (−)*	*Surplus or deficit as percentage of gross domestic product*
1913	167	167	0	—
1914	170	296	−126	−5.6
1915	244	1,046	−802	−29.5
1916	428	1,399	−971	−30.6
1917	627	1,839	−1,212	−30.0
1918	790	2,154	−1,364	−28.2
1919	962	1,401	−439	−8.7
1920	1,032	979	+53	+0.9

Source: Feinstein (1972), Tables 4 and 12.
Note: These figures exclude external loans and other capital transactions which were included in the chancellor's budget, but include national insurance contributions and benefits.

about 45 per cent during 1916–18. The internal current account deficit as a proportion of the national income ran at about 30 per cent from 1915 to 1918, and there can be little doubt that financial policy played an important part in inflation in that, had more been raised by taxation, less spending power would have remained in the hands of the public.

There was then no conception of demand management on a national income accounting basis such as Keynes was to introduce into the Treasury in 1940/41. Nevertheless, Treasury officials in 1914, thinking in terms of a limited supply of loanable funds, were quick to advise Lloyd George, then the Chancellor of the Exchequer, against relying too heavily on borrowing. They noted that in the past nearly half the cost of wars had been met from taxation. Lloyd George, who cared little for conventional financial wisdom, chose not to follow this advice, and set himself the more modest task of raising enough revenue to pay for normal expenditure in peace,

Table 3.3 Wages and Prices (1913 = 100)

Calendar year	*Average weekly wage rates*	*Average weekly wage earnings*	*Retail prices*
1913	100	100	100
1914	101	101	101
1915	108	117	121
1916	118	133	143
1917	139	170	173
1918	179	211	199
1919	215	241	211
1920	257	278	244
1921	256	260	222
1922	198	209	179

Source: Feinstein (1972), Table 65

plus a margin to pay for the interest on loans raised to pay for the war (French 1982a, p. 106). This was, to say the least, a novel conception of war finance, but it was a policy continued by his successor, Reginald McKenna, who raised it to the level of a principle, which came to be called the 'McKenna rule'.

Government borrowing need not cause an expansion in the money supply if the money borrowed is money which would otherwise have been spent or invested by private individuals. But the sums which the Government wished to borrow were greater than the non-bank public could lend from their savings. Consequently, much of the money which was lent to the Government came from the banks, either directly, or as a result of members of the public borrowing from banks in order to invest in government bonds. Monetary inflation originated when the Government borrowed from its own banker, the Bank of England, on Ways and Means advances. These advances were temporary loans of an ordinary banking kind. When, for example, in a given period, the Government spent £10 million more than it collected in taxation or loans from the public, the Bank of England would advance £10 million, by a book entry. The Government would use the advance to pay its contractors and creditors by cheque. Once the cheques were cleared, the joint stock banks would find themselves holding, collectively, £10 million more in cash at the Bank of England, while having collectively £10 million more in liabilities to depositors. The joint stock banks did not wish to hold cash reserves of more than a fraction of their liabilities, so that at the end of the period in which they had accumulated £10 million in cash, the banks would be willing to lend to their customers or to the Government up to several times the original amount. Money lent to the Government would be spent by it, and would return again to the banks, once more increasing their cash at the Bank of England, and thus repeating the process set in motion by the original Ways and Means advance. Each Ways and Means advance thus created new purchasing power many times its own amount. Even so, it was in the interests of the Government to borrow the new money from the banks or their customers rather than allow members of the public to borrow it, for in this way the Government could divert purchasing power to itself. There was no lack of cash, because from 1914 the Government resorted to the printing press, producing new paper money called currency notes, which were unbacked by gold (Sayers 1938, pp. 272–9).

An increase in the quantity of money permitted increased demand to be expressed in terms of higher prices. The chief element in demand, however, was government expenditure itself. Once there were adequate controls over civilian economic activities, in 1917–18, there were fewer opportunities for private expenditure and, therefore, there was more inducement to save. The last eighteen months of the war saw a slackening of the rate of inflation, as the Government absorbed purchasing power by selling medium-term bonds and short-term Treasury bills. The latter were issued to the banks, and fell due to be paid in three, six or twelve months. This meant, however, that the banks could obtain cash by not buying new Treasury bills when old ones matured. Consequently, the Government could not prevent a great inflationary postwar boom in 1919–20, when the banks used cash from maturing Treasury bills to lend to private borrowers (Morgan 1952, chs. 4–8).

Could the Government have relied more on taxation, as its critics (who included Philip Snowden, the future Labour Chancellor of the Exchequer) claimed? Allowance has to be made for the willingness, or otherwise, of taxpayers to contribute, for unless there had been a vast increase in the number of tax inspectors much direct taxation was in effect voluntary. As things were, the Inland Revenue was checking on, and discovering, unpaid tax for years after the war. From 1915 there was first a Munitions Levy on profits made on munitions contracts, and then an Excess Profits Duty on all profits exceeding a standard based on prewar experience, or a permitted percentage of capital invested in the business. The taxes were novel because hitherto direct taxes had been payable by shareholders, but not by companies *qua* companies. The rate of Excess Profits Duty was raised in stages, from 50 per cent in 1915 to 80 per cent in 1917, but never reached the 100 per cent charged in the Second World War. Where there was collusion between businessmen to fix prices, and until the state took over control of much of the economy in 1917–18, the tax was largely ineffective in reducing profits, even though it raised revenue. Businessmen usually regarded the tax as an expense and, where possible, would charge prices which left them with the same profit as they would have aimed at had the tax not existed (Stamp 1932, p. 216).

The sources of war-related inflation were not, of course, exclusively domestic. Wartime disruption of trade created shortages and price rises throughout the world, and Britain was more dependent on imports than any other belligerent. Britain could finance its imports by exporting goods and services, by shipping gold, by selling overseas assets, or by borrowing abroad. Britain maintained a current account balance of payments surplus down to 1917, but this did not prevent an acute shortage of dollars developing as, by the autumn of 1916, some 40 per cent of all British war purchases, for itself and for its allies, were being made in North America. Some gold was shipped, and at the end of 1915 private owners of dollar securities were invited to sell or lend them to the Treasury (a penal tax followed on income from such securities which had been retained by their owners). Dollar securities were either sold or used as collateral for loans raised in America. The export of British capital was prohibited from 1916 and, in order to attract foreign balances, the Bank of England raised short-term interest rates in London. Britain was effectively off the gold standard during the war, since gold shipments were not covered by the war risks insurance scheme. Even so, it was considered by the Treasury to be important to keep the exchange rate at something like the prewar parity of $4.86 to prevent disruption of inter-Allied finances and to maintain British prestige. Early in 1917 the shortage of dollars was such that the Treasury considered letting the exchange rate go, but once America entered the war in April 1917, US Treasury dollar loans were available to finance purchases in America and to maintain the exchange rate at $\$4.76\frac{7}{16}$ until April 1919, when Britain formally left the gold standard (Burk 1979 and 1982; Morgan 1952, ch. 9).

The State and the Trade Unions

There had been considerable industrial conflict in the boom years 1910–14. However, once war broke out, union leaders called an 'industrial truce'. Most were patriotic men who, like the Government, believed that the war would be short. In fact, the war far outlasted the truce. As prices and profits soared, unions demanded, and employers were often willing to grant, wage increases, and a price–wage spiral developed (see Table 3.3). It was, however, over the question of 'dilution' that the industrial truce broke down. Dilution meant that work hitherto reserved for members of craft unions was to be done by workers who had not served apprenticeships. Skilled workers were in short supply, and it was only by economising on such labour, often by breaking the work process down into simple stages which semi-skilled workers could cope with, that government contracts could be met. By early 1915 strikes in defence of craft privileges in the engineering and shipbuilding industries were impeding production at a time when output was of crucial importance to the outcome of the war.

In March 1915 Lloyd George, still Chancellor, asked union leaders to agree to compulsory arbitration to avoid strikes, and to the temporary use of semi-skilled or women workers on munitions contracts, for the duration of the war. The union leaders gave their assent on condition that profits on munitions contracts should be limited. Following this 'Treasury Agreement', as it was called, a National Labour Advisory Council of union representatives was set up under the chairmanship of a Labour MP, Arthur Henderson, to advise the Government on labour questions. In July 1915 the Treasury Agreement was given legal force in the Munitions of War Act, which was to apply to all industries designated by the Government as vital to the war effort. The most unpopular aspect of the Act from the point of view of the ordinary worker was that it introduced a system of 'leaving certificates' by which an employer, by withholding a certificate, could prevent a worker moving to another job. This was an attempt to prevent employers bidding against each other for scarce labour by raising wages, but workers' opposition to the system was such that it was abandoned in 1917.

Compulsory arbitration under the Act was quickly challenged by a coal strike in South Wales. Some 200,000 miners were involved at one time and, although the Government declared the strike to be illegal since 21 days' notice had not been given to allow arbitration, the men could not be forced to go underground. The Government backed down by persuading the employers to grant most of the strikers' demands. Elsewhere arbitration seems to have had some success: 10 million working days had been lost through strikes in 1914, but only about 3 million were lost in 1915 and about 2½ million in 1916. Increased industrial unrest in 1917 raised the figure to nearly 6 million (Macdonald 1960, ch. 7).

On the whole, the Munitions of War Act was acceptable to the official trade-union leadership, with the exception of the miners' leaders. Men who met in the National Labour Advisory Council could obtain a broad conspectus of the national interest. Matters appeared differently on the shop floor, where men could see differentials between themselves and less skilled workers being eroded at a time when wages were in any case lagging behind prices. Not for the last time, moderate union leaders found that it was one thing to reach agreement with government, and quite another to persuade rank-and-file members to abide by the agreement. Indeed, it was the very moderation of the official leadership which helped to pave the way for a militant shop-stewards' movement. An unofficial strike on Clydeside in 1915 led to the creation of a standing Clyde Workers' Committee, an association of shop stewards representing all grades of workers. More strikes followed, and the links between the Committee and the Independent Labour Party, which was opposed to the war, led the Government to regard the shop-stewards' movement as subversive. In March 1916 some of the Clydesiders' leaders were 'exiled' by being required to live in Edinburgh. Similar workers' committees sprang up in other munitions centres where craft traditions were strong, but the support of the Labour Party for Lloyd George's war aims, and divisions between craftsmen and other workers, seem to have prevented the shop-stewards' movement from developing the revolutionary momentum desired by some of its members (Hinton 1973).

At all events, Lloyd George was concerned to maintain industrial peace. On becoming Prime Minister in 1916, he made Henderson, the Chairman of the National Labour Advisory Council, one of his inner War Cabinet of five ministers. A Ministry of Labour was created, with a trade-union leader, John Hodge, as its first Minister, to take over industrial relations from the Board of Trade (Lowe 1982). When industrial unrest increased in 1917, Lloyd George appointed a Commission on Labour Unrest, headed by George Barnes, a trade unionist. It was this Commission which recommended the abolition of the system of leaving certificates. The Commission also endorsed the recommendation of a committee, headed by J.H. Whitley, Deputy Speaker of the House of Commons, that joint councils (later known as Whitley councils) representing employers and unions should be set up in each industry at national, district and works levels. Co-operation in industrial matters was thus not to be limited to official union leaders and big business.

On balance, government policy in 1915–18 did much to advance the cause of collective bargaining. The weaker unions found that compulsory arbitration under the Munitions of War Act forced employers to make agreements with them which made it easier to recruit members. The Whitley councils made possible collective bargaining in trades where unions had made no progress before 1914 (Lovell 1977, pp. 50–2). The main source of trade-union strength, however, was not industrial relations policy but the Government's demand for munitions and, therefore, labour. Trade-union membership rose by over 50 per cent between 1914 and 1918, but membership fell when the Government adopted deflationary economic policies after the war.

Promises of Social Reform

The increased importance of labour presented Lloyd George with a challenge in the broader political field beyond industrial relations. Participation in government enhanced the reputation of the Labour Party. The 1918 Reform Act, which trebled the electorate by removing property and residential qualifications for male voters over 21, and by enfranchising most women over 30, made it seem likely that social questions would dominate politics after the war. Nor could social questions be ignored during the war, as war-weariness by 1917 made military victory alone seem an inadequate reward for hardships undergone. Government commissions of enquiry into industrial unrest that year reported that while there was general support for the war, working people were determined there should be no return to pre-1914 social conditions. The shortage of working-class housing was a particularly strong grievance. For Lloyd George, promises of social reform, which he himself doubtless believed in, had the double advantage of appealing to the imagination of an expanded electorate while sustaining morale. A Ministry of Reconstruction was set up in 1917 with instructions to draw up programmes for postwar 'social amelioration' and economic improvement. In December 1918, one month after the Armistice, Lloyd George went to the polls, still heading a Conservative-dominated Coalition, making much of the slogan 'homes fit for heroes' (Morgan 1979).

Political concern with working-class housing was not new in 1918. A shortage of land had raised the price of urban building before 1914, thereby tending to raise rents, while increasing local authority expenditure had raised rates, further exacerbating relations between landlord and tenant (Englander 1983; Melling 1983). There was already an acknowledged shortage of working-class housing in 1914, but prewar policy was still based on Victorian legislation designed to improve public health. Local authorities were required to replace slums with new housing, and they were permitted (but not required) to add to the local housing stock to reduce overcrowding. Between 1890 and 1914, however, London County Council, by far the biggest local authority builder, had provided housing for only 25,000 people under this permissive legislation in addition to rehousing 22,000 people through slum clearance. Local authorities had to borrow for these purposes, their loans being sanctioned by central government, and even in 1914 (a peak year) sanction was sought by English and Welsh authorities for loans for a total of only 2,465 houses. In 1911 the Conservatives had proposed that the Treasury should subsidise local authority house building by a total of £1 million annually, and it seems unlikely that the Liberals would have allowed themselves to be outbid in what was becoming an important political issue (Swenarton 1981, ch. 2; Wilding 1972).

In the absence of Exchequer subsidies, 95 per cent of working-class housing before the war had been provided by private enterprise. The supply of new housing was determined by the ability and willingness of workers to pay rent, by the cost of building, and by the returns available on alternative forms of investment. As already noted, both building costs and rents were rising before 1914. Moreover, private builders could easily be crowded out by a rise in interest rates since the purchase of land and materials, and the wages of labour, must all be financed out of capital before any return on the investment would be forthcoming. Given an unregulated trade cycle, it is hardly surprising that there was not a steady supply of new housing; and given widespread poverty, it was unlikely that private building could ever cure overcrowding.

The war itself exacerbated the housing problem as private building ceased at a time when a sudden influx of labour into areas with shipyards or munitions factories produced overcrowding. When landlords attempted to raise rents, there was a wave of rent strikes, starting in Glasgow in the autumn of 1915 (Melling 1983). To avoid industrial unrest, the Government imposed rent controls. This was seen by working-class leaders as a great victory, but when rents failed to keep up with inflation, landlords were often unable to maintain their property, which was allowed to deteriorate, and there was little incentive to build new houses for rent. By 1919 it was estimated that rents would have to increase by 35 per cent if landlords were to recover their position in 1914. In 1917 the Ministry of Reconstruction's Housing Advisory Panel estimated that 300,000 houses and cottages would have to be built in England and Wales if the immediate housing shortage were to be cleared, whereas a 'normal' annual construction figure would be 75,000. Moreover, in 1917 a Royal Commission on Housing in Scotland, where overcrowding had long been a more serious problem than in England, estimated that 235,000 houses would have to be built if accumulated shortages arising from neglect in peace and war were to be tackled (Orbach 1977).

There was no prospect that private enterprise alone could clear the backlog quickly. Even when the Government decided to provide the finance, there remained the problem that wartime controls on building, and high interest rates, had led to the closure of brickyards and a reduction in the building labour force. Time as well as money was needed for the industry's recovery. Ministers, however, were more conscious of political expediency than of practical problems. Lloyd George used the bogey of Bolshevism to bring his Conservative colleagues round to support Dr Christopher Addison who, as the first Minister of Health, was responsible for the housing programme. (The new Ministry took over the supervisory functions of the Local Government Board in 1919.)

Although, as we have seen, local authorities had very limited experience of housing programmes, there was no other system of public authority which covered the whole country and was yet aware of local needs. Consequently, Addison's first 1919 Housing Act required local authorities to draw up schemes both to overcome the shortage and to raise standards of housing. An incomplete survey by 1920 suggested that 800,000 houses would be needed ultimately, and in the meantime the Government had pledged itself to build 500,000 houses in three years from 1919. Moreover, the new houses were to be of a high standard, the economic rent for which was beyond the means of the lowest-paid workers. To encourage local authorities to build, Treasury subsidies were offered to meet losses incurred beyond those covered by a 1d. rate. This meant that local authorities would, to a large extent, be spending other people's money – hardly an inducement to economy. Under a second Act in 1919, private builders were also to receive subsidies from central government to build houses to specified standards.

A huge imbalance of demand and supply was being created, yet the Government was under strong pressure in Parliament to abolish wartime controls on trade and industry and, in the case of building, controls had been removed at the end of 1918. Attempts by Addison to legislate against non-essential building in 1919 failed. The consequences were what one would expect. Prices and wages in the building industry rose rapidly, tendencies which price rings among contractors and resistance by trade unionists to dilution did nothing to diminish. Average building contract prices of local authority houses increased from about £740 in the summer of 1919 to about £930 in the autumn of 1920. There was a decline in prices thereafter as a result of a general depression in trade, but in 1921 Lloyd George's Cabinet decided that Addison's programme was too expensive and local authority building under the Act was limited to 170,000 houses. A further 4,500 subsidised houses were built by public-utility corporations. Over 39,000 subsidised houses were built by private enterprise under the second 1919 Act. Even including unsubsidised private housing, the total number of houses built between the Armistice and March 1923 was only 252,000, about half the figure the Government had promised to build in three years (Bowley 1945, pp. 23f; Marriner 1976).

Addison's Acts thus failed in their immediate objective. On the other hand, the principle that the supply of housing was a responsibility of government had been established, and much more generous Treasury grants had been made available than the £1 million annually proposed before the war. The grants for housing under the Addison Acts amounted to £3.3 million in 1920/21, £9.1 million in 1921/22, and £8 million in 1922/23 (Mallet and George 1929, p. 393; 1933, p. 558).

Another aspect of social reform where promises of improvement were only partially fulfilled was education. Under an Act introduced for England and Wales by H.A.L. Fisher, the President of the Board of Education, in 1918, the school-leaving age was raised from 12 to 14 years, and fees in state-supported elementary schools were abolished. The Act also required local authorities to provide over a period of years continuation schools where 14 to 16 year olds would receive part-time education. The annual cost of providing these schools was not large, being estimated by Fisher at only £300,000 in 1921–22, rising thereafter as more schools were built but still not more than £900,000 in 1928. However, local authorities, who would have to pay half the cost (the balance being paid by the Treasury), were not anxious to proceed. As part of an economy drive in 1921–22 the Cabinet decided to relieve local authorities of the obligation to provide continuation schools and only one authority persisted with the scheme after 1922. Economy at the expense of continuation schools was no doubt gratifying to the powerful industrialists' lobby, which had opposed part-time education after the age of 14 on the grounds that this would add to labour costs (Andrews 1976, pp. 49–54; 69–75). Secondary education for all was still a long way off, and the principle enunciated in the 1918 Act that 'children and young persons shall not be debarred from receiving the benefits of any form of education by which they are capable of profiting through inability to pay fees', did not find general application until after another world war.

The same was true of a national health service. Free treatment of venereal disease had been introduced in 1917 for civilians as well as soldiers, and this has been described by Titmuss (1976, p. 81) as 'the first instalment of a free national health service.' It was, however, very much an isolated instalment. Despite wartime concern about the poor physique of many army recruits, there was no major development in new health services in the aftermath of war. In 1920 a Council on Medical and Administrative Services under Sir Bernard Dawson, a doctor who had served as a major-general during the war, produced an interim report which spoke of 'the increasing conviction that the best means of maintaining health and curing disease should be made available to all citizens.' However, there was no final report and it was not until after the Second World War that the principle of making the best available to all found expression in the National Health Service. What did happen between 1914 and 1918 was a major expansion in welfare services for mothers and infants. The Local Government Board had proposed to local authorities just before the outbreak of war that they should provide comprehensive ante- and post-natal services, and had offered to pay half of the cost. By 1916 the Local Government Board was offering to pay for nurses, health visitors and inspectors of midwives, for the full expenses of ante-natal clinics, for the hospital treatment of infants, and also for the provision of doctors for the poor and for understaffed regions such as the north of England. Similarly, the Board of Education financed child care classes for mothers from 1915 (Thane 1982, pp. 133–38).

Historians of social policy have offered a number of explanations of why social services were victims of an economy drive in 1921–22. Abrams (1963), while accepting that the Government believed that it faced an economic crisis by late 1919, has suggested that the decisive failure of reform had occurred before there was pressure for cuts in public spending. The Ministry of Reconstruction was a research department with inexperienced staff who encountered jealous rivalry from the Local Government Board, leading to administrative delays. Moreover, the Ministry of Reconstruction did not grasp that effective social reform, especially in an expensive field like housing, involved a transfer of wealth from some members of society to other members. In Abrams' view, any economic explanation for the failure of social reform has to be supplemented by a sociological explanation of disharmony of class interests. Lowe (1978) has expressed caution against concentrating too narrowly on the years 1918–21, and has suggested that the fundamental obstacle to social reform was the continuing unwillingness of government to respond to political and economic change brought about by the war.

He points out that although a National Industrial Conference of employers and unions recommended minimum wage legislation in 1919, the creation of new trade boards was halted in 1921.

While it is clear that the abandonment of social policy objectives involved political judgement, the nature of the economic problems facing government after 1918 should not be overlooked. The study of social policy in isolation can lead to misjudgements. For example, in a standard work on the evolution of the welfare state, Fraser (1984, p. 178) states that public expenditure rose sixfold during the war, and 'the political will generated by the need to raise such enormous sums of money could equally be used to meet the peacetime needs of society.' However, most of the money for the war had been raised by borrowing, not by taxation, and a distinction has to be drawn between borrowing for a temporary emergency (war) and borrowing for continuing purposes (social services). Moreover, the twelvefold increase in the National Debt between 1914 and 1920 greatly increased the purchasing power in the hands of the public since much of the Debt was in the form of short-term Treasury bills which, once they had matured, could form the basis of bank credit expansion (see p. 43). A private spending boom, beginning in 1919, followed by a private investment boom, led to wholesale prices rising more rapidly in 1920 than at any time since early 1917 (Dowie 1975, p. 446). Government and private expenditure were competing for scarce resources, and 'the political will generated' during the war to give government priority was now lacking.

Private demand had been restrained in 1917–18 by government controls, including rationing (see pp. 37–9). After the war the Government willingly gave way to the businessmen's cry of 'back to 1914' and most controls were abandoned in 1919, even though the shortages which had given rise to them had by no means passed (Pigou 1947; Tawney 1943). The 1918 Reform Act was followed, surprisingly some might think, by the election of a Parliament the majority of which was Conservative, described in a well-known phrase as 'a lot of hard-faced men who looked as if they had done very well out of the war' (Keynes 1919, p. 91). Even if the political complexion of Parliament had been otherwise, it is doubtful if controls could have been exercised without the expertise and co-operation of the businessmen who had been recruited into government service during the war. However, once victory over Germany had removed the justification for controls on grounds of national security, businessmen had no interest in maintaining them (Cline 1982).

In the absence of wartime controls, government could respond to the problem of inflation only by trying to restrict its own expenditure to what could be raised by taxation and by engineering a rise in interest rates to discourage private investment. This was the first time that monetary policy had been used primarily to control the domestic economy rather than to maintain the exchange rate, and it is worth noting that in the circumstances even Keynes was in favour of 'dear money' in 1919. He believed that continued inflation would 'strike at the whole basis of contract, of security, and of the capitalist system generally' (Howson 1974, p. 102). High interest rates were, of course, in direct conflict with the needs of the building industry. Again, attempts to balance the budget ran counter to social policy. Even allowing for major reductions in defence expenditure, there remained a prospective budget deficit, and the nation's leading tax expert anticipated that there would be difficulty in raising revenue for the Government's spending programmes unless taxation of business profits, then regarded as a temporary wartime expedient, were made permanent (Stamp 1919). There was an 'economy' campaign in Parliament, backed by informed opinion such as the *Economist* as well as by less informed sections of the press. Attention initially focused on the war-swollen bureaucracy, and the free-spending habits it had developed during the war. As an attempt to deal with this, the Treasury's control over Whitehall was increased, the Permanent Secretary of the Treasury being recognised as head of the civil service. However, Sir Warren Fisher, whom Lloyd George appointed Permanent Secretary of the Treasury in 1919, pointed out that much more could be saved by cutting back on policy than by cutting back on civil service establishments (Burk 1982, pp. 97–102). The Treasury's arguments were accepted, and in December 1919 the Chancellor, Austen Chamberlain, announced to Parliament the Government's intention to cease borrowing, particularly on Ways and Means, and to exercise economy in public expenditure. This was a first step towards a return to the gold standard (see Chapter 4).

Social reform was thus *initially* a victim of the inflationary boom of 1919–20. But, as noted above, the cuts in housing and education *policy* came in 1921/22, by which time the boom had broken, prices were falling (Table 3.3), and unemployment was rising. Moreover, by 1920/21 the Chancellor's budget was in surplus. After 1920 the driving forces behind economy were, firstly, the belief of businessmen that only by reductions in taxation could capital be released for private enterprise and, secondly, the goal of the Treasury and the Bank of England to restore the gold standard to the prewar parity. It was in response to demands in Parliament for economy that the Government appointed a committee of business leaders, under Sir Eric Geddes, to recommend cuts in public expenditure (Cline 1974). The recommendations of the Committee were followed by cuts known to history as the 'Geddes axe', which marked the end of the expansionary phase of postwar social reform.

One element in social service expenditure which continued to expand in the early 1920s despite the Geddes axe was government contributions to unemployment insurance. An Unemployment Insurance Act, greatly extending the scope of the 1911 scheme, had been passed in 1920, but this was much too late to build up a fund capable of meeting, on a sound actuarial basis, the heavy demands made on it almost as soon as the Act was passed. A National Insurance (Munitions Workers) Act had been passed in 1916, to provide a fund for postwar unemployment, but the Act's implementation had met opposition from enough employers and trade unionists to make it a dead letter. Many workers regarded national insurance contributions as an unfair tax, and workers in occupations not previously subject to frequent unemployment believed that better arrangements could be made outside the national scheme (Whiteside 1980). Most industrial workers were brought into the 1920 Act, but a number of other groups including non-manual workers earning more than £250 a year were excluded (see note to Table 4.1 on page 65). Meanwhile, free out-of-work donations had been provided for demobilised servicemen and unemployed munitions workers, the Government fearing to throw such people on to the Poor Law. This set a precedent for state doles for unemployed workers who had not paid enough contributions to qualify for national insurance benefits, and was followed by Treasury loans to the Unemployed Insurance Fund to enable it to make payments in anticipation of unemployed workers' future contributions. Persistent unemployment after 1920 made it seem unlikely that these loans would ever be repaid (see Chapters 4 and 5). State doles, in one form or another, for the unemployed were an enduring feature of social policy from 1919.

The Impact of War on Policy

In assessing the impact of war on policy, it is useful to distinguish between immediate, but temporary, effects (e.g. the imposition of controls, including attempts to restrict the free movement of labour through the system of leaving certificates), and longer-term effects (e.g. partially fulfilled promises of social reform). Again, it is useful to distinguish between direct effects, that is attempts by government to secure resources for the war effort, and indirect effects, that is the adaptation of policy to social and economic change brought about by the war. According to which kind of effect one stresses, it is possible to argue that war had a greater or lesser impact on policy.

Discussion of this topic often takes as a starting point Andrzejewski's concept of the military participation ratio (1954, pp. 33–9; 70–4). According to Andrzejewski, the greater the participation of the lower classes in war, the greater is the tendency to social equality. This concept was taken up by Titmuss (1958), when he developed his theory that the mass mobilisation of modern wars concentrated the collective mind of the state on the needs of the people since the quality of recruits was of national importance. This implied a harmony of class interests – a notion which Abrams (1963) attacked when he drew attention to the shortcomings of social reform in 1918–20. Indeed, so far as the First World War is concerned, one can say that while there was mass mobilisation of men and industrial resources, concern about the needs of the people did not prevent the restoration of economic orthodoxy at the expense of social reform programmes after the war. Moreover, in pressing for the housing programme in 1919, Lloyd George spoke of the need to combat Bolshevism as well as the need to improve public health. Harmony of class interests was not always an obvious feature of society either during or after the war. Neither Titmuss nor Abrams attempted to quantify social reform in terms of public finance. The economists Peacock and Wiseman (1967, p. 91), however, have produced figures for what they call the displacement effect of war on public expenditure. They calculate that whereas before 1914 expenditure by central and local government on social services amounted to not much more than 4 per cent of gross national product, this proportion never fell below 8 per cent in the interwar years. War makes higher levels of taxation politically acceptable. Whereas the 'People's Budget' of 1909 had created a constitutional crisis, the war years saw a more than fivefold increase in the normal rate of income tax and a ninefold increase in the maximum rate of supertax (Mallet and George 1929).

Turning to economic policy, most wartime measures were temporary, even if links between Whitehall and industry were strengthened. The central question of a general protective tariff was not resolved until the economic crisis of 1931. The McKenna Duties of 1915 were retained, enabling the motor industry to expand with the domestic market. Again, for reasons of national security, various industries, such as optical instruments, wireless valves and certain chemicals, were protected against renewed foreign competition by the Safeguarding of Industries Act of 1921. In the words of the Act, 'no ordinary economic rules' applied to these 'key industries'. On the other hand, no protection was afforded to basic industries like steel, or to agriculture; indeed, one of the Government's economy measures in 1921 was the ending of the subsidies to maintain guaranteed minimum prices for corn. The greatest impact of war on economic policy was the indirect one of disruption of the pre-1914 international economy. British export industries did not prosper in the post-1918 world of increased foreign competition and tariffs. Many markets lost during the war were not recovered, and Britain's balance of payments was thereby weakened. The sale of overseas assets during the war, and the need to repay the £1,150 million War Debt to the United States, added to this weakness. Britain's strength as an international creditor had gone (Milward 1970, pp. 45–6), and this was to undermine the policy of returning to the gold standard.

References

Abrams, P. (1963) 'The failure of social reform: 1918–20', *Past and Present*, no. 24, pp. 43–64.

Andrews, L. (1976) *The Education Act, 1918*, Routledge and Kegan Paul.

Andrzejewski, S. (1954) *Military Organisation and Society*, Routledge and Kegan Paul.

Ashworth, W. (1960) *An Economic History of England 1870–1939*, Methuen.
Bowley, M. (1945) *Housing and the State 1919–1944*, George Allen and Unwin.
Burk, K. (1979) 'J.M. Keynes and the exchange rate crisis of July 1917', *Economic History Review*, 2nd series, vol. 32, pp. 405–16.
Burk, K. (1982) 'The Treasury: from impotence to power', in her book, *War and the State. The Transformation of British Government, 1914–1919*, George Allen and Unwin.
Cline, P. (1974) 'Eric Geddes and the "experiment" with businessmen in government, 1915–22', in K. Brown (ed.), *Essays in Anti-Labour History*, Macmillan.
Cline, P. (1982) 'Winding down the war economy: British plans for peace-time recovery, 1916–19', in K. Burk (ed.), *War and the State*, George Allen and Unwin.
Dowie, J. (1975) '1919–20 is in need of attention', *Economic History Review*, 2nd series, vol. 28, pp. 429–50.
Englander, D. (1983) *Landlord and Tenant in Urban Britain 1838–1918*, Oxford University Press.
Feinstein, C. (1972) *National Income, Expenditure and Output of the United Kingdom, 1855–1965*, Cambridge University Press.
Fraser, D. (1984) *The Evolution of the British Welfare State*, Macmillan.
French, D. (1982a) *British Economic and Strategic Planning 1905–1915*, George Allen and Unwin.
French, D. (1982b) 'The rise and fall of "business as usual"', in K. Burk (ed.), *War and the State*, George Allen and Unwin.
Harris, J. (1982) 'Bureaucrats and businessmen in British Food Control, 1916–19', in K. Burk (ed.), *War and the State*, George Allen and Unwin.
Hinton, J. (1973) *The First Shop Stewards' Movement*, George Allen and Unwin.
Howson, S. (1974) 'The origins of dear money, 1919–20', *Economic History Review*, 2nd series, vol. 27, pp. 88–107.
Keynes, J.M. (1919) *The Economic Consequences of the Peace*, reprinted in *Collected Writings of John Maynard Keynes*, vol. 2 (1971), Macmillan.
Lovell, J. (1977) *British Trade Unions, 1875–1933*, Macmillan.
Lowe, R. (1978) 'The erosion of state intervention in Britain, 1917–24', *Economic History Review*, 2nd series, vol. 31, pp. 270–86.
Lowe, R. (1982) 'The Ministry of Labour, 1916–19: a still, small voice?', in K. Burk (ed.), *War and the State*, George Allen and Unwin.
Macdonald, D.F. (1960) *The State and the Trade Unions*, Macmillan, ch. 7.
MacLeod, R. and K. (1975) 'War and economic development: government and the optical industry in Britain, 1914–18', in J. Winter (ed.), *War and Economic Development*, Cambridge University Press.
Mallet, B. and George, C. (1929) *British Budgets, Second Series, 1913/14 to 1920/21*; (1933) *Third Series, 1921/22–1932/33*, Macmillan.
Marriner, S. (1976) 'Cash and concrete: liquidity problems in the mass production of "Homes for Heroes"', *Business History*, vol. 18, pp. 152–89.
Melling, J. (1983) *Rent Strikes*, Polygon.

Milward, A. (1970) *The Economic Effects of the Two World Wars on Britain*, Macmillan.
Morgan, E. (1952) *Studies in British Financial Policy, 1914–25*, Macmillan.
Morgan, K. (1979) *Consensus and Disunity: The Lloyd George Coalition Government 1918–1922*, Oxford University Press.
Orbach, L. (1977) *Homes for Heroes: A Study of the Evolution of British Public Housing, 1915–1921*, Seely, Service.
Peacock, A. and Wiseman, J. (1967) *The Growth of Public Expenditure in the United Kingdom*, George Allen and Unwin.
Pigou, A.C. (1947) *Aspects of British Economic History 1918–25*, Macmillan.
Reader, W. (1970) *Imperial Chemical Industries: a History*, vol. 1, Oxford University Press.
Sayers, R.S. (1938) *Modern Banking*, Oxford University Press.
Stamp, J. (1919) 'The special taxation of business profits', *Economic Journal*, vol. 29, pp. 407–27.
Stamp, J. (1932) *Taxation During the War*, Oxford University Press.
Swenarton, M. (1981) *Homes Fit for Heroes: The Politics and Architecture of Early State Housing in Britain*, Heinemann.
Tawney, R.H. (1943) 'The abolition of economic controls, 1918–21', *Economic History Review*, vol. 13 pp. 1–30.
Thane, P. (1982) *Foundations of the Welfare State*, Longman.
Titmuss, R. (1958 and 1976) *Essays on 'the Welfare State'*, George Allen and Unwin.
Trebilcock, C. (1975) 'War and the failure of industrial mobilisation: 1899 and 1914', in J. Winter (ed.), *War and Economic Development*, Cambridge University Press.
Whiteside, N. (1980) 'Welfare legislation and the unions during the First World War', *Historical Journal*, vol. 23, pp. 857–74.
Wilding, P. (1972) 'Towards Exchequer subsidies for housing 1906–1914', *Social and Economic Administration*, vol. 6, pp. 3–18.
Wilding, P. (1973) 'The Housing and Town Planning Act 1919 – a study in the making of social policy', *Journal of Social Policy*, vol. 2, pp. 317–34.
Wrigley, C. (1976) *David Lloyd George and the British Labour Movement*, Harvester Press.
Wrigley, C. (1982) 'The Ministry of Munitions: an innovating department', in K. Burk (ed.), *War and the State*, George Allen and Unwin.

4

The Return to the Gold Standard

There is general agreement among economic historians that the decision in 1925 to return to the gold standard at the pre-1914 parity of $4.86 resulted in sterling being overvalued. The figure usually quoted is Keynes's estimate, based on a comparison of retail prices, that sterling was overvalued by about 10 per cent against the dollar. However, the best overall measure of overvaluation is not any one bilateral exchange rate but the effective exchange rate, that is the average rate measured against a 'basket' of currencies selected and weighted according to their importance in world trade. On this basis Redmond (1984) has calculated that the pound was overvalued by 20–25 per cent in 1925 and, although the degree of overvaluation declined thereafter, it remained over 10 per cent in 1930. The deflation necessary to raise sterling from $3.40 in 1920 to $4.86 in 1925, the effects of the higher exchange rate on British export prices, and the impact on investment of higher-than-normal interest rates necessary to defend the gold standard after 1925, might all have been expected to have increased unemployment. We have seen, however, that in 1919, when the first steps to a return to the gold standard were taken, the chief challenges facing the Treasury were inflation and the control of public expenditure, and it can be argued that it was these problems, rather than employment considerations, which determined policy. Again, it was known that a return to a fixed rate of $4.86 required downward flexibility of wages, and it is worth examining the interaction of monetary policy, employers' attempts to reduce wage costs, and trade-union resistance to wage cuts. Was it a coincidence that the General Strike of 1926 occurred the year after the return to the gold standard? Finally, whatever the economic consequences, did the gold standard policy provide the Treasury with an effective means of curbing public expenditure? A broader question is raised by the last point. To what extent can economic theory, whether the 'orthodoxy' of the 1920s or any other, act as a means of restricting political responsibility for the problems of society?

The Decision to Return to the Gold Standard

The return to the gold standard at the prewar parity was announced by the Chancellor of the Exchequer, Churchill, in April 1925. Keynes set the tone of much subsequent discussion when he wrote in his pamphlet, *The Economic Consequences of Mr. Churchill* (1925, p. 212f), that the Chancellor had been 'deafened by the clamorous voices of conventional finance' and, being incompetent to judge matters for himself, had been 'gravely misled by his experts'. In particular, Churchill's advisers had calculated, on the basis of a comparison of movements in British and American wholesale prices since 1914, that deflation to reduce British prices by 2 or 3 per cent would be sufficient to raise sterling to $4.86. Keynes reckoned that since the index of wholesale prices included a disproportionate element of import prices, the true internal price adjustment on the basis of retail prices would be 10 or 12 per cent. This view of Churchill's decision as being the product of miscalculation and of submission to the dictates of classical economics has been carefully documented by Moggridge (1972, pp. 71, 142). On the other hand, Pollard (1970, pp. 9–16, 22–5) attributed the decision to the self-interest of City financiers, who dominated the Bank of England. In 1924–25, 15 of the 26 members of the Bank's Court were connected with overseas banking; 5 were connected with shipping and insurance; and only 2 with industry. In Pollard's view, such a body could be expected to favour a return to gold on terms which would raise the prestige of the City in world financial circles, regardless of intellectual arguments about the effects of an overvalued exchange rate on industry.

While incompetence, miscalculation and self-interest were

doubtless all present in decision making in 1924–25, it is not clear why Treasury officials should have been beholden to the interests of City financiers. Still less is this likely of the Labour Chancellor of the Exchequer, Philip Snowden, who adopted and supported their policy during and after his tenure of office in 1924 (Moggridge 1972, pp. 37 and 74). In what follows it is argued that the Treasury and the Bank of England each had its own reasons for favouring a return to the gold standard and that, moreover, Treasury officials had their own views about the safeguarding of private capital, which inclined them to favour a return at $4.86. There were also international aspects which mattered more to those taking the decision than to their critics.

During the war the Bank had lost control both of domestic interest rates and of exchange-rate policy. From 1915 Treasury bills had been available on tap instead of the normal practice of being issued by weekly tender. As a result, if the Bank tried to make effective a Bank Rate out of line with Treasury bill tap rate, banks would not renew their holdings of Treasury bills, forcing the Government to borrow from the Bank on Ways and Means, and thus defeat any attempt at credit restriction. It was for this reason that the Bank and the Treasury tried to reduce the banks' holdings of Treasury bills, funding the floating debt and other short-term debt at the earliest possible date by offering higher interest for longer-dated bonds (Howson 1975, pp. 14–29). As for the exchange rate, by 1917 this was dependent on American loans, which were handled by representatives of the Treasury, and the Treasury also took powers to impose rudimentary foreign exchange controls (Burk 1982, pp. 88–9, 93–6). The Bank's chance to make out a case for the restoration of its full powers came in 1918 when the Treasury and the Ministry of Reconstruction set up a 'Committee on Currency and Foreign Exchanges after the War', with the retiring Governor of the Bank, Lord Cunliffe, as Chairman, to 'report upon the steps required to bring about the restoration of normal conditions in due course'. In its first interim report (Cd. 9182) the same year, the Cunliffe Committee expressed its belief that before the war the gold standard had prevented exchange-rate fluctuations and had operated automatically 'to check undue expansion of credit.' The Committee spelt out the conditions for an effective gold standard: firstly, the ending of government borrowing as soon as possible, with a reduction in the National Debt, especially Treasury bills;

secondly, Bank Rate should be made effective, so that the Bank could check a foreign drain of gold or a 'speculative expansion of credit'; and, thirdly, there should once more be a legal limit to the issue of paper money unbacked by gold (the fiduciary issue).

The Bank's institutional interest in re-establishing its control over monetary policy is obvious. For a Treasury official surveying the inflationary domestic credit expansion and the increasing indebtedness to America resulting from government expenditure in 1918, the *means* to restoring the gold standard must have been no less attractive than the end itself. Lloyd George's unwillingness to follow, or even to understand, official advice on public finance must have given the Treasury and the Bank a common interest in removing monetary policy from the hands of politicians. This distrust of politicians must have been reinforced by developments abroad in the early 1920s. There was inflation in France, and hyperinflation in Germany, when governments, unlike the British Government, failed to balance budgets, and trade was impeded by fluctuating exchange rates. At the international monetary conference at Genoa in 1922 the leading capitalist states indicated their intention to return to gold when possible, although unfortunately, given the different circumstances of each state, there could be no agreement as to timing or relative parities. Quite apart from recreating monetary stability in Europe, there was also the problem of the financial unity of the British Empire. The dominions which linked their currencies to sterling – Australia, New Zealand and South Africa – were pressing hard for a restoration of the gold standard by 1924 (Pressnell 1978). So too was Benjamin Strong, Governor of the Federal Reserve Bank of New York, whose co-operation was important in efforts to stabilise the international monetary system (Moggridge 1972, pp. 51–60).

For the Bank of England, the stability of exchange rates based on gold would help to revive international trade and investment. This in turn ought, other things being equal, to help the business of the City of London, but there seems to have been little or no consideration given to the adverse effects of an overvalued exchange rate on British exports and, therefore, on Britain's capacity to invest overseas. Indeed, it does not seem to have occurred to the Cunliffe Committee that Britain should return to the gold standard at anything but the prewar parity (Moggridge 1972, p. 18). In this matter the prestige of sterling and of the City seem to have been decisive.

For the state there was a temptation to accept a decline in the purchasing power of the currency, for this would reduce the burden of the war-swollen National Debt, annual charges on which were a larger element in the chancellor's budget than defence or social services in the 1920s. The Treasury set its face firmly against this temptation. Sir John Bradbury, one of the officials who took a leading role in the decision to return to gold, thought, even in 1931, that monetary management which did not maintain the value of creditors' money would lead to an unwillingness to forego consumption and, therefore, would diminish savings which, according to pre-Keynesian economic theory, would in turn diminish funds available for investment (Cmd. 3897, pp. 266f).

Ministers, however, had to face the political implications of a return to gold. Indeed, one of the reasons why the Cabinet had hesitated between March and December 1919 before accepting the Cunliffe Committee's recommendations had been fear of unemployment and social unrest. There was no doubt from the outset that what was involved was deflation and wage cuts. Even after the Cabinet had been won over, some Treasury officials advised caution (Howson 1975, pp. 11, 19, 21–2). Much would depend on the pace of events, and the Cunliffe Committee itself had expected that the transition period required for a complete return to pre-1914 conditions would be ten years. In fact the pace of events in the three years from December 1919 suggests that politicians quickly overcame their fear of social unrest. Bank Rate was raised and kept at 6 per cent or above for 18 months at a time when prices were falling, and the money supply, which had been growing rapidly in 1919, fell in 1921 and 1922. Central government itself cut expenditure and ran a series of budget surpluses. The postwar boom was in any case breaking by 1920, beginning with a fall in demand for consumer goods at the beginning of the year, followed by demand for exports. Dear money came at a time when businessmen's optimism was giving way to pessimism, and reinforced the latter (Howson 1975, pp. 10, 17–29). Unemployment rose to a then record level of an average of 12.2 per cent of the total workforce and stayed high thereafter (Table 4.1).

On the other hand, deflation seemed to be having the intended effect: the official wholesale price index fell by about half between 1920 and 1922 (Mitchell and Deane 1962, p. 477); retail prices fell by an average of 27 per cent, and average money wage rates by 23 per

Table 4.1 Unemployment, 1920–39

	(1) *Annual average percentage of insured workers unemployed*	*(2)* *Annual average percentage of total workforce unemployed*
1920	3.9	—
1921	16.9	12.2
1922	14.3	10.8
1923	11.7	8.9
1924	10.3	7.9
1925	11.3	8.6
1926	12.5	9.6
1927	9.7	7.4
1928	10.8	8.2
1929	10.4	8.0
1930	16.1	12.3
1931	21.3	16.4
1932	22.1	17.0
1933	19.9	15.4
1934	16.7	12.9
1935	15.5	12.0
1936	13.1	10.2
1937	10.8	8.5
1938	12.9	10.1
1939	10.5	—

Sources: Column 1: Department of Employment and Productivity (1971), Table 160. Column 2: Feinstein (1972), Table 58.

Note on Interwar Unemployment Statistics

During these years the official statistics for unemployment were those shown in column 1. The National Insurance Act of 1920 covered all people over 16 except those in agriculture or domestic service, established civil servants and the police, railway officials, and non-manual workers earning more than £250 a year. Workers over 64 were excluded in 1927.

A major inconsistency in the series arises from the 'genuinely seeking work' condition for unemployment benefit. This was introduced in 1921 for workers who would normally have been in insured work, but who had been unable to pay contributions. The Labour Government removed the 'genuinely seeking work' condition in 1930, and thus certainly increased the numbers of people claiming benefit, particularly married women. The condition was restored in 1931, but the figures for 1930 and 1931 should be regarded as somewhat higher than they would have been had it been in force throughout these years (by how much it is impossible to say).

Column 2 was derived by Feinstein from the 1931 Census of Population data on the total workforce, including those categories excluded from the National Insurance scheme. This has the effect of lowering the percentage figures, since the excluded groups were less subject to unemployment than the people included in the scheme. Feinstein's figures probably overstate somewhat the level of unemployment in the total workforce in the 1920s and later 1930s, since his adjustments to the official figures are based on a year when the relative differentials between unemployment for groups outside the National Insurance scheme and for those inside the scheme may have been unusually low.

Finally, it should be noted that while annual average percentages are a convenient measure of unemployment over time, they do not tell us how many people were unemployed in a given year. The size of the workforce varies over time, according to the size of the population, its composition by age and sex, and the extent to which women and juveniles are available for paid employment. Moreover, annual average figures, such as those for 1932 (17.0 per cent, or 3,400,000 people) do not record how widely unemployment was experienced, since many people were unemployed for short periods.

For further discussion of unemployment statistics see Booth and Glynn (1975), Garside (1980) and Swann and Turnbull (1975).

cent (Feinstein 1972, Table 65). By the end of 1922 sterling stood at \$4.63½ compared with \$3.40 in February 1920. Small wonder Bank and Treasury officials felt that when the time was appropriate, the extra adjustment to reach \$4.86 could be made without much extra cost. In 1925 a British Treasury committee recommended that a free gold market should be restored in London, despite evidence from representatives of the Federation of British Industries that an early return would be premature. Keynes and McKenna, the former Liberal Chancellor, gave evidence in favour of a managed currency to stabilise domestic prices, but this was rejected, apparently on grounds of political impracticality. The Conservative victory in the 1924 election encouraged speculation in favour of sterling, which rose to \$4.79, and the committee estimated that a reduction in British prices of 6 per cent would enable a rate of \$4.86 to be sustained.

The prospect of further deflation troubled the incoming Chancellor, Churchill, who, however, admitted to having a 'limited comprehension of these extremely technical matters'. From

Churchill's point of view, the problem was whether to renew legislation (due to expire in 1925) under which the export of gold was controlled, or to go back to the gold standard. Churchill knew that Sir Otto Niemeyer, his principal Treasury adviser on financial questions, would provide strong arguments to support a return to gold, whereas a failure to return would leave Churchill exposed to criticisms in Parliament from City representatives, criticisms which he would not be competent to answer. Niemeyer assured him that the gold standard would ultimately promote employment by reviving international trade, and Churchill gave his assent to a return at $4.86 (Moggridge 1972, ch. 3).

This decision completed the process of removing monetary policy from the hands of politicians. Austen Chamberlain, while Chancellor, had apparently agreed by 1921 to a return to the pre-1914 practice whereby officially the Chancellor should not have advance notice, or not more than an hour's notice, of a public announcement of a change in Bank Rate. In practice regular contacts between the Bank and the Treasury ensured that the latter knew what was going on (Sayers 1976, vol. 1, p. 119; Clay 1957, p. 129). Even so, under the gold standard it was possible for Churchill to argue, as he did in 1929, that the Government had no responsibility for the movement of Bank Rate, and that he did not control the policy of the Bank. Subsequently his Labour successor, Snowden, defended the autonomy of the Bank at the 1930 Labour Party Conference (Tomlinson 1981, p. 98; Winch 1969, pp. 92f). The gold standard was not really an automatic mechanism since it required monetary management both to return to, and to maintain, it. Nevertheless, it suited chancellors no less than bankers to uphold the principle that such management should be outside party politics.

Wage Cuts and the General Strike

The intended effect of raising Bank Rate was to reduce credit, and thereby demand and employment, leading to a reduction in prices, wages and costs. But before 1914 it had very seldom been necessary to force a general reduction in money wages, and the degree of adjustment necessary had never been so great as that attempted in the gold standard policy after 1919. Average money wages and retail prices fell by about 30 per cent between 1920 and 1923 (Feinstein

1972, Table 65), a remarkable degree of flexibility. Initially there was a good deal of resistance to wage cuts, but the number of working days lost through industrial stoppages fell sharply from 1921 (Table 4.2). Both the monetary authorities and their critics seem to have expected that deflation would continue to cut costs, especially wages, after 1925, so as to complete the adjustment to the new exchange rate. Keynes (1925, pp. 220–4) was complaining about the injustice, not the practicality, of the policy when he pointed out that export industries such as coal would be hardest hit since the higher exchange rate immediately raised their costs relative to competitors, whereas trades catering for the domestic market would be affected only indirectly. Table 4.3 shows that the downward pressure on wages between 1920 and 1925 had indeed been uneven, with those trades which traditionally had a high proportion of exports to output (coal, cotton, iron and steel and shipbuilding) experiencing the greatest cuts in money wage rates. This might have been expected to divide the trade-union movement, but in fact the troubles of the

Table 4.2 Industrial Relations

	Total union membership (000s)	*Working days lost through industrial stoppages (000s)*
1920	8,348	26,568
1921	6,633	85,872
1922	5,625	19,850
1923	5,429	10,672
1924	5,544	8,424
1925	5,506	7,925
1926	5,219	162,233
1927	4,919	1,174
1928	4,806	1,388
1929	4,858	8,287
1930	4,842	4,399

Source: Department of Employment and Productivity (1971).

Table 4.3 Indices of Weekly Money Wage Rates by Industry (1924 = 100)

	Coal	*Cotton*	*Iron and steel*	*Shipbuilding and repairing*	*Engineering*	*Railways*	*Building*
1920	187	162	202.5	175	152	127.5	145.5
1925	98.5	100	99	106	101	100.5	103
1929	87	98.5	91.5	108	104	96	101

Source: Mitchell and Deane (1962), p. 351.

miners aroused a remarkable degree of solidarity. The story of the General Strike of 1926, and of its antecedents, has often been told (e.g. Morris 1976; Phillips 1976) and need only be summarised here. The main questions raised are: why was there widespread (although by no means unlimited) support for the miners, and what were the consequences of resistance to wage cuts?

Relations between the miners and the mine owners had long been turbulent, and in 1919 the Miners Federation had demanded nationalisation of the industry. A Coal Industry Commission, representing both owners and miners, under the Chairmanship of Sir John Sankey, a judge, had reported on the industry, with Sankey and the miners' representatives recommending state ownership. Lloyd George's Coalition Government had rejected this advice, and in 1921 the state's wartime controls over the mines were removed, and the mines returned to their owners, as soon as the state found itself having to subsidise losses in the slump. The owners at once demanded wage cuts, and the prospect of a general strike loomed, for the miners had formed a 'Triple Alliance' with the Transport Workers Federation and the National Union of Railwaymen, whereby each union was to give the others mutual support. In the event, J.H. Thomas, the railwaymen's leader, withheld support, on the grounds that his members' funds should not be sacrificed if the miners' leaders were to be intransigent. This event – known in labour history as 'Black Friday' – led to victory for the owners. Events turned out rather differently in 1925, when the owners again demanded wage cuts and suggested longer hours. Under a new standing order, the General Council of the TUC was entitled to intervene in negotiations if large numbers of workers were involved in a dispute, and also to organise moral and material support if a strike occurred. The General Council gave the miners its support and, rather than face a general strike, the Conservative Government of Stanley Baldwin set up a Royal Commission into the industry, meanwhile offering a subsidy (which it had previously refused) to maintain existing wages and hours. This event was hailed by the Left as 'Red Friday'.

The Royal Commission, chaired by Sir Herbert Samuel, a Liberal politician, recommended in 1926 that mining should be reorganised under private ownership to make it more efficient. The Report also said that the government subsidy should end, and never be repeated, which meant that the only way the industry could make ends meet while it was being reorganised was to cut its wage bill. The miners' leaders, however, refused to accept lower wages or longer hours, while the owners showed little sign of seriously considering reorganisation. The General Council negotiated directly, on the miners' behalf, with Cabinet ministers, but as preparations for a general strike went ahead the Government withdrew from the talks, refusing to negotiate under duress. In the General Strike which followed in May 1926 almost every union supported the miners, and some two million workers were called out. After nine days, however, the General Council ended the strike without securing any guarantees for the miners, or, indeed, for the other strikers, against wage cuts or victimisation. The miners were left to fight on alone for another seven months before they gave in to the owners' demands.

It is sometimes said that the Government bought peace with a subsidy in 1925 so as to be better prepared to crush a general strike the following year. Research into the Government's records, however, has shown that the Government was probably almost as ready for a strike in 1925 as in 1926. Baldwin probably genuinely hoped for a compromise, but could not press the mine owners very far because of feeling in the Conservative Party (Mason 1969). Why was a subsidy not continued? A long-term subsidy for a staple industry was anathema to a Conservative government for, once the principle of subsidies was conceded, all industries would want them, and the market economy, and in particular the willingness of capitalists to take risks, would be impaired. This was probably the key issue, although it was kept in the background and others were put to the fore. The Government claimed that the trade unions were attempting to usurp the prerogative of Parliament, an issue which could rally more volunteers to man transport and other services than a call to preserve the market economy would have done.

The strike does seem to have affected Baldwin's attitude to wage cuts. He had been reported before the strike as saying that 'all the workers in this country have got to face a reduction of wages.' After the strike he said he would 'not countenance any attack on the part of employers to use this present occasion for trying in any way to get reductions in wages' (Clegg 1954, p. 22). Apparently other means of reducing industrial costs would have to be found. The Trade Disputes Act of 1927 prohibited sympathetic strikes and attempted to restrict unions' political funds by requiring members to contract in, instead of out as hitherto. The Act did not restrict unions' activities in their own industries, however, and following a brief industrial peace as unions' strike funds recovered, the number of working days lost through industrial stoppages rose again by 1929 to the 1924 level (Table 4.2). Average money wage rates in 1929 stood at the level of 1923, although retail prices had fallen by about 6 per cent.

Stable money wages at a time when prices were falling implied higher real wages, and this rise in the price of labour took place despite a large increase in the supply of labour. As a result of high Edwardian birth-rates, there were 430,000 more insurable workers in 1929 than in 1924 (Mitchell and Deane 1962, pp. 62f). Pollard (1970, p. 151) has suggested that money wage stability was a result of a bargain between unions and employers whereby the former undertook not to obstruct industry's attempts to reduce wage costs by replacing workers with capital while employers undertook not to cut wages. As evidence of collaboration, Pollard points to the Mond–Turner conferences of 1928, in which a group of employers, led by Sir Alfred Mond of ICI, and representatives of the General Council of the TUC, led by its Chairman Ben Turner, attempted to establish a permanent National Industrial Council. This body would have represented both sides of industry and would have advised the Government on economic policy, while also acting as a conciliation agency in industrial disputes. In the event nothing concrete came of the talks, which were never officially supported by any employers' organisation, but the talks symbolised the TUC's position as a mediator between labour and capital as well as between labour and government (Dintenfass 1984).

The TUC certainly remained opposed to money wage cuts, and Keynesian theory would suggest that they were right, from the point of view of aggregate demand. Wages were too high in the 1920s in the sense that British industry's competitiveness in world export markets was reduced (given the gold standard policy). On the other hand, there was no prospect of export-led growth. Britain's traditional exports were in relatively stagnant sectors of international trade. Coal faced increasing competition from oil, and all British exports were suffering from a sudden increase in foreign competition, tariffs and import substitution as a result of an increase in world manufacturing capacity during the First World War. Moreover, Britain was more reliant than other industrial countries on markets, such as the Empire or South America, where demand was determined by income from primary products. Given stagnant or falling prices for primary products in the 1920s, such markets were hardly buoyant. No doubt lower wage costs might have encouraged newer industries, such as motor vehicles or electrical goods, to expand exports, but a general reduction in wages would have reduced domestic demand upon which these consumer industries chiefly depended. What one can say is that money wage rigidity favoured the South of the country, where the new consumer industries were concentrated, and exacerbated the problems of the North and West (where export industries were concentrated).

It should not be thought that the balance of trade was the only, or even the principal, problem encountered in maintaining the gold standard. Indeed, it can be argued that the difficulty Britain encountered with its balance of payments was due less to the difference between British and American prices than to the deterioration in London's international position as a financial centre. London's short-term credit balance had been wiped out by the First World War, and London's position as leading financial centre had been altered permanently by New York's emergence as a centre of international lending during the war, a position buttressed thereafter by America's strongly favourable balance of payments. Moreover, whereas in 1914 short-term assets held by foreigners in London had been approximately matched by short-term debts of foreigners to London, by the 1920s the ratio of the former to the latter was about 2:1. Thus, even though the Bank of England held larger gold reserves than before 1914, sterling was always vulnerable to a movement of funds from London if interest rates were higher elsewhere or if fundholders felt that sterling's exchange rate would fall (Morgan 1952, pp. 342f, 367). Since allowing gold to be shipped in any quantity would reduce confidence in sterling, the only defence of the exchange rate available to the Bank, apart from limited intervention with unpublished holdings of foreign exchange or with loans from other central banks, was to raise interest rates in London. Moreover, although Britain had a balance of payments surplus on current account throughout the 1920s (except 1926), these surpluses were insufficient to finance the amount of overseas lending to which London had become accustomed before 1914. This was a source of concern not only in the City but also to those industrialists who believed that overseas lending created jobs in British export industries. The loss of competitiveness by British industry in fact made it unlikely that overseas lending would have such an effect.

Domestic monetary policy had a generally restrictive effect in most years in the 1920s (Howson 1975). While Bank Rate of $4\frac{1}{2}$ to $5\frac{1}{2}$ per cent in 1925–29 does not seem high today, it must be remembered that prices were falling then, so that interest rates were very much higher in real terms. Even firms capable of self-financing new fixed assets might prefer to hold interest-bearing securities if the return expected from physical capital were less than the interest to be earned on securities, given the expected effect of falling prices on profits. This was least likely to be the case when investment was in new products (e.g. cars or radios) or techniques (such as a shift to assembly-line production), where there was a prospect of a high rate of return on physical capital. The industries which were most affected by high interest rates were the same industries as those which suffered most from an overvalued exchange rate: coal, cotton, iron and steel, and shipbuilding. Many firms in these industries had been over-optimistic in the boom of 1919–20, and had borrowed heavily from banks to invest in new capacity which, in the event, proved to be greater than demand for their products justified. High interest rates made it difficult for these firms to reduce their overdrafts, and banks which had over-extended themselves in lending to such firms found themselves in difficulty. The Bank of England found itself involved in major schemes to rationalise the capacity of firms in cotton, shipbuilding and heavy engineering, to restore profitability and to safeguard the stability of the banking system (Sayers 1976, Vol. 1, pp. 314–27).

Employment Policy in the 1920s

There were a number of possible ways in which to raise the level of private investment in Britain. For example, the introduction of tariffs would have reserved a larger share of the British market for British firms and might have induced foreign firms to invest in Britain. Tariffs might also have encouraged retaliation, worsening the plight of Britain's export industries. Moreover, a general tariff, unlike income tax, would have raised revenue according to individuals' consumption rather than according to their means. Election results suggested widespread support for free trade, the policy of the Liberal and Labour parties. The Conservative Party did badly in general elections when it advocated tariffs, as in 1906 and 1923, but well when it pledged itself not to change the fiscal system, as in 1922 and 1924. Keynes himself was a free trader in the 1920s. Another possible means to encourage private investment was to reduce risk. Under the Trade Facilities Act of 1921 the state guaranteed loans raised by many firms in the iron and steel, engineering, electrical and building industries, for development schemes which would reduce unemployment. The Treasury never liked the state taking over the business of the banks (since it believed that the state would be left with all the bad risks), and loan guarantees were ended in 1926.

Industry could also be helped by reducing the burden of local rates. Churchill saw this as a means of offsetting the effects on exports of the higher exchange rate after 1925. Rates for Poor Law relief were greatest in areas where the export industries were concentrated, and his scheme for 'derating' industry was that firms should be relieved of three quarters of their rates, and local authorities should be recompensed by central government grants. Derating was first discussed in Cabinet in 1926, but did not become effective until the Local Government Act of 1929 (Gilbert 1970, pp. 225–8). In the view of Treasury officials, the only way Britain could be competitive on international markets, while having higher real wages than its rivals, was through more efficient business management. Business should put its own house in order, rationalising surplus capacity, but there should be no financial aid from the state, for this would only delay the unpleasant process of re-adapting to changed market conditions since 1914.

If private investment could not, or would not, provide for all the labour on offer, there was the alternative of public works. As noted in Chapter 2, temporary employment on road making, forestry and so on had been mooted before 1914 as a means of taking up the slack in the labour market in a recession. At the end of 1920 Lloyd George's Coalition Government set up an Unemployment Grants Committee which was to allocate central government funds to local authorities to encourage them to embark on public works schemes. Until the mid-1920s it was possible to regard widespread unemployment as a temporary phenomenon arising out of disruption in international markets, and correspondingly it was possible to regard increased public expenditure on roads or other social capital as a temporary measure. By 1925 it was harder to take this view, and an unusually high level of public works expenditure could be represented as stealing work from the future, so that central government funds for the purpose were reduced (Hancock 1962).

Howson (1981, pp. 279–81) has calculated the maximum possible effect of public works on employment in the 1920s. She assumed that each £1 million of government expenditure would provide 2,500 man-years of direct primary employment, plus an equal amount of indirect primary employment on transport and materials. She further assumed that increased expenditure by workers thus brought into employment would raise aggregate demand to the extent of an employment multiplier of between 1.5 and 2.0. This means, for example, that if the public works planned between December 1920 and March 1922 had been carried out, 200,500 workers would have been employed either directly or on transport and materials, and a further secondary employment of between 100,250 and 200,500 would have been created through increased aggregate demand. However, as she points out, it would have taken several years for the multiplier effect to come through, and a more realistic multiplier relating primary to total employment would be unity in the short run, and 1.5 in the long run (Thomas 1981, pp. 345–6). On this basis it would seem that public works schemes, as planned, would have had little impact on the average unemployment level of about 2 million in 1921–22, even if these schemes had not been cut down by the Geddes 'axe'. By 1928/29 central government loans and grants for employment creation were less than half the 1921/22 level (Table 4.4).

The Treasury was a consistent opponent of all special

Table 4.4 Central Government Expenditure after the Geddes 'Axe' (£m.)

	1921/22	*1922/23*	*1923/24*	*1924/25*	*1925/26*	*1926/27*	*1927/28*	*1928/29*	*1929/30*
Education	53.7	47.4	46.3	46.6	47.1	48.4	48.7	47.8	48.2
Health insurance	9.2	5.8	6.1	7.1	6.9	6.4	4.0	4.0	4.0
Health services	4.4	3.6	3.2	3.2	3.5	3.7	4.1	4.0	4.2
Housing	9.1	8.0	8.3	9.1	9.1	10.0	11.1	12.1	12.8
Pensions:									
Old age (non-contributory)	22.0	22.4	23.2	24.9	27.0	30.0	32.8	34.1	34.9
War pensions	95.8	80.6	72.6	69.9	67.3	63.6	60.2	57.1	54.5
Widows and old age (contributory)	—	—	—	—	—	4.0	4.0	4.0	4.0
Unemployment									
Insurance	7.8	12.0	12.8	13.1	13.5	10.8	12.0	11.8	19.4
Loans and grants for public works	3.8	2.3	3.0	3.5	3.6	6.1	2.0	1.8	1.9
Total for social policy	205.8	182.1	175.5	177.4	178.0	183.0	178.9	176.7	183.9
Defence	189.4	111.0	105.8	114.7	119.4	116.7	117.4	113.5	113.0
National Debt (fixed charges, interest and sinking funds)	332.3	324.0	347.3	357.2	358.2	378.6	378.8	369.0	355.0

Source: Mallet and George (1933), Tables I–III.

employment-creating schemes, partly because they conflicted with its goal of balancing the chancellor's budget but also because of a belief that government expenditure, even if financed by loans, would reduce the funds available for private investment. Treasury arguments against public works assumed that the maintenance of the gold standard would prevent the creation of new loanable funds through an expansion of bank credit. It would be difficult to prevent these new funds finding their way abroad and, in any case, foreigners, fearing a rise in British prices and a fall in sterling's exchange rate, might withdraw their funds from London. Again, the Treasury assumed that the state would not compete with private enterprise in the production of goods for sale, so that public capital expenditure was limited to roads, housing and some utilities (for which local authorities were responsible), Post Office telephones and, after the creation of the Central Electricity Board in 1927[1], transmission lines for the new national grid. If such capital expenditure were pressed on with too quickly, practical problems and profiteering would raise prices, and surplus capacity would be created. Private enterprise, guided by the market mechanism, would find better uses for savings. The Treasury, following classical economic theory, assumed that savings were always a necessary precondition for investment. As Keynes was to demonstrate in his *General Theory* (1936), this was not true when there were unemployed resources in the community, for then investment would raise the community's income and create the savings necessary for the investment. Keynes gave his support to Lloyd George's promise in 1928–29 that if returned to office, the Liberals would spend an additional £251 million on public works over two years, more than halving unemployment within a year. However, practical problems of implementing such a programme would have prevented the

1. The Central Electricity Board was created to construct, own and operate a national grid to transmit electricity. Power generation remained in the hands of municipal or private enterprise. The Board, made up largely of businessmen, was appointed by the Minister of Transport, but was largely autonomous in practice. The reasons why a Conservative government should create a state enterprise were wholly technocratic: larger, more efficient power stations required larger markets, and a national grid would allow cost reductions through economies of scale.

employment multiplier having such an effect in one year, or even in four or five years, and if Lloyd George had kept his other promises of maintaining free trade and the gold standard, much of the employment multiplier effect would have leaked abroad through imports (Cmd. 3331; Keynes and Henderson 1929; Middleton 1983; Peden 1984; Thomas 1981, pp. 337–46).

The 'Treasury view' on public works, like the gold standard, acted as a barrier to increased public expenditure. The fact that public works to cure unemployment were advocated by Lloyd George, the architect of wartime inflation, did little to inspire confidence among those for whom the maintenance of the value of money was more important than the creation of employment. As it happened, it was Labour, not the Liberals, who came to office as a result of the 1929 election, and Labour's efforts to solve unemployment were to be swamped by a world depression.

Social Policy after the Geddes 'Axe'

While the policy of returning to the gold standard seemed to represent the triumph of economic orthodoxy, a study of central government expenditure in the 1920s shows that economic orthodoxy had to make a series of compromises with social and political imperatives. Defence expenditure bore the brunt of the Geddes 'axe', being reduced by over 40 per cent between 1921/22 and 1922/23. Social expenditure fell by about 11½ per cent between these years, and by a further 3½ per cent or so between 1922/23 and 1923/24, before gradually rising again to the 1922/23 level by the end of the decade. Expenditure on education, health insurance and health services in 1929/30 remained below the 1921/22 (pre-Geddes) level, indicating a lack of political priority. Expenditures on housing, pensions (other than war pensions) and unemployment insurance, on the other hand, all rose above the 1921/22 level (Table 4.4).

Housing expenditure was back to the 1921/22 level by 1924/25 and increased by about a third by the end of the decade. An Act brought in by Neville Chamberlain, the Conservative Minister of Health, in 1923, offered a subsidy of £6 a year for 20 years for each house built to specific standards. The idea was to encourage low-priced, privately-built, housing, both for sale and for rent, in the hope that the housing market would recover, so that further subsidies for new houses would be unnecessary after two years. Local authorities could also receive subsidies under the Act, but each local authority had to make a case to the Ministry of Health showing that in its area, housing could not be left to private enterprise. As a further encouragement to private enterprise, the Rent and Mortgage Act of 1923 removed controls from all houses which became vacant. The hope that private enterprise alone would build sufficient houses for rent proved to be a vain one. Apart from the unattractiveness of a market in which many people had very low incomes, private builders had to cope with the high interest rates associated with the gold standard policy, and this offset the effect of subsidies.

John Wheatley, the Labour Minister of Health, restored to the local authorities their full powers to build. In his Act of 1924 Wheatley introduced a new Exchequer subsidy for local authority houses – £9 per house per year for 40 years in urban areas, and more in rural areas – and he extended the period of the Chamberlain subsidy to 1929. The Conservatives cut housing subsidies in 1927, and a Conservative-dominated National Government brought the Wheatley subsidies to an end in 1934. By that date over 520,000 houses had been built under the Wheatley Act and 438,000 under the Chamberlain Act. Subsidised housing thus accounted for less than half the 2,207,000 houses built in 1923–34, the balance being privately built for sale, usually to people drawing upon the funds of the rapidly growing building society movement. Wheatley's main contribution to increasing the supply of houses may well have been his 'gentleman's agreement' with the building trade unions in 1924, whereby the latter responded to his subsidy proposals by agreeing to an increase in the number of men employed in the building trades. Even so, the supply of new housing barely kept up with the increase in new households, so that there was very little replacement of obsolete housing. Moreover, the high standards demanded by the Chamberlain and Wheatley Acts meant that, even with subsidies, rents were usually too high for slum dwellers to afford (Bowley 1945, chs. 3–4). Nevertheless, the concept of housing as a social service had clearly survived the Geddes 'axe'.

Turning briefly to pensions, the one new measure in the period was Chamberlain's Widows', Orphans' and Old Age Contributory Pensions Act of 1925. This allowed for equal contributions by employers and employees, with a state subsidy of £4 million annually for ten years. The fund so created would provide insured workers between 65 and 70, or their dependants on the insured's death, with pensions without a means test. The Act was clearly intended to expand pension provision at the least possible cost to the taxpayer. The cost of non-contributory pensions under Lloyd George's 1908 Act was mounting rapidly (Table 4.4), as more and more people lived beyond the age of 70. The new pensions for old age and for widows were fixed at 10s a week, the same as non-contributory pensions had been since 1919. The Labour Party opposed the contributory principle, but the main opposition to Chamberlain came from private insurance companies, anxious about their future business (Gilbert 1970, pp. 235–51). It was an indication of the growing confidence and competence of the state in social policy that this opposition could be over-ruled.

The most volatile element in social policy was unemployment insurance. In theory this should have been self-balancing expenditure, but, as already noted, high unemployment after 1920 prevented the National Insurance Fund from accumulating a surplus. Moreover, the out-of-work donation introduced by Lloyd George's Coalition Government in 1919 had been more generous than the 1911 Unemployment Insurance scheme. The latter had paid benefits below subsistence level to the wage earner only, whereas the former had been set at subsistence level with allowances for dependants. These new features had to be included in the 1920 scheme, since to offer less for contributions than what had been given *gratis* would have provoked social unrest. Again, to prevent the mass of the unemployed being thrown on to the Poor Law, 'uncovenanted benefits' were paid out of the Insurance Fund from 1921 to workers who had not managed to pay enough contributions to qualify. Since large-scale unemployment was expected to be temporary, it was supposed that workers in receipt of uncovenanted benefit would pay contributions later. As unemployment persisted, the Unemployment Insurance Fund had to borrow more and more from the Treasury.

Attempts were made to limit the number of claims by imposing a 'genuinely seeking work' test for uncovenanted benefit. A claimant had to appear before a Local Employment Committee to provide a list of firms visited and to show a 'state of mind' that he or she preferred working for wages to living on benefit. The onus of proof was on the claimant, since committees could refuse benefit without having to show that work was available in the area. Local Employment Committees were made up of employers and trade unionists, with chairmen who were usually retired businessmen or magistrates. Appointment was by the Ministry of Labour, which made sure that committee members shared its views on the need to maintain the will to work. Altogether some three million claimants were refused benefit under the 'genuinely seeking work' test between 1921 and 1930, when the Labour Government, under pressure from its backbenchers, abolished the test. There was also a means test imposed from 1922–24 and 1925–28 (Deacon 1976). Disqualification from benefit could be used to control workers' conduct, since a claimant could be refused benefit if he were on strike or had been dismissed for 'misconduct', including 'insolence' and drunkenness (Brown 1978, pp. 141f.)

The first Labour Government of 1924 extended the 'genuinely seeking work' test to workers who had earned standard insurance benefit through contributions. This was the price a minority government had to pay for dropping the means test (Deacon 1976, pp. 36–9). Further, the Liberals and Conservatives combined to limit the period for which uncovenanted benefit (which Labour had renamed 'extended benefit') would continue to be paid out of the National Insurance Fund. This led to a review of unemployment insurance by the Blanesburgh Committee, which in 1927 recommended a merger of standard and extended (now renamed 'transitional') benefit, and claimed actuarial soundness on the grounds of an unfulfilled anticipation that unemployment would fall markedly in three years. The Conservatives' Unemployment Insurance Act of 1927 followed these recommendations. Transitional benefit was yet another attempt to separate the majority of unemployed from the Poor Law.

Workers denied insurance had recourse to the Poor Law, and in some areas they were lucky enough to find that the ratepayers had elected socialist guardians who would provide relief above the scale set by the Ministry of Health. This phenomenon was known as 'Poplarism', because of the stand taken by the guardians of Poplar, in the East End of London, against the time-honoured principles that recipients of relief should be worse off than if they had been in work, and that family income should be taken into account in assessing need (Ryan 1978, pp. 70–80). Chamberlain, as Minister of Health, took powers to replace such boards of guardians with his own commissions. Then, as part of his Local Government Act of 1929, he abolished all boards of guardians, and transferred their functions to the boroughs and counties. The local authorities were to set up Public Assistance Committees, which were forbidden to pay more relief to paupers than what they would have been entitled to under unemployment insurance. In fact, since assessment of need varied from area to area, many Public Assistance Committees did pay over that limit (Gilbert 1970, pp. 214–35).

The period of the gold standard policy was thus also one in which central government took increasing responsibility for compensating for interruption of earnings, although this was done in a way which would minimise interference with the 'natural' working of the labour market. Housing and education, the responsibility of local authorities, also attracted large central government subsidies. Even so, the expansion of social services in the 1920s was less than that promised in 1917–19. The gold standard could not be maintained if foreign financiers lost confidence in sterling and withdrew their balances from London, and a precondition of financial confidence was a balanced budget. Since Labour and the Liberals subscribed to the gold standard policy, from the point of view of encouraging international trade, no less than the Conservatives, this meant that all parties in the 1920s supported chancellors in their attempts to control public expenditure. As we shall see, even in 1931, when Labour split over the question of which cuts were to be made to balance the budget, the Cabinet did not dispute that cuts ought to be made to balance the budget and to preserve the gold standard. The pre-1931 experience of the gold standard does suggest that widespread acceptance of economic 'orthodoxy' can act as an effective means of limiting both public expenditure and government responsibility for economic misfortune.

References

Documents

Cd. 9182 Committee on Currency and Foreign Exchanges after the War, *First Interim Report*, BPP 1918, vol. VII, pp. 853–64.

Cmd. 3331 *Memoranda on Certain Proposals Relating to Unemployment*, BPP 1928–29, vol XVI, pp. 873–926.

Cmd. 3897 (Macmillan) *Report of the Committee on Finance and Industry*, BPP 1930–31, vol. XIII, pp. 219–546.

Books and Articles

Booth, A., and Glynn, S. (1975) 'Unemployment in the interwar period: a multiple problem', *Journal of Contemporary History*, vol. 10, pp. 611–36.

Bowley, M. (1945) *Housing and the State 1919–1944*, George Allen and Unwin.

Brown, J. (1978) '"Social control" and modernisation of social policy', in P. Thane (ed.), *The Origins of British Social Policy*, Croom Helm.

Burk, K. (ed.) (1982) *War and the State*, George Allen and Unwin.

Clay, H. (1957) *Lord Norman*, Macmillan.

Clegg, H.A. (1954) 'Some consequences of the General Strike', *Transactions of the Manchester Statistical Society*, 1953–54.

Deacon, A. (1976) 'In search of the scrounger: the administration of unemployment insurance in Britain 1920–1931', *Occasional Papers in Social Administration*, no. 60.

Department of Employment and Productivity (1971) *British Labour Statistics: Historical Abstract 1886–1968*, HMSO.

Dintenfass, M. (1984) 'The politics of producers' co-operation: the FBI–TUC–NCE talks, 1929–1933', in J. Turner (ed.), *Businessmen and Politics*, Heinemann.

Feinstein, C. (1972) *National Income, Expenditure and Output of the United Kingdom 1855–1965*, Cambridge University Press.

Garside, W.R. (1980) *The Measurement of Unemployment: Methods and Sources in Great Britain 1850–1979*, Basil Blackwell.

Gilbert, B.B. (1970) *British Social Policy 1914–1939*, Batsford.

Hancock, K. (1962) 'The reduction of unemployment as a problem of public policy, 1920–29', *Economic History Review*, 2nd series, vol. 15, pp. 328–43.

Howson, S. (1975) *Domestic Monetary Management in Britain 1919–38*, Cambridge University Press.

Howson, S. (1981) 'Slump and unemployment', in R. Floud and D. McCloskey (eds.), *The Economic History of Britain since 1700*, vol. 2, Cambridge University Press.

Keynes, J.M. (1925) *The Economic Consequences of Mr Churchill*, reprinted in *Collected Writings of John Maynard Keynes*, vol. 9, Macmillan.

Keynes, J.M., and Henderson, H. (1929) 'Can Lloyd George do it?', reprinted in *Collected Writings of John Maynard Keynes*, vol. 9, Macmillan.

Mallet, B. and George, C. (1933) *British Budgets, Third Series, 1921/22–1932/33*, Macmillan.

Mason, A. (1969) 'The Government and the General Strike, 1926', *International Review of Social History*, vol. 14, pp. 1–21.

Middleton, R. (1983) 'The Treasury and public investment: a perspective on inter-war economic management', *Public Administration*, vol. 61, pp. 351–70.

Mitchell, B.R., and Deane, P. (1962) *Abstract of British Historical Statistics*, Cambridge University Press.

Moggridge, D. (1972) *British Monetary Policy 1924–31: The Norman Conquest of $4.86*, Cambridge University Press.

Morgan, E.V. (1952) *Studies in British Financial Policy*, Macmillan.

Morris, M. (1976) *The General Strike*, Penguin Books.

Peden, G.C. (1984) 'The "Treasury view" on public works and employment in the inter-war period', *Economic History Review*, 2nd series, vol. 37, pp. 167–81.

Phillips, G. (1976) *The General Strike: the Politics of Industrial Conflict*, Weidenfeld and Nicolson.

Pollard, S. (ed.) (1970) *The Gold Standard and Employment Policies Between the Wars*, Methuen.

Pressnell, L.S. (1978) '1925: the burden of sterling', *Economic History Review*, 2nd series, vol. 31, pp. 67–88.

Redmond, J. (1984) 'The sterling overvaluation in 1925: a multilateral approach', *Economic History Review*, 2nd series, vol. 37, pp. 520–32.

Ryan, P. (1978) 'Poplarism 1894–1930', in P. Thane (ed.), *The Origins of British Social Policy*, Croom Helm.

Sayers, R.S. (1976) *The Bank of England 1891–1944*, vol. 1 and vol. of appendixes, Cambridge University Press.

Swann, B. and Turnbull, M. (1975) *Records of Interest to Social Scientists: Unemployment Insurance 1911 to 1939*, Public Record Office.

Thomas, T. (1981) 'Aggregate demand in the United Kingdom 1918–45', in R. Floud and D. McCloskey (eds.), *The Economic History of Britain since 1700*, vol. 2, Cambridge University Press.

Tomlinson, J. (1981) *Problems of British Economic Policy 1870–1945*, Methuen.

Winch, D. (1969) *Economics and Policy: A Historical Study*, Hodder and Stoughton.

5

The Impact of the Post-1929 Depression

The world depression which began in 1929 was as great a challenge to *laissez-faire* beliefs as the First World War had been. The market mechanism alone had proved inadequate to deal with shortages of goods and labour in 1914–18; in the post-1929 depression it failed to cope satisfactorily with a surplus of goods and labour. Falling prices and rising unemployment led to an international financial crisis in 1931–32 which ended the old economic order of the gold standard and free trade. Britain's real gross national product fell by 5.5 per cent between 1929 and 1932, but this was modest compared with a 30 per cent fall in the United States (Richardson 1967, ch. 1).

The sharp fall in world food and raw material prices (wheat prices, for example, were more than halved between 1929 and 1931) reduced the incomes of primary-producing countries. This in turn reduced demand for British exports, 40 per cent of which had gone to such countries. The output of the traditional staple industries, notably coal, cotton, shipbuilding and steel, which relied heavily upon export markets, consequently fell, and unemployment rose. On the other hand, falling prices raised the purchasing power of money incomes. Since salaried workers were least subject to unemployment, it is hardly surprising that industries catering for the middle classes recovered quickly from the depression. By 1933 residential construction was 40 per cent and electrical power output 45 per cent above the 1929 level (Richardson 1967, p. 16). The depression was felt least in the South-East of England, where there

Table 5.1 (a) Regional Variations in Unemployment (Percentage of Insured Workers)

	England							
	South-East	*Midlands*	*North-West*	*North-East*	*Scotland*	*Wales*	*Northern Ireland*	*UK average*
1929	5.6	9.3	13.3	13.7	12.1	19.3	14.8	10.4
1932	14.3	20.1	25.8	28.5	27.1	36.5	27.2	22.1
1934	8.7	12.9	20.8	22.1	23.1	32.3	23.4	16.7
1936	7.3	9.2	13.1	16.8	18.7	29.4	22.7	13.2
1938	7.7	10.0	17.7	12.9	16.8	25.9	24.4	12.9

Source: McCrone (1969), p. 100.

Table 5.1 (b) Numbers Employed in Staple Industries (000s)

	Coal	*Cotton*	*Shipbuilding*	*Iron and steel*
1929	957	555	157	124
1932	819	518	65	82
1937	792	409	135	155
1938	791	393	138	139
Change 1929–32	–138	–37	–92	–42
Change 1929–37	–165	–146	–22	+31

Source: Mitchell and Deane (1962).

was the greatest concentration of salaried workers and rentiers; unemployment was highest and lasted longest in regions where the old export industries were concentrated. Table 5.1(a) shows how this was true of Wales (coal), North-West England (cotton), Northern Ireland (linen and shipbuilding), and Scotland and North-East England (coal, shipbuilding and iron and steel).

Table 5.1(b) shows that a total of about 310,000 jobs in coal, cotton, shipbuilding and iron and steel were lost in the downward phase of the depression, 1929–32. At this stage the cause of unemployment might have been put down to a general deficiency of demand, but in 1937, after five years of recovery in the economy as a whole, a total of 333,000 fewer people were employed in coal, cotton and shipbuilding than in 1929. The bulk of these lost jobs were in coal and cotton where there had been a great decline in exports. In the case of coal, for example, a fall in total output between 1929 and 1937 of 17.5 million tons was more than accounted for by the fall of 20 million tons in exports. Iron and steel did recover in the 1930s behind tariff barriers, but the other staples were unlikely to recover fully from the depression unless there were an increase in world trade or (in the case of shipbuilding) a naval arms race.

The causes of the economic crisis of 1931 lay largely outside the control of the British Government. A world financial crisis arose because falling prices increased the real burden of debt at a time when American foreign lending, which had been crucial to international liquidity in the 1920s, was being reduced. A speculative boom on the New York stock exchange drew in funds in 1928–29, and the fall in security prices from October 1929 led to a serious banking crisis in the United States. By 1931 the United States was a net importer of capital. As countries found themselves unable to renew credits in New York to finance foreign debts, there were defaults and a scramble for international liquidity developed.

The 1931 Crisis and the Fall of the Labour Government

In the circumstances described above, it is understandable that international problems, rather than the level of domestic demand, were the focus of concern during Labour's period of office from 1929 to 1931. Ramsay MacDonald, the Prime Minister, spoke of the need for 'world confidence', and his advisers told him that the gold standard was necessary for orderly international trade and finance. As late as the summer of 1931 the Macmillan Report on *Finance and Industry*, whose signatories included Keynes and other critics of the gold standard, stated that 'it would be an immense shock to the financial world' if Britain were deliberately to devalue to make its exports more competitive (Cmd. 3897, paras. 255–57). Moreover, the ability of any creditworthy person or institution to borrow short-term funds in London had been regarded as a stabilising feature of the pre-1914 international economy.

J.H. Thomas, the Lord Privy Seal, who was in charge of unemployment policy, and Snowden, the Chancellor of the Exchequer, were agreed that the basic cause of unemployment was loss of exports. Thus, although Thomas had ideas for creating jobs through railway, road and harbour improvements, slum clearance and extensions to the national electricity grid, he agreed with the Treasury view that such schemes should be limited to those which would lower the costs of production. Again, Labour ministers were agreed that exports should be regained through increased efficiency and not through subsidies (Skidelsky 1975, ch. 9). These constraints, together with the usual administrative delays in starting public works, meant that little was achieved. Middleton (1983) has calculated that the number of jobs created, directly and indirectly, was still only about 11 per cent of total numbers unemployed in the summer of 1931. His figure is probably an overestimate, since he assumes an employment multiplier of 1.5 took effect without lags.

The bitterest critic of Labour's unemployment policy was Thomas's assistant, Oswald Mosley, Chancellor of the Duchy of Lancaster. Mosley believed (rightly as it turned out) that exports would not recover their pre-1929 level in the foreseeable future. He wanted to develop the home market, and in 1930 he drew up an ambitious programme for loan-financed public works. This, however, fell foul of Treasury objections that such a policy would reduce financial confidence and raise interest rates, and Mosley resigned (Skidelsky 1975, ch. 10). There was some substance in these objections, for early in 1931 even a rumour that the Government was about to launch a large development loan was enough to drive down the price of gilt-edged stock (Williamson 1984b, p. 122).

From the Treasury's perspective, the problem was that if the Government appeared to financiers around the world to be spending more than the nation could afford, confidence in the Bank of England's ability to maintain sterling's fixed value against gold would be lost. The Bank's reserves of gold and foreign exchange could not maintain the gold standard indefinitely if there were a run on the pound. The key to financial confidence was a balanced budget, for this would show that public expenditure was under control and that the Government was not increasing the proportion of paper pounds relative to Britain's gold reserves.

By 1931, however, future government expenditure was unpredictable. Rapidly increasing unemployment forced the Treasury to lend money to the Unemployment Insurance Fund so that benefits could be paid. Moreover, the Labour Government had made it easier to claim benefit. The Labour Party Conference in October 1929 had insisted on the abolition of the 'genuinely seeking work' test, and under the National Insurance Act of 1930 a claimant could only be disallowed if he or she refused an offer of suitable employment. Inevitably there were allegations of false claims, especially as the Unemployment Insurance Fund's deficit rose from £83 million in May 1931 to over £100 million by the late summer. Moreover, Labour had continued the transitional benefits of the 1927 Act (see p. 81) while transferring the cost of these from the Insurance Fund to the Exchequer. A rapid increase in the numbers of married women receiving transitional benefit was criticised by the Government's opponents as a sign of laxity. MacDonald's response was to delay action by setting up a Royal Commission on unemployment insurance late in 1930, but this merely enabled the Treasury to demonstrate publicly how borrowing for unemployment benefits was unbalancing the budget. In a desperate effort to reduce the number of claimants, the Government brought in regulations to exclude most married women from transitional benefit (Deacon 1976, pp. 69–86).

Although the weakness of sterling in 1931 was by no means solely the result of action, or inaction, on the unemployment problem, the Government's failure to balance the budget turned a financial crisis into a political crisis, which in turn exacerbated the financial crisis. As in 1924, Labour lacked a majority in Parliament, and was dependent upon the support of the Liberals who, however, remained in opposition, joining with the Conservatives in calls for economies to balance the budget. Such pressure was not unwelcome to Snowden, who was trying to preserve the gold standard by curbing spending proposals of Cabinet colleagues. Early in 1931 he invited Sir George May, formerly secretary of the Prudential Assurance Company, to head a committee which was to make recommendations on all possible reductions in government expenditure. May believed that since 1918 all parties had tried to win electoral support by making lavish promises of 'reforms' and that the time had come to restore the political balance in favour of the advocates of strict economy (Cmd. 3920, pp. 12–13).

It was common ground among the Government's economic advisers at this time that remedies for the depression included restoration of financial confidence by reforming unemployment insurance and by balancing the budget without increasing direct taxation. Cuts in government expenditure were not, however, the only way to do this. Keynes and other economists advised MacDonald to balance the budget by imposing a revenue tariff, and by March 1931 Keynes was urging action soon, as a crisis of confidence was very near (Marquand 1977, p. 590). MacDonald nonetheless procrastinated. The threatened crisis came in the summer, beginning with a Central European banking crisis which led foreigners to draw upon their liquid assets in London. This in turn led to a loss of confidence in sterling, and gold flowed out of London from 16 July. The Bank of England defended the gold standard by seeking credits from central banks in New York and Paris and by raising Bank Rate. On the very day the credits were announced, 1 August, the

May Report was published, and its contents entirely offset any beneficial effects of the Bank's actions. The Report placed the Government's finances in the worst possible light. The estimate of the budget deficit of £120 million for 1931/32 included a Sinking Fund of £52 million – that is a contribution towards repayment of the National Debt – at a time when no other important country tried to do such a thing. With more reason, the Report included the Unemployment Insurance Fund as a revenue liability, but the May Committee's demand that borrowing for the Fund should cease was something that not even the Treasury had called for in its evidence to the Royal Commission on Unemployment Insurance (Peden 1983, p. 381). The May Committee recommended that unemployment benefit be cut by 20 per cent to save £66.5 million. A further £30 million could be saved by other expenditure cuts, including reductions in public employees' pay. Stress was laid on the fact that falling prices had raised the purchasing power of wages and unemployment benefit, but May did not take account of the corresponding increase in the real income of holders of the National Debt (Cmd. 3920, pp. 14–21, 215–23).

Keynes's advice to MacDonald was that reducing government expenditure would reduce economic activity and therefore revenue. Since the gold standard could no longer be defended, Keynes suggested a devaluation of at least 25 per cent, with no return to the gold standard until the policies of other countries were clear (Howson and Winch 1977, pp. 88–90). Devaluation was a technical question on which it was the Bank of England's responsibility to advise, but the Bank had deliberately cultivated a mystique on financial matters, and ministers seem not to have had a clear understanding of the whole range of options before them (Sayers 1976, p. 387; Williamson 1984a). The tension was such that the Bank's Governor, Montague Norman, had a nervous breakdown. Snowden, together with the Conservative and Liberal opposition, insisted on larger cuts in expenditure than the majority of the Cabinet would stand for. There was a proposal to raise a loan in New York, but Morgan's, the bankers advising the Government, made clear that such a loan could only succeed if the budget had the approval of the Bank of England and the City of London. The TUC leaders, on the other hand, opposed cuts in wages and unemployment benefit, and demanded a special tax on fixed-interest securities. The majority of the Cabinet felt that the unity of the Labour movement was paramount, and

MacDonald resigned on 24 August (Clay 1957, pp. 391–95; Marquand 1977, pp. 611–37). At all events, even once MacDonald had formed a National Government with the Conservatives and Liberals, and had imposed expenditure cuts of £70 million and obtained a foreign loan, the gold standard had to be suspended on 21 September 1931. At the time this was regarded as a great blow. Britain, however, had preserved its financial reputation by doing everything possible to defend the gold standard, and it was now in a position to take what advantage it could of a floating exchange rate.

The Economic Policy of the National Government

The National Government remained nominally in being for the rest of the decade. As MacDonald was succeeded as prime minister by the Conservatives Stanley Baldwin in 1935 and Neville Chamberlain in 1937, it became indistinguishable from a Conservative government, and its economic policies were dominated by Chamberlain even while he was Chancellor of the Exchequer (1931–37). The Government was criticised by Keynes and others for its allegedly unimaginative approach to unemployment and economic management, but research since the 1970s into 'behind-the-scenes' deliberations of senior civil servants and their economic advisers in the 1930s has softened such judgements (Winch 1983, pp. 64–65). In fact, economic policy after 1931 was a remarkable mixture of orthodoxy and innovation.

Fiscal policy remained orthodox in that the Chancellor aimed to balance his budget, even though he sometimes failed to do so. There was no deliberate attempt to reflate the economy through deficit finance. Nevertheless, the Treasury did wish to restore prices to their pre-depression level. As Figure 5.1 shows, wholesale prices had fallen by about 25 per cent, and the cost-of-living index by over 12 per cent by 1932, whereas wage rates had fallen by less than 5 per cent. The rentier and the consumer had gained from falling prices, while manufacturers had been discouraged by falling profits, so that the working classes as a whole had lost as much from unemployment as they had gained from increased real wages. In the light of experience of the 1920s, Treasury officials accepted that money wages could not be reduced significantly. They aimed, therefore, to raise businessmen's expectations of profit by raising wholesale prices (and by

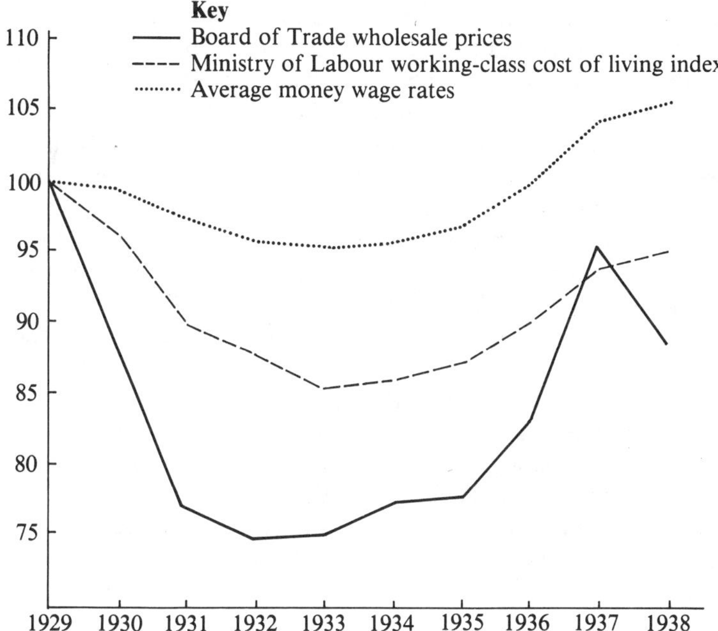

Source: Mitchell and Deane (1962), pp. 345 and 478–9.

Figure 5.1 Prices and Wages (1929 = 100)

reducing taxes) while hoping that money wages would remain unchanged (Howson 1975, pp. 86, 94). The chosen instruments of policy were low interest rates (to reduce the cost of investment) and sterling depreciation, tariffs and price-fixing agreements (to raise prices). Rationalisation of industry into more profitable units was also encouraged. Public works were at first abandoned as an instrument of policy and, although they were reintroduced later, together with some experiments in regional policy, the basic strategy adopted in 1931–32 remained unchanged until the war.

The apparent contradiction between attempting to balance the budget while hoping to raise wholesale prices is explicable in terms of financial confidence. Balanced budgets provided an assurance that there would be no general inflation. Interest rates could then be reduced, and this itself would help to balance the budget since the largest single item in the budget was payment of interest on the National Debt. It was hoped that economic recovery would come through private investment rather than government expenditure. Much depended upon business confidence, something which is neither wholly rational nor subject to quantification by economic historians. It was believed in Whitehall that private investment in industry was superior to public works from the points of view of wealth creation and international competitiveness. Prior to 1935, at least, the Treasury still seems to have believed that public expenditure would tend to divert money away from private enterprise, unless the public expenditure were financed by new money created by the Bank of England, and that, if additional credit were to be created, it would be better used by private enterprise (Peden 1984). The Government's reluctance to interfere with private industry often gave economic policy an appearance of being piecemeal but, given the Government's own assumptions, there was more logic and coherence to its policy than some accounts written before the 1970s would suggest. We turn now to the effects of different aspects of policy.

Fiscal Policy

As noted in Chapter 4, it is possible by using the concept of the employment multiplier to estimate how many jobs could be created by government expenditure. The expenditure of incomes of those engaged on public works and their immediate suppliers will, after an interval, raise employment generally by a multiplier usually now taken to be about 1.5. Employment will only be increased, however, if government expenditure is a net addition to expenditure within the community. This point is best explained with reference to the Keynesian income–expenditure identity: $Y = C + I + G + X - M$, where Y is the national income, C is consumption (i.e. private expenditure on current goods and services), I is private investment, G is government expenditure, X is exports and M is imports. When an economy is at less-than-full employment, as was obviously the case in Britain in the 1920s and thirties, an increase in G will not only create jobs directly but will also raise Y. The additional flow of income in the community should raise both C and I, and thereby create additional employment, which in turn will raise the community's income and expenditure, and thereby create further employment (and so on). The process is not an infinite one, however, since at each stage some proportion of the increased income will be saved, some proportion will be spent on imports, and some part of the purchasing power will be lost through higher prices. The extent to which direct government expenditure creates indirect, or secondary, employment in addition to direct, or primary, employment varies with circumstances. For example, uncertainty about the future may lead to people saving a higher proportion of their incomes, as precautionary balances, while investors hold back until they can be more sure of their returns. The manner in which G is financed also matters. If the increase in G is financed out of taxation, Y will rise, but only in so far as the incomes taxed would have been saved and not spent or invested. Equally, if G is financed by borrowing money which would otherwise have been taken up by private investors, the increase in G is merely a substitute for an increase in I. An increase in G will be most effective in raising Y, and thereby the demand for labour if the expenditure is financed from newly-created bank credit or from savings which would not otherwise have been invested. Even then, it is important to remember that G has different components. For example, central government expenditure on roads might simply replace local authorities' expenditure on roads. Moreover, even as increased G tends to raise Y, the rise may be offset by a fall in X (if, for example, increased domestic demand diverts manufacturers from exports markets) or if there is a rise in M (if increased demand sucks in imports). Finally, the extent to which a rise in Y will raise employment depends upon (a) the movement of wages (a rise in the price of labour will affect the demand for it) and (b) the extent to which the location and skills of unemployed workers match the new demand for labour.

It follows, therefore, that one cannot assume that employment would necessarily have been raised in proportion to deficit expenditure. Nevertheless, other things being equal, budget deficits and surpluses published at the time suggest that fiscal policy had a mildly reflationary effect during most of the downward phase of the trade cycle (1929–32) and a mildly deflationary effect during the upward phase (1932–37). The published figures are misleading, however, in that, for example, the Chancellor's budget omitted employer and employee contributions to the health and unemployment insurance funds, but included government contributions. Again, sums borrowed under the Defence Loans Act during 1937/38–1939/40 were treated as revenue, so that a surplus of almost £29 million was produced in 1937/38, even though £65 million had been borrowed for defence. Middleton (1981) has made the necessary adjustments to the budget figures to bring them into line with modern fiscal accounting. There is the further complication that deficits or surpluses reflected not only what fiscal policy was doing to the economy, but also what changes in economic activity were doing to the budget. Tax yields and expenditure on unemployment relief at given rates were determined by whether the economy was moving into or out of depression. Economists therefore estimate the direction of fiscal policy by using the concept of the constant employment budget. This involves estimating what government revenue and expenditure would have been, given the same tax rates and expenditure plans, had private demand been enough to maintain a previous level of employment. The constant employment budget balance is the difference between this hypothetical revenue and expenditure. Middleton (1981) calculated that had employment levels been maintained at the 1929 level, all budgets from 1929/30 to 1936/37 would have been in surplus. On

Table 5.2 The Constant Employment Budget Surplus

	Middleton (at 7.6–8.0 per cent unemployment) (£ m. at current prices)	*Thomas (at 7.4 per cent unemployment) (£ m. 1938 prices)*
1929/30	+ 17.4	+ 40.8
1930/31	+ 47.1	+ 65.2
1931/32	+ 106.7	+ 101.9
1932/33	+ 124.5	+ 166.8
1933/34	+ 174.2	+ 152.5
1934/35	+ 138.0	+ 144.7
1935/36	+ 85.8	+ 103.4
1936/37	+ 37.4	+ 85.2
1937/38	− 3.7	+ 44.7
1938/39	− 80.7	− 19.2

this basis budgets became increasingly deflationary as the depression deepened between 1929 and 1932. Thomas (1981), using somewhat different estimating procedures and assumptions, has produced similar results (Table 5.2).

There are, nonetheless, problems in using the concept of the constant employment budget. In particular, there is always a lag before the full effect of fiscal policy is felt on employment, so that a counterfactual history should estimate the effects of a budget on subsequent years. Moreover, one should in principle disaggregate the effect of different elements within the budget. For example, the proportion of income saved (and therefore taken out of the flow of incomes) would vary between high-income recipients of interest on the National Debt and low-income recipients of state benefits. In the absence of a model which would enable one to calculate the different effects of different elements within the budget, any measurement of the effects of fiscal policy must be imperfect. What one can say is that the calculations by Middleton and Thomas show that such deficits as occurred between 1929/30 and 1937/38 fell far short of what would have been required to restore the 1929 level of employment. It was only from 1937/38 or 1938/39 that loan-financed defence expenditure had an unambiguously reflationary effect on the economy.

Monetary Policy

The Treasury regarded a reduction in Bank Rate as the principal means of counteracting a depression (Howson 1975, pp. 90–5; Peden 1984, pp. 177–8). The Treasury had wished to help industry by lowering interest rates since 1923, but two other policy objections had conflicted with this goal: defence of the gold standard and funding of the National Debt.

It was no longer necessary to attract foreign funds to London by raising Bank Rate after sterling was allowed to float in September 1931. Indeed, for the rest of the 1930s the Treasury and the Bank of England regarded inflows of foreign money as potentially destabilising, both because these might raise the exchange rate and the domestic money supply more than the authorities wished, and because foreign money might be withdrawn at inconvenient times. The Exchange Equalisation Account was set up in 1932 as a Treasury fund to be used to smooth out fluctuations caused by capital movements (Howson 1980). The Bank of England managed the Account, with the advice and consent of the Treasury – an arrangement which marked the end of the era in which British international monetary policy had been controlled by an independent central bank.

In practice the Account was used to keep the exchange rate down. Once sterling had depreciated from $4.86 in September 1931 to $3.40 in March 1932, speculators felt that the only direction sterling could go was upwards. The Treasury, however, favoured a rate of $3.40 since this would raise import prices, reduce the real burden of the National Debt, and help exporters (Howson 1975, pp. 84–6). As matters turned out, it was not possible to hold sterling at $3.40. The Roosevelt Administration in the United States also wished to raise prices and to help its exporters, and tried to do so by devaluing the dollar against gold in 1933/34 (Drummond 1981, pp. 139–57, 181–4). Thereafter sterling was generally above $4.86 until British rearmament and the prospect of war in Europe caused confidence in sterling to decline against the dollar in 1938–39 (Howson 1980, pp. 22–32).

British exporters thus enjoyed only a brief respite from American competition in international markets in 1932–33. Moreover, some countries, such as Japan, depreciated their currencies more than Britain did. On the other hand, other countries, such as France, persisted for a time with fixed exchange rates based on gold. Redmond (1980) has calculated that sterling's effective exchange rate was still 4 to 5 per cent below the 1929–30 level from the American devaluation in 1934 until after the devaluation of the franc in 1936, but that by 1937 sterling was actually more overvalued than in 1929–30. The floating pound does seem to have helped to arrest the fall in Britain's share of world export trade, which had occurred under the gold standard, for Britain's share of world export trade remained almost constant over the 1930s. On the other hand, in spite of sterling's depreciation, the proportion of British exports going to foreign countries outside the sterling area fell from 43.8 per cent in 1932 to 37.9 per cent in 1935. The main long-term benefit of the floating pound would seem to have been the release of domestic monetary policy from the need to maintain a fixed exchange rate. One other aspect of policy which had an impact on domestic investment following suspension of the gold standard was restriction of foreign investment. Exchange controls were imposed from September 1931 until March 1932, and thereafter there was an unofficial embargo on new foreign capital issues in London. Although informal, the embargo seems to have been fairly effective (Cairncross and Eichengreen 1983, pp. 83–103).

The primacy of domestic monetary policy was in marked contrast to the 1920s, when Bank Rate had sometimes been raised to 6 or 7 per cent to maintain the exchange rate. Bank Rate was reduced from 6 per cent at the beginning of 1932 to 2 per cent six months later – the level at which it was to remain, except for a brief period at the outbreak of the Second World War, until 1951. The Treasury thereby achieved its goals of a cheap money policy and a reduction in the burden of the National Debt on the budget. A major conversion operation in March 1932 replaced 5 per cent War Loan 1929–47 (which made up over a quarter of the National Debt) with 3½ per cent War Loan 1952 or after. Cheap money was part of an attempt to manage the economy by encouraging investment, and to that extent the Treasury agreed with the Macmillan Committee that in the case of financial institutions Britain might 'well have reached the stage when an era of conscious and deliberate management must succeed the era of undirected natural evolution' (Howson 1975, pp. 90–5, 142; Cmd. 3897, para. 9). On the other hand, the Treasury still wished to reduce the volume of floating debt (Treasury bills), and funding operations tended to counteract cheap money. Although the money supply grew on average by 6 per cent a year from 1932 to 1936, compared with 2 per cent a year from 1926–28, there were sharp reductions from time to time as private-sector holdings of Treasury bills were reduced. Commercial banks used these bills as secondary reserves, and a shortage of bills meant that bank lending did not expand as fast as the rise in the demand for credit. From the end of 1936 the growth in the money supply slowed down and longer-term interest rates began to rise (Howson 1975, pp. 95–103; 130–5). Cheap money's contribution to economic recovery was thus much less consistent than a fixed Bank Rate might imply.

Nevertheless, cheap money seems to have been a useful, if permissive, factor in economic recovery. A decline in mortgage rates from 6 to 4.5 per cent provided considerable stimulus for housing demand, while builders could finance their operations more cheaply on credit. A rapid growth in the number of privately built houses for sale or rent, from 131,000 in 1931 to 288,000 in 1934, owed something to demographic trends (which increased the number of households), rising real incomes and a rapid development in the building society movement. Even so, a dear money policy could have offset all these factors, and cheap money kept the housing boom going once prices began to rise (Nevin 1955, ch. 8). Investment in manufacturing was back at the 1929 level by 1934 and a boom developed in 1936–37 (Table 5.3). However, given that investors need the prospect of profits, as well as lower costs of borrowing, one should not assume that monetary policy was solely responsible for the boom.

Tariffs and Imperial Preference

Despite the McKenna Duties and the Safeguarding of Industries Act (see Chapter 3), Britain was still essentially a free-trade economy when the National Government took office. Only about 2 or 3 per cent of the total value of imports in 1930 were affected by protective duties. There had been a substantial body of business opinion in favour of protection since the First World War, but electoral opinion had apparently favoured free trade. However, the prospect of a large Conservative majority in favour of protection after the election in the autumn of 1931 led to a surge of imports to forestall the expected

Table 5.3 Gross Domestic Fixed Capital Formation (£ m. at 1930 Prices)

	Dwellings	*Manufacturing*
1929	130	73
1932	128	54
1933	168	55
1934	188	80
1935	179	79
1936	178	91
1937	167	112
1938	165	98

Source: Feinstein (1965), p. 38.

raising of tariff barriers. The protectionists in the Government, led by Neville Chamberlain, seized the opportunity to rush through the Abnormal Importations (Customs Duties) Act, and duties of up to 50 per cent were imposed on a wide range of manufactures and horticultural products in November and December. There followed the Import Duties Act, which came into operation in April 1932 with a general tariff of 20 per cent. Raw materials, some food (including wheat and meat) and Commonwealth and colonial products not previously subject to tariffs were exempt (Capie 1983).

The Import Duties Act was followed in the same year by the Ottawa Agreements, which were intended to secure as large as possible a share of British Empire markets, including the United Kingdom, for Empire countries. However, the National Government's goals of expanding Britain's industrial exports and protecting its farmers conflicted with the dominions' hope that Britain would take more of their agricultural products, and the dominions and India continued to protect their infant industries. Thus the Ottawa Agreements tended to provide imperial preference by increasing duties or introducing quotas on non-Empire goods, rather than by making large-scale mutual tariff concessions. The proportion of British exports going to the Empire rose from 43.5 per cent in 1931 to 48.0 per cent in 1937, the equivalent figures for imports being 28.6 and 39.1 per cent. Some diversion of trade had thus been achieved, but Empire markets were not a major factor in Britain's economic recovery (Drummond 1974; Richardson 1967, p. 262).

Britain became more self-sufficient in the 1930s. The volume of industrial production, as measured by annual indices, rose by 45.6 per cent in the upswing of 1932–37, but imports rose by only 20 per cent (Richardson 1967, p. 244). However, it is hard to say how much this was a result of tariffs and how much the result of a reduced effective exchange rate of sterling. The most thorough examination of the effects of the tariff (Capie 1978, 1983), however, suggests that these may have been more significant than nominal rates of 20–33⅓ per cent of volume would suggest. Capie has used the concept of effective protection which is defined as:

$$\frac{\text{Nominal duty on value of manufactures} - \left(\text{Nominal duty on inputs} \times \text{Share of inputs in value of output}\right)}{\text{Share of value added in value of output}}$$

In Britain's case imported inputs, mainly raw materials, and value added in the production process were typically about equal, so that, where there was no duty on inputs, effective protection was about twice the nominal rate. On the other hand, a 20 per cent tariff on steel raised the price of shipbuilders' inputs, so that the latter industry, which had no tariff of its own, suffered from 'negative protection' at an effective rate of −6 per cent. The picture that emerges from Capie's calculations is a complex one. Some industries, such as chemicals, cotton and some clothing, enjoyed high effective protection, but some, such as building and the lighter steel trades, suffered from negative protection. Since the last two made an important contribution to Britain's economic recovery, one should be cautious about according tariffs a wholly beneficial role.

Agricultural and Industrial Policy

Protection made possible widespread price-fixing in agricultural products, thereby shielding farmers from the full effect of the fall in world prices. The Agricultural Marketing Act of 1931 had enabled two-thirds of producers of any agricultural commodity to prepare a scheme for organised marketing, including price maintenance. Price maintenance could only be effective, however, if there were control of output and of imports, and the only marketing board established under the Act dealt with hops, which already had a protective duty. The Agricultural Marketing Act of 1933, on the other hand, authorised boards to control output and empowered the Government to support any scheme with a tariff or import quotas. Subsequently, Milk, Potato, and Bacon and Pig Marketing Boards were established. The depression made subsidies a permanent feature of British agriculture. The Wheat Act of 1932 gave farmers a standard guaranteed price, with the taxpayer paying the difference between this and the market price. Experience of sugar shortages in 1914–18 had already led to the British Sugar Subsidy Act of 1925, which had provided for subsidised purchases by refineries, on a diminishing scale over ten years, in the hope that the domestic beet sugar industry would become commercially viable. The fall in world prices in 1929–32 removed all possibility of this, and the Sugar Industry Act of 1936 reorganised production by establishing the British Sugar Corporation Ltd. This combined elements of public and private enterprise: some directors were appointed by the Government, some by shareholders, and, in view of the subsidy, profits were controlled. Agricultural policy, in short, represented a clear breach of *laissez-faire*. The annual cost of subsidies and protection was variously estimated at £32 million to £41 million, at a time when government revenue was less than £1,000 million. Even so, the effects of a massive world agricultural depression could not be wholly removed. Profits were low and much agricultural land was neglected (Pollard 1983, pp. 82–8).

Industrial policy also moved away from total reliance on unregulated markets. There developed in the period after 1929 what has been called 'industrial diplomacy' between civil servants and businessmen, as governments sought to protect business from the slump and to promote recovery. There was a conflict between Whitehall's *laissez-faire* attitudes and the needs of economic policy, and this was resolved by favouring intervention which would help to put industry back on its own feet, and by avoiding permanent commitments. So far as possible, industrial policy was kept apart from parliamentary politics, to prevent Parliament from becoming a forum in which economic interests bargained for political favours (Roberts 1984). This attitude influenced the appointment of the Import Duties Advisory Committee, which was set up in 1932 to advise the Board of Trade on tariff levels. Not one of the Committee's members was an industrialist, and its Chairman was the same Sir George May whose report had advocated reductions in public expenditure in 1931.

By implication, policy was guided by a desire to avoid rather than to move towards corporatism, which may be defined as the unification of self-governing industries by a national committee representing them and other interests, including the state (Carpenter 1976, p. 3). MacDonald experimented with an Economic Advisory Council in 1930, bringing together industrialists, trade unionists and economists with ministers to 'make continuous study of developments in trade and industry', including the effects of legislation and fiscal policy. However, the experiment was not continued in its original form after 1932 (Howson and Winch 1977). Legislation enforcing self-government of industry was passed only when an industry itself had agreed upon proposals. Since most businessmen disliked compulsion, such legislation was the exception rather than the rule.

The term 'rationalisation' itself came to be increasingly fashionable in the depression, and could mean anything from disposal of surplus capacity to amalgamations to integrate industrial processes and to permit use of the most up-to-date techniques. The Treasury saw rationalisation as a means of enabling industry to achieve profitability without subsidies (Peden 1984, p. 176). The Governor of the Bank of England saw rationalisation as a means of helping industry, and thereby relieving certain banks from the threat of bad debts, without political interference. The Bank was involved in the formation of the Lancashire Cotton Corporation in 1929–30, the Securities Management Trust (1929) and the Bankers' Industrial Development Company (1930). By these means, funds were raised by banks and industry for the disposal of surplus capacity (Sayers 1976, ch. 14). For example, the Bankers' Industrial Development Company helped to set up the National Shipbuilders Security Ltd., which levied 1 per cent on the sales of participating firms, and used the proceeds to purchase and dismantle redundant shipyards. The most notorious case was Palmer's shipyard at Jarrow, where closure in 1934 had left the town with unemployment of over 70 per cent.

The biggest challenge to the principle of voluntary reorganisation by industry was coal mining. The 1930 Coal Mines Act established a Coal Mines Reorganisation Commission, but this only succeeded in arousing the hostility of colliery owners to the principle of compulsion. The 1930 Act also provided for the fixing of output and prices by district committees of colliery owners, and, like all quota schemes, this tended to safeguard inefficient firms. Price-fixing certainly did not encourage amalgamations (Kirby 1973a). It was not until 1938 that the National Government nationalised mineral royalties, and thereby gave a new Coal Commission powers to lease mining rights in a manner which would promote amalgamations. War, however, prevented anything being done (Kirby 1973b).

The efforts of the Lancashire Cotton Corporation were supplemented in 1936 by the Cotton Spinning Industry Act. This set up a Spindles Board, financed by a compulsory levy on the industry as a whole, to buy and scrap spindles. Reduced capacity restored profitability, but even so in 1939 only 75 per cent of spinning capacity and 68 per cent of weaving capacity were employed (Kirby 1974). The need for further measures was indicated by the Cotton Industry (Reorganisation) Act of 1939, which was intended to reorganise the industry as a whole, and not just the spinning section, but again war intervened.

In the cases of cotton and iron and steel, the Government granted tariffs on the understanding that the industries would reorganise themselves. The general tariff was indeed followed by the formation of the British Iron and Steel Federation in 1934. This took over from sectional associations the function of fixing prices; it used tariffs as a bargaining weapon in negotiations with foreign cartels on import quotas, and it engaged in bulk buying of pig iron and scrap overseas. (On the other hand, protection for British producers of pig iron and semi-finished steel raised the cost of inputs for more specialised steel firms.) The Import Duties Advisory Committee proved to have no real powers to insist on amalgamations, however, and the iron and steel industry was too fragmented by conflicting interests to agree on much except tariffs and the need to avoid government control. The National Government for its part was reluctant to create a precedent for a Labour government by enforcing amalgamations, and civil servants rightly doubted their own competence to deal with complex industrial problems (Tolliday 1984). The steel industry increased its capacity from 11 million tons in 1929 to 14 million tons in 1939, but this was a result of protection and of rearmament orders, not the result of amalgamations which would have enabled integrated steel works to be built on the scale of those in the United States (Burn 1940).

The efficiency of industry depends not only on new capital investment but also on the adaptability of labour. The latter depends upon mobility, training and trade-union organisation and attitudes. A lack of working-class housing (discussed below) discouraged mobility. Mass unemployment left many young workers without apprenticeships, while the skills of the older unemployed often became obsolete. Yet the Ministry of Labour's industrial training schemes were on too small a scale to maintain the unemployed as an efficient reserve army of labour. The Ministry also failed to do anything to prevent new industries in southern Britain, being bedevilled by the same fragmented trade-union structure, and consequent demarcation diputes, as had marked older industries in the North. If the development of new consumer industries was creating an industrial structure more recognisably like our own than that of the Victorian age, it was equally true that many of the weaknesses of the new industrial structure were allowed to develop as a result of *laissez-faire* policies (Alford 1981).

This was particularly true of the location of industry. The uneven distribution of unemployment as a result of the decline of particular industries in the North and West, and the tendency of firms to set up new factories in the South, was already apparent by the late 1920s (see Table 5.1(a)). Initially policy was to move unemployed workers to industry. Between 1929 and 1938 the Industrial Transference Board assisted the movement of 200,000 adults and 70,000 juveniles, by advancing fares and removal expenses. The peak years were 1929 and 1936 when there were jobs to move to, but from 1937 the emphasis of policy was switched to moving industry to the workers (Pitfield 1978).

The first experiment in regional policy was the Special Areas (Development and Improvement) Act of 1934, which was intended to be a temporary measure 'to facilitate the economic and social improvement' of designated areas of high unemployment. Two commissioners were appointed, one for England and Wales and one for Scotland, and £2 million earmarked for their use, but since they were not allowed to provide funds for profit-making enterprises, little was achieved. Criticism, not least by the Commissioner for England and Wales, Sir Malcolm Stewart, gradually forced the Government to accept that the location of industry could not be left to market economics alone (Booth 1978). In 1936 the Bank of England, with government backing, set up the Special Area Reconstruction Association Ltd., which was to lend to small businesses which could hope to be profitable in the Special Areas in the long run but which could not obtain credit from other financial institutions. Finally, the Special Areas (Amendment) Act of 1937 allowed the Special Areas commissioners to help any firm by letting premises, or by temporary contributions towards rent, rates and taxes, while the Treasury was empowered to make loans. Regional policy had some impact, as Table 5.4 shows. Even so, the impact was limited by the lack of controls on building factories in congested

Table 5.4 Percentage of Total Number of Factories Opened in Great Britain

	1934	*1935*	*1936*	*1937*	*1938*
Special Areas	2.7	0.8	2.2	4.4	17.1
Greater London	49.2	41.8	47.3	39.1	40.6

areas (McCrone 1969, ch. 3). The report of a Royal Commission on the Distribution of the Industrial Population (the Barlow Report), published in 1940, drew attention to the economic, social and strategical disadvantages of congestion in the Greater London area (Cmd. 6153, para. 426). Indeed, congestion was no less a regional problem than unemployment.

The Overall Effect of Economic Policy

From the autumn of 1932 to mid-1937 the Board of Trade's index of total industrial output rose by 64 per cent. So substantial a recovery would seem to be a vindication of the National Government's policy. However, although the 1937 peak of industrial output was some 30 per cent above the 1929 peak, the index fell by over 10 per cent in the twelve months to September 1938, a fall equal to about half that of 1929–32. These figures suggest that the extent of recovery in 1932–37 was largely a reaction to the slump and that what the economy was experiencing was an extreme form of an unregulated trade cycle (Capie and Collins 1980).

Nevertheless, the growth of manufacturing production in 1932–37 was unprecedented. Kaldor (1982, pp. 20–2, 26–7, 33–4) has ascribed this largely to increased protection from the general tariff and short-term effects of exchange depreciation, although he allows that the building boom, induced by cheap money, must have been a contributory factor. If Kaldor is right about the significance of tariffs for recovery, then the recession of 1937–38 could be explained equally well in terms of the exhaustion of import-substitution effects. A protective tariff provides a once-and-for-all impetus to industrialists, but once foreigners' share of the existing domestic market has been reduced, further expansion depends upon an increase in domestic demand or an increase in exports. In a country like Britain, which is dependent upon imports of raw materials, some increase in exports is necessary if an increase in domestic demand is not to cause a balance of payments problem. As it happened, the growth of exports in 1935–37 was regarded by contemporaries as encouraging, but a slump in the United States in 1937–38 reduced British exports, so that recovery could not be sustained once the domestic boom had exhausted itself.

The Treasury's hopes that manufacturers' profits could be

restored, and investment encouraged, by raising wholesale prices to the 1929 level, while wages remained steady, were only partially fulfilled. Certainly wholesale prices rose more rapidly than wage rates in 1932–37, but the wholesale price index was still below the 1929 level in 1937, whereas average money wage rates were above the 1929 level. In 1938 the wholesale price index fell while average money wage rates rose (see Figure 5.1). Nevertheless, down to 1936 money wage rates were remarkably stable, a fact no doubt largely due to high unemployment. There may also have been a 'money illusion' created by the fact that the Ministry of Labour's cost-of-living index was based upon pre-1914 working-class consumption patterns, and was therefore heavily weighted towards food. The fall in world food prices in 1929–32, and the fact that most overseas food suppliers depreciated their currencies with sterling, meant that the cost-of-living index did not rise appreciably until five years after sterling's initial depreciation in 1931.

A monetary policy which permitted a private investment boom in 1933–37 was certainly a great improvement on the monetary policy associated with the gold standard. The problem was that a fiscal policy of attempting to balance the budget meant that there was no planned stimulus of public expenditure to take up the slack once the private investment boom had spent itself. It was not until 1937 that the Treasury accepted Keynes's idea of varying public works expenditure to offset changes in the trade cycle. Even then the expected maximum degree of variation between any two years – £50 million after a delay of a year – was regarded as too small to have much impact (Peden 1984). Perhaps the most promising sign regarding public works policy by 1936–37 was that the Government had recognised the need to direct public expenditure towards areas of high unemployment. Expenditure on rearmament, which had certainly not been foreseen in 1932, gave the Government the means to direct large contracts to factories in such areas (Peden 1980, pp. 11–17).

Thomas (1983) has estimated that rearmament, beginning in 1935 when unemployment stood at 2.44 million, had created about a million additional jobs by 1938. The figure of one million is something of an overestimate, since Thomas neglects the opportunity cost of export orders foregone (by general engineering firms, for example, as well as by the aircraft industry). Moreover, it should be stressed that lags, while aircraft and munitions factories were being built, and the fact that government expenditure was not financed out of loans until 1937/38, meant that about half the additional jobs were not created until 1938, that is once the post-1932 recovery was over. Even so, loan-financed rearmament acted as a major brake on the recession of 1937–38, although such expenditure did not wholly offset the fall in exports. The main beneficiaries were iron and steel, engineering and coal, and the areas which benefited most included areas which had previously suffered from heavy unemployment (Central Scotland, North-East England and Wales), as well as the Midlands and South-West of England (where the aircraft industry was located). On the other hand, armaments do not produce an economic return, and 25 to 30 per cent of the cost of armaments produced in Britain represented the cost of imported raw materials. It is hardly surprising that from 1937 until the outbreak of war Britain had a balance of payments deficit which could not have been sustained indefinitely (Peden 1979, pp. 62–3, 84–5, 91, 96–9).

Recent studies, using an explicitly Keynesian framework to analyse the possible effects of civilian public works in the early 1930s, have concluded that the programme suggested by Lloyd George in 1929 would have been too small to deal with the subsequent increase in unemployment, whereas a programme which would have been sufficient for that purpose would have run into balance of payments problems (Glynn and Howells 1980; Thomas 1981). Only by closing the economy, as Nazi Germany did, through state controls of trade and capital movements could these problems have been overcome. Middleton (1982, 1983) has drawn attention to a different aspect of inadequate state powers to carry out a massive public works programme. A much higher proportion of capital investment than today was in the hands of the private sector, and within the public sector most capital investment was carried out by local authorities, which were often slow to respond to changes in central government policy. In any case, major causes of unemployment – reduced exports and decline in particular industries and regions – could not have been cured simply by raising aggregate demand through increased public investment (Booth and Glynn 1975). Nevertheless, public investment could have reduced, even if it could not cure, unemployment. Moreover, public expenditure could have been used to distribute income more evenly, whereas cheap money tended to favour the most creditworthy, and therefore the better-off, sections of the community.

Unemployment, even at the peak of recovery in 1937, still stood at 8.5 per cent of total employees (or 10.8 per cent of insured employees) and this must be included in any criticism of economic policy. It has, however, been argued that the persistence of higher-than-normal unemployment was a consequence of *social* policy. Unemployment benefits were more generous, relative to current wages, than before 1914, and Benjamin and Kochin (1979) have produced econometric equations in support of the view that such benefits reduced the incentive to work. Indeed, they suggest that had there been no unemployment insurance system, insured unemployment would have fallen by 5 to 8 percentage points to 'normal' levels, except in the depths of the depression. Benjamin and Kochin certainly overstate their case. Their failure to account for regional variations in unemployment (Collins 1982) can be explained only by an assumption of labour mobility which the lack of working-class housing in areas where industry was expanding does not entitle them to make. Again, even if the unemployed had been forced to seek casual jobs, as before 1914, more powerful trade-union organisation since the First World War would have made it difficult for the unemployed to price themselves into regular employment. While it would be surprising if more generous unemployment relief had not reduced the desperate search for low-paid or irregular work (itself a major cause of poverty before 1914), it is difficult to accept Benjamin and Kochin's monocausal explanation of abnormal unemployment. Some part of the explanation must lie in the incomplete success of the National Government's market-orientated economic policy.

The 'Onward March' of Social Policy

Early in 1932 Sir Richard Hopkins, a leading Treasury official, forecast that 'the onward march (even under a severe economic policy) of the cost of education, widows' pensions, housing and other things' would soon be resumed (Peden 1983, p. 381). Certainly the economy campaign of 1931/32 had no permanent impact. Total expenditure by central and local government on education, housing and civil pensions rose from £221.8 million in 1931/32 to £248.3 million in 1935/36. Of these, only expenditure on education fell even temporarily. Indeed, despite a 10 per cent cut in unemployment

Table 5.5 Gross Expenditure on Social Services: Central and Local Government (£ m. at Current Prices)

	1930/31	*1931/32*	*1932/33*	*1933/34*	*1934/35*	*1935/36*
Unemployment and public assistance	144.1	164.0	161.8	147.6	148.3	150.8
Education	104.2	103.3	100.8	101.7	105.7	117.7
Public health	55.6	56.9	58.7	58.6	60.5	63.5
Housing	37.5	40.2	42.6	44.8	46.1	48.2
Civil pensions	72.1	78.3	81.2	83.9	85.6	88.4
War pensions	49.2	47.0	44.5	42.8	41.2	40.5
Total	462.7	489.7	489.6	479.4	487.4	503.1
Social service expenditure as percentage of gross domestic product	11.1	12.7	13.1	12.6	12.1	12.0

Sources: Hicks (1970) p. 383; Feinstein (1972), T 13.

insurance benefits in 1931, a rise in the numbers of the unemployed and a fall in GDP meant that the proportion of national income going to unemployment relief, and to social services generally, rose in 1931/32 and 1932/33 (Table 5.5). Such a phenomenon under a severe economic policy has not been unknown in more recent times.

It was possible to increase expenditure upon social services, even while balancing the budget, because of the fall in interest rates in 1932 and the fall of unemployment from 1932/33 to 1936/37. After the successful conversion of War Debt in 1932, the sum which the Chancellor had to find in his budget for payment of interest on the National Debt fell from £296 million in 1931/32 to £215 million in 1933/34 (Hicks 1970, p. 379).

The relief of unemployment remained a major political problem. The economy measures of 1931, besides cutting insurance benefits, limited standard benefit to 26 weeks. Transitional benefit, or transitional payment as it was now called, for those not entitled to standard benefit, was to be administered by the Public Assistance Committees (PACs) of the local authorities, and a stringent family means test was to be applied. The means test took account of all household income, and payment was according to a household assessment of need. For families unaccustomed to Poor Law procedures it was an experience which left bitter memories. Moreover, local administration resulted in wide divergences in scales and conditions. Chamberlain saw a 'danger of relief being put up for auction by the parties' at local and national elections, at a time when unemployment was a common experience and an even more widespread fear, and when abnormal unemployment was expected to continue for years to come (Booth 1978). The Treasury also stressed the need to maintain financial confidence by showing that in future, unemployment insurance would be actuarily sound, and that the unemployment payments would be under firm control, so that 'another 1931' would not recur.

Chamberlain's solution was the Unemployment Act of 1934. Part I dealt with compulsory insurance. Contributions were fixed by an independent Unemployment Insurance Statutory Committee (chaired by Sir William Beveridge) at 10d. each for employee, employer and government, with the intention that the Fund would not have to borrow at the current level of unemployment (then about 17 per cent of insured employees). Since unemployment fell after 1934, it proved possible to reduce the Fund's debts, which had been fixed at £105 million in 1934, to £77 million by 1939, while also reducing contributions to 9d. in 1936 and increasing benefits (Gilbert 1970, pp. 179–80).

Part II of the Unemployment Act dealt with workers who had not paid enough contributions, or who had exhausted insurance benefit. A new Unemployment Assistance Board (UAB) took over from the PACs about 728,000 people receiving transitional payments and also over 200,000 able-bodied people who had been receiving poor relief on the rates. The UAB was to pay means-tested subsistence benefit according to national scales, and not according to the generosity or otherwise of local PACs. As it happened, the UAB rates proved to be lower than those paid by some PACs, and there were demonstrations by the unemployed when the UAB opened its offices in January 1935. The UAB was supposed to be an independent body, removed from local or parliamentary politics, but, with a general election in prospect, the Government had to intervene. The Minister of Labour, Oliver Harvey, hurriedly announced a standstill arrangement whereby the unemployed were to be paid either the old PAC scales, or the new UAB scales, whichever were more favourable to the applicant, until more generous UAB scales were introduced in 1936–37 (Briggs and Deacon 1973; Gilbert 1970, pp. 180–92; Stevenson 1983, pp. 203–9). It should not be thought, however, that the situation of the unemployed was in any way enviable: a survey of the long-term unemployed at the end of 1936 revealed widespread hopelessness, often combined with pathetic attempts to maintain respectability on inadequate means (Pilgrim Trust 1938).

Education was not accorded a high priority by the National Government (Dean 1971). Teachers' salaries were reduced between 1931 and 1935, and fees were charged according to parental means from 1932 for what had been free places in state-aided secondary schools. About 75 per cent of children left school at 14, and the best rewards in society continued to go to those who could afford school and university fees. The Hadow Report of 1926 had recommended the division of elementary education into primary and secondary stages, but successive governments left local authorities to decide the speed with which the Report was implemented. Financial stringency meant that even in 1939 one-third of children over 11 years old in the elementary system in England and Wales were in schools which had not been reorganised on Hadow lines. The

Hadow Report had also recommended the raising of the school leaving age to 15, and the approach of the 1935 election led the National Government to promise to do so. However, the Education Act of 1936 allowed pupils to leave before 15 if they found 'beneficial' employment, and the Act was not to come into force until September 1939, by which time a 'bulge' in the numbers of children of school age would have passed. In the event the Act was abandoned on the outbreak of war (Carr-Saunders and Jones 1937, pp. 112–26; Middleton and Weitzman 1976, pp. 152–201). Lack of interest in education may have had an adverse effect on the quality of the labour force. Certainly there were far fewer students receiving technological instruction in Great Britain than in Germany (Albu 1980, pp. 67–73). On the other hand, the 1930s can be seen as a period of progress in education: falling school rolls, themselves a result of the decline in the birth-rate, improved the ratio of teachers to pupils, while falling prices (and reduced salaries) offset the effects of cuts in public expenditure on the schools themselves in 1931–32 (Vaizey 1958, pp. 26, 31–2, 40, 70).

The public health services remained as fragmentary in the 1930s as before. Most were in the hands of local authorities, and National Health Insurance continued to be administered by many competing approved societies, all paying statutory benefits, but most also providing 'extras'. Generalisations about progress or otherwise are therefore difficult. Chamberlain's Local Government Act of 1929 had given local authorities powers to transform former Poor Law infirmaries into municipal hospitals of a high standard, but outside Greater London and certain other areas little had been achieved ten years later. There was a national shortage of hospital beds, and about a third of those available were in voluntary hospitals. Voluntary hospitals were supported by private health insurance, but, like most other hospitals, they found it difficult to cope with rising costs as medical science advanced. Public institutional treatment for most infectious diseases was available practically universally, but there was little indication of any tendency for cases of infectious diseases among school children to decline (PEP 1937a). There was, however, a significant improvement in the survival rates of infants, deaths in the first year of life falling from 65.6 per 1,000 in 1932 to 50.4 per 1,000 in 1939 in England and Wales. The comparable figures for Scotland were 81.1 and 68.5, reflecting harsher conditions, especially in housing. The maternal mortality rate, which in England and

Table 5.6 Numbers of Houses Built in England and Wales (000s)

	Jan. 1919–March 1930	*April 1930–1940*
Local authority	529.4	633.6
(of which for slum clearance or decrowding)	—	(329.4)
Private enterprise	947.2	2,084.2
(of which built with state subsidies)	(411.3)	(21.9)
Total built	1,476.6	2,717.8

Sources: Bowley (1945), p. 271; Becker (1951), p. 322.

Wales had been constant at about 4.0 per 1,000 births for many years, fell between 1935 and 1939 to 2.5 per 1,000 births, chiefly, it seems, as a result of improvements in obstetrical care and in attendance at public ante-natal clinics (Winter 1979).

Health, of course, depended upon housing as well as medical services. There were two main developments in housing policy in the 1930s. The first, initiated by the Labour Government, encouraged local authorities to concentrate on slum clearance. The second, initiated by the National Government, aimed to restore the private market as the normal means of satisfying demand for housing. The results are shown in Table 5.6. At first sight these figures suggest that housing policy in the 1930s was remarkably successful. However, attention has to be paid to the distribution of housing.

The Housing Act of 1930, introduced by the Labour Minister of Health, Arthur Greenwood, offered to local authorities a subsidy which varied according to the number of people rehoused from slums. The hope was that this form of subsidy would make local authorities more willing than hitherto to rehouse large poor families. The National Government followed this with the Housing Act of 1933, which abolished the Wheatley subsidy (see p. 79), thereby leaving slum clearance as the only form of building subsidised by central government funds. A further stage in this return to the pre-1914 'sanitary' policy was the 1935 Housing Act, which required local authorities to prepare plans to end overcrowding in their areas (Bowley 1945, pp. 135–68). Local authorities' own housing policies varied enormously according to local conditions and politics (Daunton 1984; Melling 1980). There was, however, a general problem of competition for building resources as the private housing boom of the 1930s was supplemented by rearmament work. The Ministry of Health, advised by the Treasury, decided in 1937–38 that slum clearance would have to be slowed down, and subsidies were reduced. No attempt was made to curb private building, apparently for fear of opposition from the National Government's supporters (Bowley 1945, pp. 166–8; Peden 1979 pp. 83–4, 90).

Both private builders and local authorities benefited from cheap money, but, in the absence of subsidies, effective demand for housing was determined by ability to raise a mortgage or to pay economic rent. Chamberlain expected that the depression-induced fall in building costs would make it possible for private enterprise to build unsubsidised houses which the poor could afford. However, rents which would cover the cost of building new houses did not fall sufficiently for this to happen, and the Government itself recognised the shortage of low-cost housing by suspending decontrol of rents of smaller working-class houses. Inevitably, the middle classes benefited most from the housing boom. By 1939 there was no longer an absolute shortage of houses in England and Wales, but not enough suitable houses had been built to keep pace with the increasing number of households and many working-class people had to make do with multiple occupation of large pre-1914 houses vacated by the middle classes (Becker 1951; Bowley 1945, pp. 169–79; Gilbert 1970, pp. 200–3).

In Scotland matters were much worse. Slums and overcrowding had long been a greater problem there (in 1911 47.7 per cent of the population had lived in flats or cottages with only one or two rooms, whereas in England and Wales only 7.1 per cent had lived in such cramped accommodation). Nevertheless, London governments in the interwar period were content to apply broadly the same housing legislation to Scotland as to England. Scotland also suffered more than England from the depression (Table 5.1(a)). As a result, only

311,500 houses were built in Scotland between 1919 and 1939, and in 1943 321,000 houses there were officially classified as unfit for human habitation. It was estimated in 1936 that 22.6 per cent of Scottish households were overcrowded, compared with only 3.8 per cent in England (Bowley 1945, pp. 261–8; Crammond 1966, pp. 18–24). Northern Ireland had a Parliament which was responsible for its own housing policy, but the Government there believed that the housing problem was temporary and could be solved by private enterprise. In the event, local authorities in the province provided only one-twelfth of new housing in the interwar years (compared with one-quarter in England and Wales) and there was evidence of a decline in the quantity and quality of the housing stock available to those who could not buy or could not afford to pay high rents (Murie *et al.* 1971).

The social services of the 1930s represented the results of a haphazard piling up of measures over 30 years. Both the popularity of most services, and the need for an overhaul, were apparent to informed opinion (PEP 1937b, pp. 32–3). Nevertheless, underlying much administrative muddle there were some general principles. Where a social service, for example a hospital, was provided for a local community, that community had to contribute to the cost through the rates, a principle that worked against poor areas even though there were usually matching central government grants. Where a social service was provided for an individual or his dependants, he was required either to have contributed to national insurance or to undergo a means test. There were no such 'welfare state' principles such as universal coverage by national insurance or the provision of optimal services in health and education on a national scale. Social services were intended to be a minimum which could be supplemented by self-help. Workmen continued to contribute more in aggregate to voluntary insurance and other self-help schemes than to national insurance (Briggs 1981, p. 362), and the middle classes were excluded from national insurance. Social expenditure financed by progressive taxation effected a redistribution of income from rich to poor which, in 1937, raised the income of the working classes by 8–14 per cent (Barna 1945, p. 233–4). It does not seem to have been deliberate policy, however, to redistribute incomes in this way, and great inequalities of wealth remained.

There was, on the other hand, renewed concern in the 1930s with what before 1914 had been called 'national efficiency', although that term was no longer used in political debate. Neville Chamberlain was particularly interested in the Government's National Fitness Campaign in the late 1930s, and in 1939 the British Medical Association voted in favour of the extension of national insurance to dependants (Thane 1982, pp. 195–6). Contemporary concern with unsatisfactory social conditions has rightly been echoed by social historians (Constantine 1983; Stevenson 1984), but generally social conditions were much better than ever before. This is reflected in the way Rowntree adjusted his poverty standard between 1899 and 1936 (see pages 11–13). What was particularly worrying from the standpoint of national efficiency, however, was the extent to which poverty was experienced by children. A survey in Birmingham suggested that 14 per cent of families and 30 per cent of children in the city had inadequate diets. Matters were undoubtedly worse in less prosperous communities. The size of families in relation to family income was still a major determinant of poverty, and there was a strong movement, led by Eleanor Rathbone, which called for family allowances for all, including people in work, so as to reduce the economic burden of having children. Arguments about child poverty were reinforced by the concern felt in some circles that the decline in the birth-rate would lead to a decline in Britain's population, and therefore its standing as a great power. However, apart from restoring cuts made in 1931 in income-tax child allowances, in 1935, and raising them in 1936, the National Government took no action to help people in work. Since few wage earners then paid income tax, it would seem that even these steps to help parents were really designed to please the National Government's middle-class voters (Macnicol 1980).

The End of *Laissez-Faire*?

There was no response in Britain to the post-1929 depression which could be compared to the vast programmes of public works projected in Roosevelt's 'New Deal'. As one Whitehall official remarked in 1935, at a time when Lloyd George was calling for a British 'New Deal':

> In the United States . . . gambling holds much the same place in national life as cricket does in ours. Nothing, therefore, is more natural than that the American government should indulge in a gamble while a British

> government has to keep a straight bat and sometimes to stone wall. Such tactics may not appeal to those spectators who have more enthusiasm than knowledge of the pitch, but it is to be hoped that the barracking will not affect the batsmen. For the state of England is not such that they can afford to take great risks.[1]

The official then went on to point out that Britain, unlike the United States, was not a self-sufficient country with ample gold reserves who could ignore the effect of public works on the balance of payments.

Britain did not take a gamble in the 1930s. Under the National Government, business confidence was not to be disturbed by government departing from the 'rules of the game' whereby government confined itself to establishing conditions in which private enterprise could flourish. Nevertheless, unstable world economic conditions meant that from 1931 government had to begin to manage the economy consciously in order to improve prospects for private investors. Management of the currency – by the Treasury as well as the Bank of England – and tariffs were used to this end. Fiscal orthodoxy, and a reluctance to intervene directly in business decisions, remained as relics of *laissez-faire*, but price-fixing by agricultural producers, and by some industrial producers, was encouraged. An unregulated free market was no longer seen as a sufficient condition for prosperity, even if private enterprise was expected to provide the main thrust of recovery.

Unemployment policy was directed to maintaining social peace while economic recovery was awaited. The unemployed were maintained at bare subsistence level, but otherwise little was done to prepare them for future employment. Other aspects of social policy represented the logical development of Edwardian social reform, and there was no serious attempt to use the decline in demand for private goods as an occasion to use unemployed resources for public welfare. Only a very tentative counter-cyclical public works programme was being mooted in 1937. Despite considerable departures from *laissez-faire* principles in economic policy, and to a lesser degree in social policy, Britain had still some way to go before it would have a managed economy or a welfare state.

---

1. Memorandum by Sir Frederick Leith-Ross, in Treasury Papers, series 188, file 117, Public Record Office, London.

References

Documents

Cmd. 3897 (Macmillan) *Committee on Finance and Industry, Report,* BPP 1930–31, vol. XIII, pp. 219–546.

Cmd. 3920 *Report of the* (May) *Committee on National Expenditure,* BPP 1930–31, vol. XVI, pp. 1–282.

Cmd. 6153 *Royal Commission on the Distribution of the Industrial Population* (Barlow) *Report*, BPP 1939–40, vol. IV, pp. 263–592.

Books and Articles

Albu, A. (1980) 'British attitudes to engineering education: a historical perspective', in K. Pavitt (ed), *Technical Innovation and British Economic Performance,* Macmillan.

Alford, B. (1981) 'New industries for old? British industry between the wars', in R. Floud and D. McCloskey (eds.), *The Economic History of Britain since 1700,* vol. 2, Cambridge University Press.

Barna, T. (1945) *Redistribution of Incomes Through Public Finance in 1937,* Oxford University Press.

Becker, A.P. (1951) 'Housing in England and Wales during the business depression of the 1930s', *Economic History Review,* 2nd series, vol. 3, pp. 321–41.

Benjamin, D.K., and Kochin, L.A. (1979) 'Searching for an explanation of unemployment in interwar Britain', *Journal of Political Economy,* vol. 87, pp. 441–78.

Booth, A. (1978) 'An administrative experiment in unemployment policy in the Thirties', *Public Administration,* vol. 56, pp. 139–57.

Booth, A., and Glynn, S. (1975) 'Unemployment in the interwar period: a multiple problem', *Journal of Contemporary History,* vol. 10, pp. 611–36.

Bowley, M. (1945) *Housing and the State 1919–1944,* George Allen and Unwin.

Briggs, A. (1981) 'Social history 1900–45', in R. Floud and D. McCloskey (eds.), *The Economic History of Britain since 1700,* vol. 2, Cambridge University Press.

Briggs, E. and Deacon, A. (1973) 'The creation of the Unemployment Assistance Board', in *Policy and Politics,* vol. 2, pp. 43–62.

Burn, D. (1940), *The Economic History of Steelmaking, 1867–1939,* Cambridge University Press.

Cairncross, A., and Eichengreen, B. (1983) *Sterling in Decline: The Devaluations of 1931, 1949 and 1967,* Basil Blackwell.

Capie, F. (1978) 'The British tariff and industrial protection in the 1930s', *Economic History Review,* 2nd series, vol. 31, pp. 399–409.

Capie, F. (1983) *Depression and Protectionism: Britain between the Wars,* George Allen and Unwin.

Capie, F., and Collins, M. (1980) 'The extent of British economic recovery in the 1930s', *Economy and History,* vol. 23, pp. 40–60.

Carpenter, L. (1976) 'Corporatism in Britain 1930–45', *Journal of Contemporary History,* vol. 11, no. 1, pp. 3–25.

Carr-Saunders, A., and Jones, D.C., (1937) *A Survey of the Social Structure of England and Wales,* Oxford University Press.

Clay, H. (1957) *Lord Norman,* Macmillan.

Collins, M. (1982) 'Unemployment in interwar Britain: still searching for an explanation', *Journal of Political Economy,* vol. 90, pp. 369–79.

Constantine, S. (1980) *Unemployment in Britain between the Wars,* Longman.

Constantine, S. (1983) *Social Conditions in Britain 1918–1939,* Methuen.

Crammond, R.D. (1966) *Housing Policy in Scotland,* Oliver and Boyd.

Daunton, M.J. (ed.) (1984) *Councillors and Tenants: Local Authority Housing in English Cities, 1919–1939,* Leicester University Press.

Deacon, A. (1976) 'In search of the scrounger', *Occasional Papers on Social Administration,* no. 60.

Dean, D. (1971) 'Conservatism and the national educational system 1922–40', *Journal of Contemporary History,* vol. 6, no. 2, pp. 150–65.

Drummond, I. (1974) *Imperial Economic Policy, 1917–1939,* George Allen and Unwin.

Drummond, I. (1981) *The Floating Pound and the Sterling Area,* Cambridge University Press.

Feinstein, C.H. (1965) *Domestic Capital Formation in the United Kingdom,* Cambridge University Press.

Feinstein, C.H. (1972) *National Income, Expenditure and Output of the United Kingdom, 1855–1965,* Cambridge University Press.

Gilbert, B.B. (1970) *British Social Policy 1914–1939,* Batsford.

Glynn, S., and Howells, P. (1980) 'Unemployment in the 1930s: the "Keynesian" solution reconsidered', *Australian Economic History Review,* vol. 20, pp. 28–45.

Hicks, U. (1970) *The Finance of British Government 1920–1936,* Oxford University Press.

Howson, S. (1975) *Domestic Monetary Management in Britain 1919–38,* Cambridge University Press.

Howson, S. (1980) *Sterling's Managed Float: The Operations of the Exchange Equalisation Account, 1932–39,* Princeton University Press.

Howson, S. and Winch, D. (1977) *The Economic Advisory Council, 1930–1939,* Cambridge University Press.

Kaldor, N. (1982) 'Keynes as an economic adviser', in A.P. Thirlwall (ed.), *Keynes as a Policy Adviser,* Macmillan.

Kirby, M. (1973a) 'The control of competition in the British coal mining industry in the Thirties', *Economic History Review,* 2nd series, vol. 26, pp. 273–84.

Kirby, M. (1973b) 'Government intervention in industrial organization: coal mining in the nineteen-thirties', *Business History,* vol. 15, pp. 160–73.

Kirby, M. (1974) 'The Lancashire cotton industry in the inter-war years: a study in organizational change', *Business History,* vol. 16, pp. 145–59.

McCrone, G. (1969) *Regional Policy in Britain,* George Allen and Unwin.

Macnicol, J. (1980) *The Movement for Family Allowances, 1918–45,* Heinemann.

Marquand, D. (1977) *Ramsay MacDonald,* Jonathan Cape.

Melling, J. (ed.) (1980) *Housing, Social Policy and the State,* Croom Helm.

Middleton, N., and Weitzman, S. (1976) *A Place for Everyone,* Victor Gollancz.

Middleton, R. (1981) 'The constant employment budget balance and British budgetary policy, 1929–39', *Economic History Review,* 2nd series, vol. 34, pp. 266–86.

Middleton, R. (1982) 'The Treasury in the 1930s: political and administrative constraints to acceptance of the "new" economics', *Oxford Economic Papers,* vol. 34, pp. 48–77.

Middleton, R. (1983) 'The Treasury and public investment: a perspective on inter-war economic management', *Public Administration,* vol. 61, pp. 351–70.

Mitchell, B.R. and Deane, P. (1962) *Abstract of British Historical Statistics,* Cambridge University Press.

Murie, A., Birrell, W., Hillyard, P., and Roche, D. (1971) 'Housing policy between the wars: Northern Ireland, England and Wales', *Social and Economic Administration,* vol. 5, pp. 263–79.

Nevin, E. (1955) *The Mechanism of Cheap Money,* University of Wales Press.

Peden, G.C. (1979) *British Rearmament and the Treasury, 1932–1939,* Scottish Academic Press.

Peden, G.C. (1980) 'Keynes, the Treasury and unemployment in the later nineteen-thirties', *Oxford Economic Papers,* vol. 32, pp. 1–18.

Peden, G.C. (1983) 'The Treasury as the central department of government 1919–1939', *Public Administration,* vol. 61, pp. 371–85.

Peden, G.C. (1984) 'The "Treasury view" on public works and employment in the interwar period', *Economic History Review,* 2nd series, vol. 37, pp. 167–81.

PEP, Political and Economic Planning (1937a) *Report on the British Health Services.*

PEP, Political and Economic Planning (1937b) *Report on the British Social Services.*

Pilgrim Trust (1938) *Men Without Work,* Cambridge University Press.

Pitfield, D.E. (1978) 'The quest for an effective regional policy, 1934–37', *Regional Studies,* vol. 12, pp. 429–43.

Pollard, S. (1983) *The Development of the British Economy,* Edward Arnold.

Redmond, J. (1980) 'An indicator of the effective exchange rate of the pound in the nineteen-thirties', *Economic History Review,* 2nd series, vol. 33, pp. 83–91.

Richardson, H.W. (1967) *Economic Recovery in Britain, 1932–9,* Weidenfeld and Nicolson.

Roberts, R. (1984) 'The administrative origins of industrial diplomacy: an aspect of government–industry relations, 1929–1935', in J. Turner (ed.), *Businessmen and Politics,* Heinemann.
Sayers, R. (1976) *The Bank of England, 1891–1944,* vol. 2, Cambridge University Press.
Skidelsky, R. (1975) *Oswald Mosley,* Macmillan.
Stevenson, J. (1983) 'The making of unemployment policy, 1931–1935', in M. Bentley and J. Stevenson (eds.), *High and Low Politics in Modern Britain,* Oxford University Press.
Stevenson, J. (1984) *British Society 1914–45,* Penguin Books.
Thane, P. (1982) *Foundations of the Welfare State,* Longman.
Thomas, M. (1983) 'Rearmament and economic recovery in the late 1930s', *Economic History Review,* 2nd series, vol. 36, pp. 552–79.
Thomas, T. (1981) 'Aggregate demand in the United Kingdom 1918–45', in R. Floud and D. McCloskey (eds.), *The Economic History of Britain since 1700,* vol. 2, Cambridge University Press.
Tolliday, S. (1984) 'Tariffs and steel, 1916–1934: the politics of industrial decline', in J. Turner (ed.), *Businessmen and Politics,* Heinemann.
Vaizey, J. (1958) *The Costs of Education*, George Allen and Unwin.
Williamson, P. (1984a) 'A "bankers ramp"? Financiers and the British political crisis of August 1931', *English Historical Review,* vol. 99, pp. 770–806.
Williamson, P. (1984b) 'Financiers, the gold standard and British politics, 1925–1931', in J. Turner (ed.), *Businessmen and Politics*, Heinemann.
Winch, D. (1983) 'Britain in the 'thirties: a managed economy?', in C.H. Feinstein (ed.), *The Managed Economy: Essays in British Economic Policy and Performance since 1929,* Oxford University Press.
Winter, J.M. (1979) 'Infant mortality, maternal mortality, and public health in Britain in the 1930s', *Journal of European Economic History,* vol. 8, pp. 439–62.

6

War and Postwar 1939–51

The war which broke out in September 1939, like the First World War, raised a host of supply problems which could not be resolved satisfactorily by market forces alone. Once more, government had to take steps to control the economy and limits had to be placed on personal liberty. From May 1940 the country was governed by a coalition of Conservatives, Labour and Liberals under Churchill, and Labour ministers played a prominent part. Since many controls were continued after the war ended in 1945, and since Labour was almost continuously in office from 1940 to 1951, the war and immediate postwar years can be seen as a single period from the point of view of economic policy.

The Second World War, like the First, gave rise to a number of ambitious plans for postwar social policy. In some respects the prospects for fulfilment of these plans seemed better after 1945 than after 1918: Labour won the 1945 election and there was no depression as there had been after 1920. On the other hand, the war had so weakened the economy that it was difficult to create the 'welfare state' which Labour had promised in 1945. As always, the impact of war on social policy has to be considered over a longer period than the war itself.

The War Economy: Supply

It was not known in 1939 whether or when it would be possible to obtain the same scale of supplies from the United States as in

1915–18. Britain, in common with the other Allies, had defaulted on its war debts to the United States in the post-1931 crisis, and Congress had passed the Johnson Act in 1934 which forbade new loans to governments in default. As a result, Britain's gold and dollar reserves were at first husbanded carefully in the hope of making them last for the three-year war which Anglo–French war plans envisaged. Such caution had to be thrown to the winds once Britain stood alone in the summer of 1940, and orders in America were increased in the hope that the United States, which was still neutral, would continue supplies once Britain was no longer able to pay for them. The United States did in fact do this under the Lend–Lease Act of March 1941, whereby new requests for supplies, which the United States itself did not need, were 'lent' for the duration of the war. Existing orders had to be paid for, however, and Britain had to sell off the best of its overseas investments to raise dollars. Britain also ran up huge sterling debts with other countries. Overseas financial policy enabled Britain to devote its own economic resources to maximising war production, at the expense, *inter alia,* of exports but, as we shall see, its external financial position was seriously weakened (Sayers 1956, chs. 9–15).

Control of production was by the physical allocation of productive capacity, with manpower being the key unit of account. The Treasury, which had earlier claimed to be the supreme co-ordinating department, had its functions confined after 1940 to dealing with the budget and with overseas finance.

Businessmen were recruited into government departments, as in the First World War, and trade associations acted as agents of the Government. Responsibility for gathering economic information and advising on economic problems also lay with statisticians and economists, drawn mainly from academic life. Some were attached to the Prime Minister's Statistical Section, rather more were in the War Cabinet's Central Statistical Office and Economic Section, while others were in government departments. While the advice of economists had been available to governments before, notably through the Economic Advisory Council's Sub-Committee on Economic Information in the 1930s, it was the war which saw the integration of economists into Whitehall (Booth and Coates 1980).

State intervention in the economy drew upon First World War experience in many respects. The railways were placed under government control and the mercantile marine was directed by a new Ministry of Shipping. To save shipping space, the Ministry of Agriculture directed farmers to concentrate on the production of bulky products, such as grain, and guaranteed markets and prices. There were subsidies to encourage investment in tractors (the number of which quadrupled between 1939 and 1946) and the ploughing up of pasture. Food subsidies allowed higher prices to be offered to farmers than were charged in shops. As a result, farmers' average net money income rose by about 360 per cent between 1938 and 1946, whereas national income as a whole rose by about 75 per cent at current prices (Nash 1951, pp. 200–21; Pollard 1983, pp. 205–7).

Usually there was little direct control of manufacturing industry, apart from the royal ordnance factories and royal dockyards. Instead, the Government exercised control by drawing up programmes and subsequently by allocating raw materials, machine tools and labour, by licensing building and other investment, and by using its position as the dominant purchaser to fix contract prices (Hancock and Gowing 1949). Alternative sources of demand were suppressed through taxes, and from 1941 the Board of Trade organised 'concentration' schemes to shut down or convert factories in 'less essential' industries, reducing output of consumer goods to the minimum thought to be necessary to maintain civilian morale. Concentration schemes proved difficult to administer, and often released less labour and plant than expected, but they nonetheless made a sharp contrast with government hesitancy about prewar 'rationalisation' (Allen 1951; Hargreaves and Gowing 1952, pp. 202–24).

In coal mining the control of output and pithead prices was at first left to the owners' district executive boards. It was only when worsening industrial relations, absenteeism and falling output brought about a coal crisis in 1942 that a Ministry of Fuel and Power was set up to administer the industry centrally. Even so, output, which had fallen from 232 million tons in 1939/40 to 207 million tons in 1941/42, continued to decline, amounting to a mere 191 million tons in 1944/45. Output per manshift was adversely affected by the ageing of experienced miners and by the wearing out of equipment which could not be replaced (Court 1951).

A shortage of manpower in coal mining, such as developed after 1940, had been unexpected, but even before the war there had been shortages of some key categories of skilled labour for armaments production. Such labour could be attracted from civilian industries by raising wages in the munitions industries, as in the First World War, but this could cause cost-push inflation. On the other hand, the trade unions were opposed to industrial conscription. Churchill's solution was to put Ernest Bevin, who had been one of the leaders of the General Strike, in charge of the Ministry of Labour and National Service. The danger of invasion in 1940 made exceptional measures politically possible and the Emergency Powers Act of that year gave Bevin authority to direct anyone over sixteen years to do any work. Even so, Bevin used his authority sparingly.

Under the Essential Works Order No. 302 of March 1941 workers in any factory or undertaking scheduled by the Ministry of Labour could neither leave nor be dismissed without the Minister's consent. As with leaving certificates in the First World War, the purpose was to prevent production being disturbed by labour turnover. Bevin, however, insisted that all affected workers should enjoy adequate wages, conditions of work and welfare, and there was never the same resentment as leaving certificates had caused. Conscription of labour was introduced by age, skill and sex, but while some workers were directed to particular industries, notably the 22,000 'Bevin boys' who were selected by lot to work in the coal mines, powers to direct labour were not usually necessary. This was because the Government steadily reduced alternative forms of employment through concentration schemes or control of investment or raw materials. Conscription of women was delayed until the end of 1941, when Bevin felt public opinion was ready for a measure which even Hitler did not introduce in Germany (Bullock 1967, chs. 1–6; Gowing 1972; Ince 1946; Inman 1957, chs. 7–8).

Bevin's main problems arose from industrial relations. Acting on the advice of his Joint Consultative Committee, representing the TUC and the British Employers' Confederation, he issued the Conditions of Employment and National Arbitration Order No. 1305 in July 1940. This prohibited strikes and lockouts, except when the Minister of Labour chose not to refer a dispute to compulsory arbitration. Whenever possible, Bevin encouraged the use of existing negotiating machinery. Nevertheless, dilution, especially in engineering and shipbuilding, raised endless problems, while the miners were determined to improve their position relative to other wage earners, having fallen behind in the interwar years. Strikes were more frequent than in 1914–18 or 1927–39, but they tended to be resolved more quickly, so that the average annual loss of working days in 1939–45 was under 2 million, compared with over 4 million in 1914–18. Coal mining accounted for half the total working days lost through strikes in 1943, and two-thirds in 1944. It was, as always, impractical to impose statutory sanctions against large numbers of strikers. The classic example was a strike at Betteshanger Colliery in Kent. Although over a thousand miners were fined, the fines remained unpaid and the men refused to return to work until their leaders, who had been imprisoned, were released (Inman 1957, pp. 392–402; Macdonald 1960, pp. 123–6).

The identification of the official trade-union leadership with government controls made it vulnerable to a shop-stewards' movement, as in 1915–18. This development was checked, however, partly by the danger of invasion in 1940, partly by Bevin's promotion of the workers' interests in the use of his powers, and partly by Hitler's invasion of Russia in 1941, which won over Communists to the cause of maximising production. Even so, the negotiation of dilution agreements at plant level, and efforts to improve productivity through joint production committees representing management and labour, strengthened the authority of shop stewards, with a lasting effect on the trade-union movement (Brown 1983, pp. 143–6; Inman 1957, pp. 374–92). One is reminded that, however great the powers which government takes to control production, there must be communication with, and consent from, the shop floor.

The War Economy: Control of Inflation

There is a myth that the Second World War showed that government could solve unemployment. Since over 4.5 million people were recruited into the defence services during the war, the disappearance of unemployment, which had stood at 1.25 million on the eve of the war, was hardly surprising. Civilian employment, measured in full-time job equivalents, actually *fell* by 8.8 per cent between 1939 and 1945 (Table 6.1). It was possible to maintain 5 million people in the defence services – and, therefore, out of productive employment – only because the United States and other countries contributed to their upkeep. What the war did demonstrate was the range of devices which government could use to control, or at least to

Table 6.1 Distribution of Manpower at June Each Year*

	(1) Defence services (millions)	*(2) Civil employment (millions)*	*(3) Percentage of (2) which was female*	*(4) Insured unemployed (thousands)*
1939	0.48	18.00	26.9	1,270
1940	2.27	17.76	29.9	645
1941	3.38	17.75	33.3	198
1942	4.09	17.88	36.8	87
1943	4.76	17.44	38.8	60
1944	4.97	16.97	39.0	54
1945	5.09	16.42	38.3	103

Source: Central Statistical Office (1951), Table 9.

Note: *Men aged 14–64; women aged 14–59. Two women in part-time employment counted as one full-time equivalent.

disguise, inflation when the economy was at over-full employment.

A Treasury memorandum of 1929 on 'The Course of Prices in a Major War' had looked to the control of food prices to prevent a vicious spiral of rising prices and wage demands. The official cost-of-living index attributed 60 per cent of working-class expenditure to food (an anachronistic proportion, reflecting Edwardian consumption patterns) and it was hoped that, if food prices could be held steady, the index would not rise much and wage restraint would thereby be encouraged. The Treasury at first preferred rationing to reduce demand for food rather than subsidies to prevent price rises. By 1941, however, the advantages of food subsidies as a counter-inflation policy were felt to justify an increasing burden on the Exchequer (Hammond 1951, vol. 1, ch. 7; Nash 1951, pp. 221–38). The cost-of-living index was also held down by rent controls and by price controls on clothing. Price controls, of course, also required rationing. The cost of clothing and essential consumer goods was held down by a 'utility' scheme, whereby designs were standardised into easily-produced forms.

Table 6.2 Wages and Prices (1938 = 100)

	(1) *Average weekly wage rates*	*(2)* *Average weekly wage earnings*	*(3)** *Retail prices (official wartime index)*	*(4)* *Retail prices (post-war index for essential items)*	*(5)* *Drink and tobacco prices*
1939	101	—	—	103	109
1940	112	130	121	117	141
1941	122	142	129	129	163
1942	131	160	130	137	205
1943	137	176	129	142	239
1944	144	179	131	145	248
1945	151	178	132	148	243

Source: Feinstein (1972), Tables 62 and 65; and Pollard (1983), p. 211.

Note: *First half of 1939 = 100.

Table 6.3 Approximate Percentage Shares of Net National Product

	Government expenditure			
	War	*Civil*	*Consumer's expenditure*	*Net non-war capital formation*
1938	7	10	78	5
1939	15	9.5	73.5	2
1940	44	8	64	–16
1941	54	7	56	–17
1942	52	8	52	–12
1943	56	7	49	–12
1944	54	7	51	–12
1945	49	7	54	–10

Source: Pollard (1983), p. 214.

Table 6.2 shows the extent to which inflation was disguised. The official wartime index showed a 32 per cent increase in retail prices over 1938–45, whereas Feinstein's index (1972, T140) for 'essential items' shows a 48 per cent increase. Average wage rates and weekly earnings rose much faster than either retail price index, but all the Second World War indices rose more slowly than those for the First World War (Table 3.3). An increase of less than 50 per cent in prices for essential items in 1938–45 was a great improvement on the increase of 100 per cent in 1913–18. The fact that wage rates rose on average by 51 per cent in 1938–45 compared with 79 per cent in 1913–18 does suggest that food subsidies and price controls did have some success in dampening down wage demands. The main cost lay in food subsidies, which rose from about £16 million in 1939/40 to £96 million in 1941/42 and £196 million in 1944/45 (Nash 1951, pp. 232–3).

Price fixing, rationing and wage restraint could all contribute to counter-inflation policy, but they could not in themselves be sufficient to prevent inflation. The problem of war finance was how to make about half of the total national output of goods and services available to the Government without inflation. Table 6.3 shows how the Government's share of net national product increased over

1939–43. The cost of the war was met partly by running down capital assets (for example, by firms not using depreciation funds to replace worn-out equipment). Even so, aggregate civilian consumption had to be reduced, and in real terms it had been cut by 20 per cent by 1943, compared with 14 per cent in 1914–18. Social justice demanded heavy taxation of the rich, through supertax and excess profits duty, but some reduction in working-class demand was also necessary. In a series of articles in *The Times* in November 1939, later published as *How to Pay for the War* (1940), Keynes used a national income accounting framework to estimate the sources available to finance projected government expenditure, and the extent to which private consumption would have to be cut if there were to be no excess demand. This was the converse of his use of macroeconomic analysis in his *General Theory* of 1936, in which he had shown how unemployment could be reduced by reflation. In the absence of any official national income statistics, Keynes could give only very rough figures, but he suggested that the sources available for additional government expenditure *and* current private consumption in the coming financial year amounted to £1,625 million. This was made up of £825 million from increased output, £150 million from diversion of industry's depreciation funds, £300 million from diversion of normal new investment, and £350 million from selling gold and foreign investments and from borrowing abroad. If projected government expenditure of £1,850 million were not to cause inflation, private consumption would have to be reduced by £225 million *plus* the £825 million earned from increased output. In calculating new levels of taxation, Keynes made allowance for increased new savings, including national insurance and pension fund contributions. This left £950 million to be found in other ways. The Chancellor had already increased taxation by £400 million, and another £100 million could be raised from increased sales tax on non-necessities, like tobacco, but there remained an 'inflationary gap' of £450 million. Left to itself, this gap would be closed by an inflationary rise in national income, which would pull up both revenue and savings. This, Keynes argued, would benefit those who received inflated profits, which could then be lent to the Government, as in 1914–18. Instead, he suggested a scheme of 'deferred pay' to fill the gap. In effect £450 million would be raised by compulsory savings in proportion to income, repayment being deferred until after the war.

The trade unions were opposed to compulsory savings, even though Keynes had linked his scheme with further schemes for family allowances and price fixing of basic rations. Moreover, compulsory savings might discourage voluntary savings. Compulsory savings, or 'post-war credits' as they came to be called, were nevertheless introduced in the 1941 budget, although they never assumed the importance which Keynes had intended. The annual average sum raised was only £121 million (Sayers 1956, pp. 80–5). Keynes had thought that post-war credits could be returned whenever a depression, like that of the early 1920s, threatened, but in fact the post-1945 years were marked by a long boom. Personal post-war credits were repaid only to old age pensioners and certain other special cases, and then only in much depreciated money, so that it is doubtful if such a counter-inflation policy would ever be acceptable to the British public again.

What made the 1941 budget a landmark in public finance was that it was the first time the chancellor's budget was worked out within a national income accounting framework, as Keynes had suggested, instead of being simply a cash balance sheet of central government income and expenditure. The Chancellor, Sir Kingsley Wood, was very conservative – he first entered the pages of this book as the spokesman of commercial insurance interests against Lloyd George (page 30). Unlike Lloyd George in 1914, Wood grasped the need for a stabilisation budget. Keynes had been brought into the Treasury as an adviser in July 1940 and officials, who had once opposed his ideas for reducing unemployment through public expenditure, proved to be more willing to consider his ideas for estimating and closing the 'inflationary gap'. About the same time the Secretary of the Cabinet, Sir Edward Bridges, himself an ex-Treasury official, had been persuaded that accurate national income statistics were essential for economic planning, and he had authorised James Meade, Richard Stone and others in the War Cabinet Offices to prepare the first official national income accounts. These first figures were necessarily less than perfect, but they made possible a better appreciation of the budgetary problem than before. National income plus provision for depreciation was estimated for 1941/42 at £7,329 million, of which the Government intended to take £3,700 million for its net domestic expenditure. Revenue at current rates of taxation was estimated at £1,636 million; 'impersonal' savings (company reserves, insurance premiums, etc.) at £900 million and personal savings at £700 million, leaving an 'inflationary gap' of about £500 million. The Chancellor proposed to raise £250 million in new taxation (of which half would be postwar credits), while hoping that the national savings movement could increase personal savings by £200–£300 million (Sayers 1956, ch. 3).

The ability to raise taxation was thus an essential element in counter-inflation policy. Direct taxation accounted for an increasing proportion of revenue from 1941. Excess profits duty, charged at 60 per cent at the outbreak of war, had been raised to 100 per cent in 1940 (although, to retain some incentive to enterprise, 20 per cent postwar credits were allowed on this tax from 1941). The standard rate of income tax, which had been 5s. 6d. in the pound before the war, was raised to 10s. in 1941 and, with surtax in addition to income tax, top income earners paid 19s. 6d. in the pound. The main innovation, however, was the introduction of 'pay as you earn' (PAYE) in 1943. Before the war the payment of income tax had been largely a middle-class activity and payments were usually made half-yearly or yearly. Rising money wages during the war brought many workers into the ambit of income tax for the first time and PAYE was devised to enable them to spread payments through the year (Sayers 1956, pp. 99–111). Indirect taxation also had a role to play. With necessities cheap and scarce, more and more was spent by the public on drink, tobacco and entertainment. Since none of these items affected the official cost-of-living index, their price could be forced up through sales taxes to absorb surplus purchasing power (Table 6.2).

The proportion of government expenditure financed by borrowing from the British public fell after 1941. Moreover, of the £15,237 million raised in this way, only £770 million was derived from the printing press, that is by increasing the fiduciary bank note issue. The rest came from savings. This was possible because the Government's direct controls over investment suppressed most alternatives to the purchase of government bonds. In addition, firms were encouraged to use idle funds to take up tax reserve certificates (in readiness for tax liability) or 90-day Treasury bills. The cash reserves of the clearing banks were mopped up with Treasury deposit receipts, whereby the banks were required to lend to the Government for six-month periods. Rationing reduced the public's ability to spend and some surplus cash was attracted by the national savings movement. The Treasury and the Bank of England accepted the advice of Keynes and others not to offer high interest rates, which would have raised the burden of the National Debt, as in 1914–18 (Sayers 1956, pp. 153–62, 188–225). Conducting '3 per cent war', however, meant that few people would lend to the Government for more than short periods. As a result, suppressed wartime inflation left a postwar inheritance of pent-up demand backed by liquid funds – a circumstance which made continuation of wartime controls necessary.

Even during the war there were ample signs of inflation in the form of queues and black markets. The system of rationing through coupons could not be policed adequately (Reddaway 1951) and worked as well as it did only because public opinion was firmly in favour of 'fair shares for all'. The control of inflation, in so far as it was successful, depended as much upon public willingness to accept sacrifices as upon new fiscal techniques.

Wartime Origins of the 'Welfare State'

The upheaval of war had a number of implications for social policy and these were by no means wholly favourable to an extension of social services. The raising of the school leaving age to 15 years was abandoned when war broke out. The slum clearance programme, already retarded by rearmament, came to a halt, as did almost all other house building after 1941. It is even possible that the extension of national health insurance to workers' dependants, and the introduction of family allowances, were delayed. The Conservatives had been concerned before the war about their prospects in an election in 1940 and their research department had suggested the inclusion of these measures in their manifesto (Ramsden 1980, pp. 91–2). On the other hand, Macnicol (1980) has shown that as late as 1940 there was considerable hostility to family allowances from the TUC, which saw them as a device for justifying low wages, and that there was no enthusiasm for family allowances within the Government either. All one can say is that one has to be cautious about ascribing changes in social policy to war alone; electoral politics are also significant.

Interpretation of the impact of war has until recently been strongly influenced by Richard Titmuss's official history of *Problems of Social Policy* (1950). Titmuss argued that the hazards of war were universal and that prewar principles of selectivity could no longer be applied. Bomb victims could not be treated like recipients of poor relief. The Unemployment Assistance Board, which became simply the Assistance Board, was used to pay out hardship allowances, rather than leave these to local Public Assistance Committees, which were associated in the public mind with the Poor Law. When inflation reduced the value of old age pensions, the Assistance Board was empowered to pay supplementary pensions based on need, and by 1941 the Board was dealing with ten times as many pensioners as unemployed men. As Minister of Labour, Bevin insisted on abolishing the household means test, and the Determination of Needs Act of 1941 substituted an assumed contribution from non-dependent members of a family. Titmuss stressed cross-party support for welfare policies. According to him (pp. 506–17), the condition of inner-city children evacuated to more prosperous areas shocked public opinion and moved the Government to take 'positive steps'. Cheap or free school meals and milk were made available to all children and not, as hitherto, only to the 'necessitous'. Free milk, orange juice and cod liver oil were provided for all expectant mothers and for children under five years. In all these ways, Titmuss argued, the 'war-warmed impulse of people for a more generous society' created favourable conditions for planning 'social reconstruction' after the war.

This interpretation of the shift from selective to universal principles was followed in a number of textbooks on social policy (Bruce 1968, pp. 292–6; Fraser 1973, pp. 192–8; Marshall 1970, pp. 74–5), although not in more recent work (Thane 1982, pp. 263–7). It was Harris (1981, pp. 247–9) who pointed out that Titmuss, like all official historians of the war, had been excluded from studying plans for postwar policy, and that this meant ignoring the crucial questions such as how the social services would be paid for, or how unemployment would be controlled, after the war. Since it is much easier to have generous impulses than it is to agree on how to carry them out, study of wartime services alone is an inadequate basis for generalisations about a consensus in favour of a 'welfare state'.

The focus for discussion of postwar social planning was the Beveridge Report on *Social Insurance and Allied Services* (Cmd. 6404). The Report appeared in December 1942, at a time when ultimate victory could be foreseen and when new incentives had to be found to maintain the war effort. Despite this, the Government was cautious, if not openly hostile, to Beveridge's proposals for universal social insurance, without means test, against interruption of earnings due to unemployment, ill health or old age. It was true that the Anglo–American peace aims in the 'Atlantic Charter' of 1941 had included a reference to 'social security', but Churchill thought that such plans should be substantially left until after the war. As Harris (1977) has shown, the Beveridge Report had been very much Sir William Beveridge's own handiwork. His committee had been expected to deal with technical questions related to workmen's compensation for industrial disease or injury, and with anomalies in social insurance, such as the well-known one whereby a man whose earnings were interrupted because of unemployment received a higher rate of benefit than if he were sick. Beveridge, however, had gone beyond his terms of reference and had called for an attack on Disease, Ignorance, Squalor and Idleness as well as Want – the five giants on the road of reconstruction, as he called them in Bunyanesque language. In particular, he stated that no satisfactory scheme of social security could be devised unless there were family allowances, comprehensive health and rehabilitation services, and avoidance of mass unemployment. Indeed, the actuarial soundness of Beveridge's plan depended upon the average rate of unemployment being no higher than the lowest level in the 1930s; that is 10 per cent of the interwar insured labour force or 8.5 per cent of the wider body of insured employees in the new scheme (Cmd. 6404, pp. 120, 154–65, 185–6). Uncertainty whether unemployment could be controlled, and memories of the political consequences of an actuarially unsound unemployment insurance fund in 1931, no doubt contributed to the Treasury's critical reception of the Report.

Nevertheless there can be little doubt that the Report was extremely popular with the general public and, following a backbench revolt in Parliament, the Government felt compelled to commit itself to Beveridge's plan, at least in principle. Widespread support for universal social insurance without means test *may* have been the result of what Titmuss called a 'war-warmed impulse of people for a more generous society'. On the other hand, the fact that so many people in the armed forces and munitions industries could not but be uncertain about their own postwar employment, in the light of post-1918 experience, must have been a factor. In the interwar years the unemployed had always been a minority of the electorate; in the war those who felt threatened by unemployment may well have been a majority. Moreover, the associated prospect of universal health insurance may well have been attractive to people who had been finding the cost of private health insurance a burden.

Key interest groups were also generally in favour of Beveridge's ideas. The evidence presented to Beveridge's committee showed that hardly any trade unions opposed extensions of national insurance and even business witnesses generally favoured more intervention by the state in matters relating to national efficiency (Harris, 1981, pp. 251–60). The one business group clearly adversely affected by Beveridge's proposals were the industrial insurance companies which had helped to administer national health insurance since 1912. Beveridge not only recommended their exclusion from this, but he also proposed that national insurance should cover workmen's compensation and funeral grants, thus taking away business from the companies. These seem, however, no longer to have had the influence they had had in Lloyd George's time, and the state no longer needed their administrative expertise. Wartime experience had created new attitudes about what the state could achieve. All this does not mean, however, that there was necessarily a consensus in favour of a 'welfare state' except in the most general terms. Looking at Beveridge's five giants in turn, one finds that sometimes proposals were agreed for differing motives, or on an inadequate basis, and that sometimes there were serious disagreements between Conservative and Labour members of the Coalition Government.

Prewar social surveys had shown that the cost of bringing up children was a frequent cause of want and there had long been a lobby in favour of state allowances for each child. Beveridge was sympathetic to arguments that this would cure poverty and reverse the fall in the birth-rate, but he also saw family allowances as a means of maintaining work incentives. Unemployment relief took family size into account, whereas wages did not, so that unless allowances were paid to people in work a man might be better off unemployed. This seems to have been the argument which convinced Whitehall. The Coalition Government introduced the Family Allowances Bill in 1945, providing for payment of allowances, without a means test, for the second and each subsequent child. However, whereas Beveridge had recommended a subsistence level of 8s. a week, allowances were fixed at 5s. a week, thereby releasing government from an obligation to raise allowances with the cost of living (Macnicol 1980, pp. 183–202).

The heart of the Beveridge Report was the proposed amalgamation of all existing state insurance and pension schemes into one which would provide subsistence benefits whenever an insured person's earnings were interrupted. Beveridge's estimate of 'subsistence' was less than Rowntree's 'human needs' standard, which had been devised in 1936 to establish a poverty line. Moreover, although rents varied widely over the country, Beveridge included only a small, fixed sum for this purpose. Even so, as in the case of family allowances, the Government refused to commit itself to the subsistence principle. Otherwise the 1944 White Paper on *Social Insurance* (Cmd. 6550) generally followed Beveridge's proposals for expansion of national insurance. This meant, incidentally, that workmen's compensation, which had previously been paid for wholly by employers' insurance contributions, would now be paid for in part by employees' and Exchequer contributions (Kincaid 1975, pp. 48–59).

For all its reservations on Beveridge's main proposals, the Government did agree in principle with his assumption that there should be a comprehensive health service available to all, without any conditions of insurance contributions. The trouble was that it proved to be impossible during the war for the details of such a service to be agreed, either between political parties or with the interest groups involved. Certainly war had increased the state's role. Greatly exaggerated prewar estimates of numbers of casualties in air raids had led to the provision of 80,000 Emergency Hospital Service beds, compared with 78,000 beds in voluntary hospitals and 320,000 in local authority hospitals. Moreover, the Emergency Hospital Service gradually extended its operations from war casualties to treatment of sick people transferred from inner city hospitals and then to other evacuees. In discussions in 1943–45 on a future national health service, however, both Conservative ministers and the British Medical Association showed themselves to be determined to safeguard private practice and the independence of the voluntary hospitals. In particular, there were deep differences between successive Conservative ministers of health, Ernest Brown and Henry Willink, who were responsible for health services in England and Wales, and the Labour Secretary of State for Scotland, Tom

Johnston, who was responsible for health services north of the border. For example, Johnston successfully opposed the idea of maintenance charges for patients in hospital. The 1944 White Paper on *A National Health Service* (Cmd 6502), which was signed by Willink and Johnston, left much undecided and was avowedly only a consultative document (Pater 1981, pp. 20–103).

War certainly made government more concerned with education, although it would seem that this had at least as much to do with concern over shortcomings revealed in technical education, and their implications for national efficiency, as with social equality. The Government's Green Book, *Education After the War* (1941), did note Churchill's social ideal of 'establishing a state of society where the advantages and privileges, which had been enjoyed only by the few, should be far more widely shared', but neither the Green Book nor the subsequent Education Act of 1944 made any mention of the public schools, where privilege was greatest. On the other hand, there was an unambiguous statement in the Green Book that there was 'an urgent need, in the interests of the industrial and commercial prosperity of the country, to secure an improved system of technical and commercial training' (Middleton and Weitzman 1976, pp. 391, 407–8). The minister principally responsible for the 1944 Act was the Conservative, R.A. Butler, and he gained support from successive Conservative chancellors, Wood and Sir John Anderson, who felt that educational reform would be a lesser evil than Beveridge's expensive social security scheme. The 1944 Act raised the school leaving age to 15 and required the completion of the Hadow scheme of 1926 for the reorganisation of elementary schools into primary schools and secondary schools. Fee paying was abolished in all local authority secondary schools, but not in the 200 or so direct-grant grammar schools. Butler was anxious to retain the distinctive character of the latter, partly for the direct-grant schools' own sake and partly to avoid too sharp a contrast between the state sector and public schools for the well-off. Both retention of fees in direct-grant schools and the decision not to fix a date for raising the school leaving age to 16 years divided the House of Commons. Such cross-party consensus as there was on education was preserved only by vague promises of 'parity of esteem' between different forms of education. The Board of Education planned to provide three different kinds of school: grammar, technical and 'modern', children being selected at the age of eleven according to whether they had an 'academic' or 'practical' bent. Clearly 'parity' would depend upon, *inter alia*, allocation of resources, that is upon the social and economic priorities of postwar governments (Gosden 1976, pp. 237–387; Middleton and Weitzman 1976, pp. 207–311).

The social and economic questions which caused greatest public anxiety in 1944, according to Home Intelligence reports, were housing and jobs. Some 222,000 houses had been destroyed by bombing and two houses in every seven had been damaged in some way, while house-building virtually ceased after 1941. To meet the housing shortage arising from the war, Churchill promised 500,000 prefabricated, temporary, houses immediately after the war – a target which proved to be twice what was possible because the design chosen was steel intensive, and steel was in short supply. Housing also required land. In 1942 the Uthwatt Report proposed that development rights in all land which had not yet been built on should be nationalised and that local authorities should have increased powers of compulsory purchase. There was party feuding on these issues and, although the 1944 Town and Country Planning Act did increase powers of compulsory purchase in blitzed, slum and overspill areas, it was on the question of land, according to Michael Foot, that the wartime Coalition broke. Little consensus was suggested by subsequent events. Labour's 1947 Town and Country Planning Act imposed a 100 per cent levy on value created by permission to develop land, but the levy was repealed by the Conservatives in 1953 (Addison 1975, pp. 177–8, 247–8, 252–3, 267, 273–4).

After 1942 Beveridge turned his attention to the giant 'Idleness', and by 1944 his strictly unofficial 'report' on *Full Employment in a Free Society* was nearly ready for publication. The Government was determined to pre-empt Beveridge's proposals and it hurried out its White Paper on *Employment Policy* (Cmd. 6527). In it the Government avoided a commitment to full employment and instead accepted the maintenance of 'a high and stable level of employment' as *one* of its primary responsibilities. No legislation was proposed, on the grounds that employment could not be created by government alone. Success, it was underlined, would depend upon, firstly, international collaboration to ensure expanding export markets; secondly, upon British industry's ability to compete in these markets and in the home market; thirdly, upon stability of prices and wages, so that increased demand would expand output and employment; and, fourthly, upon a willingness and ability of workers to move from one job to another. Public investment would be planned to offset fluctuations in private investment, and, as a second line of defence, private consumption would be maintained, perhaps through variations in social insurance contributions or rates of taxation. It was made clear, however, that while the chancellor's budget need not balance every year, it should balance over a longer period, and that none of the paper's main proposals involved deliberate planning for a budget deficit. Research into the drafting of *Employment Policy* shows that it papered over deep differences between the economists of the Economic Section, who favoured deficit finance as a solution to unemployment, and traditional Treasury officials, who stressed the need to preserve rules of public finance which would inhibit ministers from running deficits indefinitely. Treasury officials were also much more inclined than the economists of the Economic Section to stress the problem of structural unemployment arising out of the distribution of industry (Booth 1983; Peden 1983; Rollings 1985).

Keynes was obviously sympathetic to attempts to apply to policy the concepts of macroeconomic analysis which he had expounded in his *General Theory* in 1936, but even he agreed with Treasury officials that domestic economic policies could not offset completely a loss of export markets. For that reason he thought that Beveridge went too far in his *Full Employment in a Free Society* in setting an objective of an average level of 3 per cent unemployment (Peden 1983, p. 295). Given this, and given officials' doubts about deficit finance, it is far from clear that the 1944 White Paper indicated a consensus in favour of the full employment policies pursued in the 30 years after the war. The White Paper did indicate a stage in Whitehall's adoption of macroeconomic analysis of demand, but in the immediate postwar years Labour was concerned with planning the supply side of the economy.

From this review of five main areas of postwar planning – social insurance, national health, education, housing and employment policy – it is difficult to find much support for the thesis that war created a lasting consensus in favour of a 'welfare state'. This is not to deny Titmuss's contention that war did require a more universalist approach to social problems, or that, as Addison (1975) argued, there was a convergence during the war of the main political parties towards a 'Butskellite'[1] centre. This convergence, however, would seem to have been a response to electoral opinion at the time of a widespread, but temporary, feeling of insecurity.

The Problem of the External Balance

Whichever party had won the 1945 election would have faced tremendous external constraints on its policies. Britain's overseas liabilities (excluding Lend-Lease) had increased from £542 million in June 1939 to £3,354 million in June 1945, while its reserves of gold and US and Canadian dollars had risen by only £121 million to £624 million between August 1939 and June 1945. Moreover, further borrowing would be necessary to finance essential imports since Lend-Lease ended with the war. The diversion of industry to war production meant that in 1945 exports were only 46 per cent of the 1938 volume. Moreover the sale of overseas assets had reduced income from abroad from £168 million in 1938 to £50 million in 1945, during which period prices had approximately doubled (Sayers 1956, pp. 491, 495–7). Like much of the rest of the world, Britain was critically short of dollars with which to pay for essential purchases in North America. The United States and Canada granted Britain lines of credit of $3,750 million and $1,250 million respectively, and the United States lent a further $650 million to enable Britain to settle outstanding Lend-Lease claims. The Labour Government hoped that these credits would see Britain through until more normal trading patterns were restored, but there were strings attached. By the Anglo–American financial agreement of 1945 Britain had to make sterling convertible for current transactions a year after Congress had ratified the agreement. The British Government was also required to recommend to Parliament a policy of adherence to the Bretton Woods agreement of 1944, that is to maintain stable exchange rates. It was not clear how the sterling–dollar rate could be maintained once sterling was convertible, unless world trade was such that demand for dollars did not lead to a

1. A coinage from the names of R.A. Butler and Hugh Gaitskell, representing respectively the left of the Conservative Party and the right of the Labour Party.

greater conversion of sterling into dollars than Britain's meagre gold and dollar reserves could withstand. Article 9 of the Anglo–American financial agreement prevented Britain from reducing demand for dollars by using tariffs or quotas to discriminate against American imports. A reduction in dollar expenditure, therefore, would require a reduction in *all* imports (Van Dormael 1978, ch. 20). Wartime controls over imports were retained but, beyond a certain point, public opinion would not accept a reduction in living standards.

Postwar inflation in the United States reduced the real value of the American credit by about a quarter by the time Britain was due to make sterling available in July 1947. Moreover the terms of trade turned against Britain, that is the price of its imports rose more rapidly than the price of its exports. Since the Government was reluctant to reduce imports, the dollar credits were used up more quickly than expected. Convertibility gave other countries a chance to exchange sterling for scarce dollars, and had quickly to be abandoned. The dollar crisis of 1947 forced the Government to cut imports, including food, to the minimum believed to be consistent with health and morale. At the same time there was an export drive, at the expense of production for home consumption (Cairncross 1985, ch. 6; Clarke 1982, pp. 81–5). Help was at hand in the form of Marshall Aid. Fears of Communist subversion in Western Europe led the United States to underwrite a European Recovery Programme. This greatly eased the dollar problem, as did the fact that after 1947 the United States turned a blind eye to discrimination against imports from America. Even so, recipients of Marshall Aid were expected to stand on their own feet as quickly as possible, and Britain was refused further aid after 1950.

Long-term external equilibrium required an increase in output to reduce imports or to increase exports. The Agricultural Act of 1947 continued the wartime policy of subsidies and price-fixing, so as to encourage farmers to grow dollar-saving crops, with some success (Britton 1952). Industrial output was held back by shortages of coal, steel and manpower. The downward trend of coal production had continued after the war and industry was brought to a standstill in a coal crisis early in 1947. This reduced exports by at least £100 million, equivalent to a quarter of Britain's current balance of payments deficit that year, and at the time was estimated to have cost twice as much (Cairncross 1985, ch. 13). Industrial manpower was in short supply partly because of the greatly increased size of the armed forces. The Labour Government was no less determined than a Conservative one would have been to maintain Britain's position as a great power, and conscription was retained after the war as British forces were deployed in various trouble spots in Europe, Asia and Africa.

Lack of industrial output meant that it made little sense prior to 1949 to devalue sterling. The time to devalue would be when British industry had recovered sufficiently to be in a position to expand exports. There was no need to devalue to reduce imports, since these were subject to physical controls. Premature devaluation would simply create inflationary pressures. In the winter of 1948–49, however, economists in Whitehall suggested that the time was approaching when sterling should be devalued so as to increase the price incentive to export to dollar markets. Labour ministers, who had little regard for the price mechanism, ignored this advice. What forced their hand was a recession in the United States, which reduced export earnings of dollars, causing a drain on the reserves, and thereby increasing speculative pressure on sterling. Instead of allowing the pound to float, as in 1931, the Government devalued from $4.03 to $2.80, a rate which was believed to preclude any danger of a second devaluation. The rate was indeed held for 18 years and, assisted by devaluations by other countries, went far towards balancing trade between the dollar and non-dollar world. Devaluation did, however, involve a real cost, since more exports were required to pay for a given level of imports and, since the economy was at full employment, this meant a cut in domestic consumption (Cairncross 1985, ch. 7).

There was also a danger of inflation. Import prices rose by 17 per cent between June 1949 and June 1950, while export prices rose by only 5 per cent. Then in June 1950 the Korean War broke out. Fear of a general war led to stockpiling of, or speculation in, food and raw materials, further forcing up their prices relative to British industrial exports. At the same time the Labour Government embarked on a rearmament programme which was beyond Britain's industrial capacity. Consequently, the budgets of 1950 and 1951 sought to reduce demand by curbs on consumption, investment and social service expenditure (Cairncross 1985, ch. 8; Dow 1964, pp. 54–61; Williams 1979, pp. 242–83).

Thus, throughout its period in office the Labour Government was at the mercy of external pressures and events which it could do little to control. This alone would have been a serious impediment to economic planning. There were, however, as we shall see, other impediments.

Labour's Planned Economy

The experience of the inflationary boom of 1919–20 meant that there was general agreement, even among Conservatives, that there should be no rapid decontrol of the war economy after 1945. Whereas Conservatives saw controls as a temporary expedient, however, Labour intended to retain as many controls as were necessary to avoid unemployment and to ensure a fair distribution of goods and services in the long run. Labour believed that a planned economy would work better than a market economy. The success of the war economy was sometimes used to justify this belief, although economists like Hayek (1944) and Robbins (1947) warned that economic problems were not at all like those in war. In war the Government had been the main consumer of goods and services and it had been possible to allocate priorities according to the single objective of winning the war. In peace, however, production would have to respond to competing demands of many consumers. On the other hand, the Government was reluctant to rely on the price mechanism as a means of allocating scarce goods and resources, and preferred rationing, even though controls, especially those over labour, would be less acceptable in peace than in war.

The state's powers inherited from the war were: financial and physical controls over investment and the allocation of raw materials; controls over imports and foreign exchange; consumer rationing and price controls; and controls over the movement of labour and restrictions on strikes. At first, controls over investment were used to direct new factory building to areas which had experienced high unemployment before the war. The development areas designated by the Distribution of Industry Act of 1945 received 51 per cent of new industrial building in 1945–47, although they had only 20 per cent of the population. As unemployment remained low, however (averaging less than 2 per cent nationally), regional policy was relaxed, and the development areas received only 17 per cent of new industrial building in 1948–50 (McCrone 1969, pp. 112–13). Control over investment was also at first a key element in counter-inflation policy, but building controls had little effect since licences were granted freely, except for private house-building. Controls over imports and foreign exchange were essential in dealing with the dollar shortage. The Government itself was responsible for 64 per cent of imports in 1946 and a further 32 per cent were controlled. In 1951 the figures were 38 per cent and 16 per cent respectively. Food rationing was actually extended; bread, which had not been rationed during the war, was put on ration in 1946, and potatoes in 1947. As shortages eased, however, controls, which had been designed to cope with scarcity, became less and less necessary. Most were either dropped, as with much consumer rationing in 1948–49, or became hardly more than nominal, although there was some reversion to direct controls during the Korean War inflation (Dow 1964, pp. 144–77; Worswick 1952a).

Wartime controls over labour were too drastic to be used in peace. The ban on strikes remained theoretically in being until 1951 but could not be enforced. Trade-union leaders agreed in 1947 to a renewal of government powers to direct labour in 'exceptional cases', but the number of workers actually directed was very small and these powers were allowed to lapse in 1950. The Essential Work Orders, which prevented workers moving from their jobs, were retained for agriculture and mining until the same date. An alternative to controls would have been to use higher wages to attract labour to where it was needed. However, the Government feared that this would set off wage-inflation and urged restraint in pay claims (Wilson 1952, pp. 237–47). In any case, the housing shortage would have limited labour's ability to move in response to higher wages.

The decline in wartime controls was, in theory, offset to some extent by Labour's nationalisation programme. The Bank of England was nationalised in 1946, as was civil aviation. The coal industry was nationalised from 1st January 1947; railways, ports, canals and long-distance road services from 1st January 1948; electricity and gas in 1948–49; and steel in 1951. It is less than certain, however, that nationalisation contributed much to effective planning of the economy. Labour had been committed since 1918 to public ownership of the means of production and distribution, but little preparatory work had been done. Details of administrative structure, finance, compensation of private stockholders, pricing policy and relations with workers and consumers had still to be worked out when Labour came to power. Leading members of the Cabinet expressed doubts whether steel should be nationalised in the 1945–50 Session, and the House of Lords' rejection of the steel bill in 1949 delayed nationalisation until after the 1950 election (Morgan 1984, pp. 94–121; Pelling 1984, pp. 77–91). Some nationalisation made no difference. For example, the Treasury, not the Bank, had had the final word in monetary policy since 1931. Where nationalisation did make a difference, the results were often disappointing, at least in the short run. The case for a strong central authority to reorganise the coal industry into larger, more economic, units had been made by a committee of mining technicians (in the Reid Report) at the end of the war, but the Report had not proposed state ownership and many of the best managers left when the National Coal Board was set up. All nationalised industries were initially no more than the sum of the individual enterprises taken over, and rationalisation took time. The overworked British Transport Commission never succeeded in its task of creating a 'properly integrated system of public inland transport'. On the other hand, the railway and other executives lacked authority under the Commission to put their own house in order. The Government itself made managerial decisions difficult by interfering in pricing policies (Kelf-Cohen 1973).

Ministers were not always clear about what could be achieved by economic planning. The senior member of the Cabinet who most clearly saw that planning involved deciding priorities between claims on scarce resources of manpower, capital equipment, fuel, raw materials and foreign exchange, was Sir Stafford Cripps, who was successively President of the Board of Trade (1945–47), Minister of Economic Affairs (1947) and Chancellor of the Exchequer (1947–50). Cripps recognised that in normal times the people of a democratic country would not give up their freedom of choice to the government, and that decisions which determined production were dispersed among thousands of organisations and individuals (Cmd. 7046, paras 8–9; Clarke 1982, pp. 77–80). As Cairncross (1985) has pointed out, however, both Cripps and his colleagues were slow to draw the obvious conclusion that the price mechanism should be relied upon to allocate resources. Ministers preferred at first to ration goods which were scarce at the existing price, instead of allowing a rise in price to encourage increased production. Price fixing, and its concomitant, rationing, clogged the government machine with endless petty detail. On the other hand, important aspects of how plans were to be achieved were sometimes neglected. In 1947 Cripps set export targets for 1948 for no less than 153 classes of goods. No doubt his exhortations made industry more export conscious but, since individual firms were not told what their own contributions should be, it was largely by chance that any target was achieved.

The Government's own organisation was not conducive to effective co-ordination of planning before 1947. Overall responsibility was at first given to Herbert Morrison, Lord President of the Council, but his time was largely taken up with nationalisation and he was ill early in 1947. There was no effective ministerial oversight until Cripps was appointed Minister of Economic Affairs, and it was not until Cripps became Chancellor of the Exchequer at the end of 1947 that the Treasury became the department with overall responsibility for economic policy. Until then, the Treasury and the Economic Section of the Cabinet Office had disputed the right to prepare the final draft of the Government's annual *Economic Surveys*, which made forecasts and set targets for the economy as a whole. It was also not until 1947 that a chief planning officer, Sir Edwin Plowden, was appointed to head a Central Economic Planning Staff in the Cabinet Office.

The biggest obstacle to effective long-term planning was events. Successive forecasts in *Economic Surveys* were upset by the external pressures discussed in the previous section. Not all crises, however, were external or unavoidable. The coal crisis, which had such serious consequences for industry and exports in 1947, has been described by Cairncross (1985, ch. 13) as 'a striking example of incompetence in industrial planning by a government dedicated to economic planning'. Holding down coal prices meant that the only signal of an impending shortage was a fall in stocks, to which only the Government could react. The Minister of Fuel and Power, Emanuel Shinwell, at first failed to grasp the seriousness of the situation and, when he did, acted perversely by depriving industry of current supplies of coal in order to build up stocks of coal at power stations. The margin of shortfall in coal output and distribution in the winter of 1946–47 was small. Timely economies in consumption and more vigorous recruitment of miners could have avoided the closure of industry. Coal output was a subject at many cabinet meetings, but ministers seemed to lack the numeracy necessary to appreciate statistical analysis.

Management of the economy at the macroeconomic level was a rough and ready affair in 1945–51. Many economists recruited during the war returned to academic life and the Treasury had no professional economist of its own for some years after Keynes died in 1946. The detachment of the Economic Section of the Cabinet Office from departmental duties meant that it could only influence policy when ministers were willing to listen. It was only gradually that ministers and civil servants acquired a nodding acquaintance with the concepts of Keynesian demand management and, in any case, the national income statistics available at first were crude (Cairncross 1985, ch. 3).

For all that, Labour's management of the economy was not unsuccessful in terms of employment and prices. Large liquid funds in the hands of the public after the war meant that there was little immediate danger of a deficiency of domestic demand. The interruption of coal supplies in 1947, however, caused widespread, if brief, unemployment, and ministers feared that if there were no Marshall Aid, there would be 1.5 million unemployed because there would be no dollars to pay for raw materials. Full employment was largely the result of American willingness to solve the world's dollar problem. The United States Government also threw its influence against measures which had restricted trade in the 1930s, such as high tariffs and competitive devaluations. The Labour Government played its part by holding down domestic consumption, so as to achieve a fast growth of exports, and this in turn reduced the dollar shortage. Investment was encouraged by a continuation of cheap money policy – indeed, Hugh Dalton, the Chancellor of the Exchequer from 1945 to 1947, tried unsuccessfully to reduce the long-term rate of interest from 3 per cent to 2½ per cent (Cairncross 1985; Dow 1964, pp. 223–7).

Control of inflation was the most striking achievement. Import prices rose by 125 per cent over 1945–51, yet retail prices rose by only 38 per cent. The rise in weekly wage earnings was greater, 46 per cent, but this was not high considering the powerful wage-bargaining position of trade unionists (figures from Feinstein 1972, T. 139–40). Rising prices of food, for which demand was inelastic, could have set off greater wage demands, so food subsidies were retained. However, the rising cost of food subsidies – £450 million in

1948/49 – was in conflict with efforts to reduce aggregate demand through a budget surplus. Food subsidies also released personal disposable income for other purposes (Nash 1951), and this tended to raise prices of consumer goods, which were still in short supply. A buoyant domestic market for consumer goods might lead to a slackening in the export drive. Yet increased exports and reduced imports were necessary to put off a devaluation which would raise food prices. This reasoning, or something like it, led to food subsidies being pegged after 1948, and food prices were allowed to rise.

Ministers were inclined to try to counter inflation by increasing output. At first a manpower budget was used to show the 'inflationary gap' between planned output and labour supply but, once demobilisation was complete, the manpower budget soon faded into the background. As direct controls weakened, the emphasis was switched to curbing aggregate demand through fiscal policy. Dalton raised additional taxes in November 1947 to curb inflation, but in general it was possible to follow a passive fiscal policy of retaining high taxation even after war-related expenditure fell. Cripps, despite his talk of the need for austerity, reduced taxes on consumption and the largest increase in taxation came in 1951 when Hugh Gaitskell, his successor, raised revenue to pay for rearmament. There was no attempt to 'fine-tune' the economy, as in the 1950s and sixties, but a less austere fiscal policy would have been inflationary (Dow 1964, pp. 28, 198–202, 210).

The success of counter-inflation policy rested heavily on the co-operation of trade unionists. The wartime National Joint Advisory Council was reconstituted in 1946 to deal with labour problems, and attempts were made to educate the public. A White Paper on *Economic Considerations Affecting Relations between Employers and Workers* (Cmd. 7018) was issued in January 1947 to draw attention to the importance of productivity and international competitiveness. A further White Paper in February 1948, *Statement on Personal Incomes, Costs and Prices* (Cmd. 7321), warned that 'until more goods and services are available for the home market, there can be no justification for any *general* increase of individual money incomes'. A conference of trade-union executives, summoned by the TUC, accepted the White Paper's call for wage restraint, but insisted on the need both to maintain wage differentials *and* to raise wages where the latter were below a 'reasonable standard of subsistence'. Of course an attempt to raise low wages while maintaining differentials was logically bound to lead to a general increase in money incomes. Nevertheless, the White Paper policy does seem to have moderated wage demands. In the 18 months before devaluation in September 1949, wage rates rose by an annual rate of increase of 2.8 per cent, while retail prices rose by an annual rate of increase of 3.3 per cent. Following devaluation, the Government appealed for, and the General Council of the TUC recommended, a wage standstill. This was to be conditional on the cost of living being held to within 5 per cent of its pre-devaluation level, and in fact retail prices rose by only 2 per cent in the first post-devaluation year. Nevertheless, the standstill was approved by only a narrow majority of a conference of trade-union executives in January 1950, and anomalies and exceptions forced the General Council to end the standstill in June. As subsequent experience was to affirm, wage restraint could not last for long (Cairncross 1985, ch. 14; Worswick 1952b).

The ultimate failure of wage restraint reminds one that the TUC cannot control its members, but can merely make recommendations. The same is true of employers' organisations. This is an important limitation to the Middlemas thesis of 'corporate bias' in British politics. According to Middlemas (1979), the period from 1914 to 1945 saw government raise the TUC, the British Employers' Confederation and the Federation of British Industries to the status of 'governing institutions'; in return these organisations came to share the government's views of the national interest. The latter may be so, but true 'governing institutions' would have had sanctions on their members.

By 1950–51 Labour's original hopes of a planned economy backed by direct controls were fading. The problem of inflation was proving unexpectedly persistent and counter-inflation policy involved running a series of budget surpluses. Since taxation was still high, a budget surplus could only be achieved by curbing public expenditure. Both inflation and attempts to curb public expenditure were to have implications for social policy.

Labour's Welfare State

The phrase 'welfare state' was in common usage after 1945 but, like so many political expressions, it was rarely defined. It is difficult, therefore, to judge whether Labour succeeded in creating a 'welfare state'. It would be generally agreed, however, that a 'welfare state' is one where market forces are modified to the extent that individuals are assured of a basic income, as of right, whether or not they are in work, and where all citizens have equal access to the best standards of health services, housing and education (Briggs 1961, p. 228). In assessing Labour's social policies, however, account must be taken not only of abstract principles, but also of what was possible in the circumstances. Twenty-eight per cent of Britain's total net assets had been wiped out during the war, compared with 15 per cent in the First World War, and even in 1951 the nation's total real wealth was hardly at all greater than in 1913 (Matthews *et al.* 1982, pp. 129–30). There was little enough surplus income for redistribution, and living standards, austere as they were, were maintained only with American assistance, which was intended to support economic, not social, reconstruction. Labour's election manifesto in 1950 stated frankly that 'new commitments for further expansion of our social services can only be accepted as production goes up; indeed more production will be necessary to underpin the immense changes on which we have already embarked (Hess 1981, p. 308).

Labour was committed to the Beveridge Report, and the Government acted with all reasonable speed. The new Ministry of National Insurance was given only 10 months in which to set up a national system of certification, payment and record of family allowances for nearly 3 million families. Under the National Insurance Act of 1946 old age pensions, payable on retirement to men over 65 and women over 60, were paid in full from 1946; Beveridge, on the other hand, had proposed that pensions should be paid only in part, with a gradual levelling up to standard national insurance benefits over 20 years, as contributions accumulated. All other benefits under the Act were payable from 1948. The Ministry of National Insurance took over unemployment insurance from the Ministry of Labour and national health insurance from about a thousand Approved Societies. State funeral benefits were introduced for the first time, payable on the death of an insured contributor. In addition the National Insurance (Industrial Injuries) Act of 1946 revised workmen's compensation along the principles of the Beveridge Report, but with the additional provision of industrial pensions related to the degree of injury where disability was likely to be permanent or prolonged (Gregg 1967, pp. 42–8).

All this was a considerable legislative and administrative achievement, but were the benefits adequate? Labour held to the Coalition Government's decision to pay family allowances of 5s. per child for second and further children, rather than Beveridge's recommended 8s., on the grounds that free school meals and milk would make up the difference. The benefits for sickness, unemployment and retirement under national insurance were 26s. per week for a single recipient and 42s. for a couple. This was an increase on existing benefits for a single person of 2s. for unemployment, 8s. for sickness and 16s. in the pension. Under trade-union pressure, industrial injury benefits were fixed at 45s. per week, well above the rate for other benefits. The Prime Minister, Attlee, admitted that national insurance benefits would sustain only a 'very modest standard of life'. Even so, Labour ministers do seem to have believed that benefits would be adequate. James Griffiths, the Minister of National Insurance, claimed that he was enacting the principle of a national minimum standard, and a cabinet paper showed he intended benefits to be 'justified broadly in relation to the present level of the cost of living', with periodic reviews. Yet the figure of 42s. for a couple had been arrived at by taking Beveridge's extremely rigorous figure for subsistence in 1938, and adding 31 per cent to allow for the change in prices. By the time benefits came to be paid in 1948, however, retail prices had risen 75 per cent above the level of 1938. Since there was no automatic cost-of-living adjustment, inflation had destroyed the subsistence basis of national insurance before the scheme had begun (Feinstein 1972, Table 65; Hess 1981, pp. 300–7; Morgan 1984, pp. 170–3; Thane 1982, p. 254).

Beveridge had envisaged a limited rôle for means-tested national assistance benefits for those who failed to fulfil the contributions for national insurance or who refused suitable employment. In his view, national assistance must always be less desirable than insurance benefit, and should therefore be subject to proof of needs and a means test (Cmd. 6404, p. 141–2). The National Assistance Act of 1948 incorporated these ideas, although it was also intended that the work of the Assistance Board in helping individuals or families whose resources were inadequate should continue. The new National Assistance Board took over most functions of the old Public Assistance Committees and it was claimed that the Poor

Law had been abolished. However, the retention of the means test meant that national assistance was still associated with the implied shame of public assistance. This feeling was particularly strong among the old, which was unfortunate given that, by 1949, 48 per cent of total national assistance payments were made to supplement retirement pensions. As inflation reduced the value of benefits under national insurance, so the proportion of those in want applying to the National Assistance Board increased (Gregg 1967, p. 267; Hess 1981, pp. 307–8).

Even so, Labour's claim to have abolished poverty received some support from a survey of York by Rowntree in 1950. Using substantially the same rigorous poverty line as in his survey of the same city in 1936, Rowntree found that the proportion of the working class living in poverty was 2.77 per cent, whereas the proportion would have been 22.18 per cent had welfare legislation remained unchanged (Rowntree 1951, pp. 39–40). The national minimum was a meagre one, however, and sickness and old age could still bring great reductions in income, even if long-term unemployment among healthy workers was now rare. Destitution might almost have been abolished, but the subsistence principle, even if it had not been distorted by inflation, left open a strong possibility that the poor would become relatively poorer as the prosperity of those in employment increased.

The National Health Service Act of 1946, and its implementation on the Appointed Day in 1948, was a considerable achievement of Aneurin Bevan, the Minister of Health. Bevan's original national health proposals differed from those of Willink, his Conservative predecessor, chiefly in respect of the degree of the Ministry's control over hospitals and doctors, and in the emphasis given to group partnerships of doctors in local health centres. Whereas Willink had wished to preserve the independence of voluntary hospitals, Bevan took over all local authority and voluntary hospitals, except those not necessary for the National Health Service (NHS). Bevan's biggest problem was with the British Medical Association which, as late as February 1948, organised a poll of its members which resulted in a vote of 8:1 against the Act. Bevan was aware of the need to meet the medical profession on some points. In particular, he was willing to allow private beds in NHS hospitals so as to attract the best specialists into the service. He met the general practitioners' fears for their independence by promising that there would be no whole-time salaried medical service. In the end the doctors and consultants were given a larger place in the administration of the NHS than Willink had envisaged. Moreover, for all Bevan's talk of local health centres, there were to be few resources available to build these for many years (Morgan 1984, pp. 154–63; Pater 1981, chs. 5–8).

The National Health Service Act created a new service only in a legislative sense. There were no more hospitals, doctors or dentists on the Appointed Day than there had been on the previous day. Any additional provision would cost money, quite a lot as it turned out. There was very little realisation of the demand for treatment which a free health service would release, still less of the way in which the advance of medical science would make that demand almost limitless. The Beveridge Report had included an estimate by the Government Actuary that a comprehensive health service for Great Britain might cost £170 million a year, with the suggestion that the cost of further development would be offset by a fall in demand as the population became healthier as a result. This figure seems to have been the basis of the Government's estimate in 1946 of £110 million as the cost of the NHS in England and Wales, after deducting contributions from local authorities and the national insurance fund. The actual cost to the Exchequer turned out to be £305.2 million in 1949/50 and £336.5 million in 1950/51. Almost three times as many prescriptions were issued in 1949/50 as in 1947. Bevan resisted any violation of the principle of a free service, but in 1951 charges were introduced for dentures and spectacles. Bevan resigned in protest, splitting the Labour Party. Ironically the charges probably had little effect on demand, for most people who had done without proper dentures or spectacles before 1948 had been issued with them by 1951. A free service undoubtedly did much to ease discomfort among the population. On the other hand, given the uneven distribution of general practitioners and hospitals before 1948, it would clearly not be possible to provide the best possible medical service for all citizens for many years (Watkin 1978, pp. 28–34; 56–9).

The housing shortage had been one of the main issues in the 1945 election and Bevin had gone so far as to promise that Labour would build 4 or 5 million houses (Addison 1975, p. 267). Even 4 million houses in five years would have required an increase in building of 120 per cent over the average for the boom years in the 1930s (Table 6.4). Yet an almost complete cessation in house-

Table 6.4 Houses and Flats Completed (Including War-Destroyed Houses Rebuilt)

	Permanent houses (000s)	*Temporary houses (000s)*	*Total (000s)*	*Of which for public authorities (%)*
England and Wales				
1934/35–1938/39 (annual average)	334.0	—	334.0	21
1941/42–1944/45 (annual average)	7.6	—	7.6	64
1945 (Apr–Dec)	1.4	8.9	10.4	91
1946	51.1	70.9	122.0	76
1947	127.5	34.4	161.9	75
1948	206.4	10.7	217.2	85
1949	171.8	—	171.8	85
1950	172.3	—	172.3	84
1951	171.9	—	171.9	87
1948–1951 (annual average)	180.6	N/A	183.3	85
Scotland (annual averages)				
1934–38	24.5	—	24.5	67
1941–44	3.5	—	3.5	92
1945–1947	6.0	8.2	14.2	95
1948–1951	23.9	N/A	25.8	95
Northern Ireland (annual averages)				
1934/35–1938/39	2.6	—	2.6	14
1941–1944	—	—	—	—
1945–1947	0.6	0.9	1.5	81
1948–1951	6.7	N/A	7.6	63

Source: Annual Abstract of Statistics (1952).
Note: N/A = data non-applicable.

building after 1941 meant that the building industry was as little prepared for the demands placed upon it as in 1919. Predictably, Labour's achievement fell far short of promises. Only in 1948 were housing completions in England and Wales significantly more than half the annual average for 1934/35–1938/39, and the fact that completions in Scotland and Northern Ireland were better than before the war largely reflected these regions' poor prewar records. What Labour did do was to restrict building for purchase and to encourage local authority building with grants and low-interest loans. One consequence of this was the creation of an electorally significant body of subsidised council house tenants.

Bevan's record as a housing minister was criticised by all parties, it being alleged that he was too preoccupied with NHS matters. Certainly the Scottish Office seems to have got off to a quicker start with its housing programme, and in 1951 housing in England and Wales was removed from the Ministry of Health and given to the new Ministry of Local Government and Planning. Bevan's main problem, however, was a lack of steel for prefabricated, temporary, houses and a lack of bricks and imported timber for traditional permanent houses. There were, moreover, the competing needs of the hospital and school-building programmes. Bevan preferred high quality houses to 'prefabs', and construction of the latter virtually ceased after 1948. Initially too many building licences were issued and growing numbers of half-built houses in 1946 were evidence of poor planning. The dollar crisis of 1947 curbed imports of timber, and subsequently there were cuts in public investment in response to inflationary pressures and balance of payments problems. The number of housing completions in England and Wales actually declined after 1948 and there was still a serious shortage of housing in 1951 (Cairncross 1985, pp. 451–9; Morgan 1984, pp. 163–70).

The 1944 Education Act had transformed the old Board of Education into a ministry with powers to impose duties on local education authorities. However, Labour's first Minister of Education, Ellen Wilkinson, had few ideas of her own on education. She spent most of her time on practical difficulties of emergency training of teachers and of building temporary hutments in order to raise the school leaving age to 15 in 1947. Since grammar schools retained their existing staffs and buildings, the gulf between them and other schools remained. There simply were not the resources available to ensure that all pupils received the best standards of education possible. Indeed, if the Treasury had had its way, the raising of the school leaving age would have been postponed. The Labour Government believed that it was creating equality of opportunity, but it did so within the traditional educational framework. It was not until 1951 that the Labour Party committed itself to comprehensive education (Gosden 1983; Vernon 1982, ch. 10).

Labour's social services fell short of an ideal 'welfare state' partly because of economic circumstances. Full employment of resources imposed choices between social services and other forms of expenditure, and between different forms of social services. For example, new factories were built at the expense of hospitals, houses and schools, and new accommodation for 14–15 year olds in secondary schools was at the expense of nursery schools. Defence absorbed more resources than one might have expected, but even so by 1949 money outlay on social services had increased by more than twice as much, compared with 1938, as outlay on defence and National Debt interest. Within social services expenditure, however, Labour's commitment to universalist principles helped to ensure that the redistributive effect would be small. When free social services, like the NHS, were of the same quality as private services, the effect was to release a proportion of income of people in higher income groups, whereas people in lower income groups benefited from services in kind which they would otherwise have foregone. This tended to *increase* the disparity in disposable incomes. The finance of the welfare state came from national insurance contributions, taxes and local rates. It was estimated in 1949 that the cost to families with a taxable income of under £500 – a group covering 80 per cent of the population – was more than the total social expenditure on an average family of four. This was because of the regressive nature of national insurance contributions and because of the high taxation on drink and tobacco. Labour's welfare state could thus be seen as largely working-class self-help organised by the state (Briggs 1952, pp. 369–77).

State and Society at Mid-Century

By 1950 the foundations of both the managed economy and the welfare state had been laid. Government had accepted unprecedented responsibility for economic stability and social welfare. Labour ministers, unlike the 1944 White Paper, did not hesitate to talk about the need to maintain full employment, and in 1951 the Government told the United Nations Economic and Social Council that 3 per cent was the maximum level of unemployment which would be tolerated. In social policy, social justice and considerations of national efficiency seemed to have come together in a welfare state run on universalist principles. All this was a far cry from *laissez-faire* principles, even if the principle of 'less eligibility' remained enshrined in the operations of the National Assistance Board.

It is far from clear what rôle the Second World War had played in these developments. The fact that the war had been preceded by historically high levels of unemployment reinforced the arguments for change, and even the Conservatives accepted that there could not be a return to prewar economic policies. It is difficult, therefore, to distinguish between the effects of the post-1929 depression and the war itself. The war gave rise to an exaggerated belief in the power of the state to control the economy and to cure unemployment. The war had firmly established economists in Whitehall, and economists who had adopted Keynes's *General Theory* showed little doubt that demand management was practicable. On the other hand, that theory itself was born of the depression.

The welfare state was a product of long-term as well as short-term influences. The value of social policy in maintaining social order and in raising national efficiency had been recognised before 1914. Some social services at least had become electoral assets – a fact deplored by the May Report in 1931 in its analysis of why social service expenditure was on an upward trend. Unemployment relief, one of the most potent reasons for increased social service expenditure, was a problem of depression, not war. Nevertheless, the Second World War does seem to have encouraged a more universalist approach to social welfare. Increases in social services during wartime could not easily be withdrawn, while uncertainty about the postwar world encouraged people to look to the state for continued social security. War, however, also reduced the real wealth of the community, which made it difficult to find the bricks and mortar to build a welfare state. This was a problem which could be solved with time and economic recovery – but only if the majority of the electorate continued to favour social service expenditure.

References

Documents

Cmd. 6404 *Social Insurance and Allied Services, Report by Sir William Beveridge*, BPP 1942–43, vol. VI, pp. 119–417.
Cmd. 6502 *A National Health Service*, BPP 1943–44, vol. VIII, pp. 315–99.
Cmd. 6527 *Employment Policy*, BPP 1943–44, vol. VIII, pp. 119–50.
Cmd. 6550 *Social Insurance Part 1*, BPP 1943–44, vol. VIII, pp. 463–526.
Cmd. 7018 *Statement on Economic Considerations Affecting Relations between Employers and Workers*, BPP 1946–47, vol. XIX, pp. 1195–1204.
Cmd. 7046 *Economic Survey for 1947*, BPP 1946–47, vol. XIX, pp. 473–508.
Cmd. 7321 *Statement on Personal Incomes, Costs and Prices*, BPP 1947–48, vol. XXII, pp. 1007–1010.

Books and Articles

Addison, P. (1975) *The Road to 1945: British Politics and the Second World War*, Jonathan Cape.
Allen, G.C. (1951) 'The concentration of production policy', in D.N. Chester (ed.), *Lessons of the British War Economy*, Cambridge University Press.
Beveridge, W. (1944) *Full Employment in a Free Society*, George Allen and Unwin.
Booth, A. (1983) 'The "Keynesian revolution" in economic policy-making', *Economic History Review*, 2nd series, vol. 36, pp. 103–23.
Booth, A., and Coates, A.W. (1980) 'Some wartime observations on the role of the economist in government', *Oxford Economic Papers*, vol. 32, pp. 177–99.
Briggs, A. (1952) 'The social services', in G.D.N. Worswick and P. Ady (eds.), *The British Economy 1945–50*, Oxford University Press.
Briggs, A. (1961) 'The welfare state in historical perspective', *Archives Européennes de Sociologie*, vol. 2, pp. 221–58.
Britton, D.K. (1952) 'Agriculture', in G.D.N. Worswick and P.H. Ady (eds), *The British Economy 1945–50*, Oxford University Press.
Brown, H. Phelps (1983) *The Origins of Trade Union Power*, Oxford University Press.
Bruce, M. (1968) *The Coming of the Welfare State*, Batsford.
Bullock, A. (1967) *The Life and Times of Ernest Bevin, Vol. 2, Minister of Labour 1940–1945*, Heinemann.
Cairncross, A. (1985) *Years of Recovery: British Economic Policy 1945–51*, Methuen.
Central Statistical Office (1951) *Statistical Digest of the War*, HMSO.
Clarke, R. (1982) *Anglo–American Economic Collaboration in War and Peace* (ed. Cairncross, A.), Oxford University Press.

Court, W.H.B. (1951) *Coal*, HMSO.
Dow, J.C.R. (1964) *The Management of the British Economy 1945–60*, Cambridge University Press.
Feinstein, C.H. (1972) *National Income, Expenditure and Output of the United Kingdom*, Cambridge University Press.
Fraser, D. (1973) *The Evolution of the British Welfare State*, Macmillan.
Gosden, P. (1976) *Education in the Second World War*, Methuen.
Gosden, P. (1983) *The Education System since 1944*, Martin Robertson.
Gowing, M.M. (1972) 'The organisation of manpower in Britain during the Second World War', *Journal of Contemporary History*, vol. 7, pp. 147–67.
Gregg, P. (1967) *The Welfare State: An Economic and Social History of Great Britain from 1945 to the Present Day*, Harrap.
Hammond, R.J. (1951) *Food, Vol. 1, The Growth of Policy*, HMSO.
Hancock, W.K. and Gowing, M.M. (1949) *The British War Economy*, HMSO.
Hargreaves, E.L. and Gowing, M.M. (1952) *Civil Industry and Trade*, HMSO.
Harris, J. (1977) *William Beveridge, A Biography*, Oxford University Press.
Harris, J. (1981) 'Some aspects of social policy making in Britain during the Second World War', in W.J. Mommsen (ed.), *The Emergence of the Welfare State in Britain and Germany*, Croom Helm.
Hayek, F.A. (1944) *The Road to Serfdom*, Routledge and Kegan Paul.
Hess, J. (1981) 'The social policy of the Attlee Government', in W.J. Mommsen (ed.), *The Emergence of the Welfare State in Britain and Germany*, Croom Helm.
Ince, G. (1946) 'The mobilisation of manpower in Great Britain for the Second World War', *Manchester School*. vol. 14, pp. 17–52.
Inman, P. (1957) *Labour in the Munitions Industries*, HMSO.
Kelf-Cohen, R. (1973) *British Nationalisation 1945–1973*, Macmillan.
Keynes, J.M. (1940) 'How to pay for the war', reprinted in *Collected Writings*, vol. 9, Macmillan.
Kincaid, J.C. (1975) *Poverty and Equality in Britain: a Study of Social Security and Taxation*, Penguin Books.
McCrone, G. (1969) *Regional Policy in Britain*, George Allen and Unwin.
MacDonald, D.F. (1960) *The State and the Trade Unions*, Macmillan.
Macnicol, J. (1980) *The Movement for Family Allowances, 1918–45*, Heinemann.
Marshall, T.H. (1970) *Social Policy*, Hutchinson.
Matthews, R., Feinstein, C. and Odling-Smee, J. (1982) *British Economic Growth 1856–1973*, Oxford University Press.
Middlemas, K. (1979) *Politics in Industrial Society*, André Deutsch.
Middleton, N. and Weitzman, S. (1976) *A Place for Everyone*, Victor Gollancz.
Morgan, K.O. (1984) *Labour in Power 1945–1951*, Oxford University Press.

D.N. Chester (ed.), *Lessons of the British War Economy*, Cambridge University Press.

Pater, J.E. (1981) *The Making of the National Health Service*, King Edward's Hospital Fund for London.

Peden, G.C. (1983) 'Sir Richard Hopkins and the "Keynesian revolution" in employment policy, 1929–45', *Economic History Review*, 2nd series, vol. 36, pp. 281–96.

Pelling, H. (1984) *The Labour Governments 1945–51*, Macmillan.

Pollard, S. (1983) *The Development of the British Economy 1914–1980*, Edward Arnold.

Ramsden, J. (1980) *The Making of Conservative Party Policy*, Longman.

Reddaway, W.B. (1951) 'Rationing', in D.N. Chester (ed.), *Lessons of the British War Economy*, Cambridge University Press.

Robbins, L. (1947) *The Economic Problem in Peace and War*, Macmillan.

Rollings, N. (1985) 'The "Keynesian revolution" and economic policy-making: a comment', *Economic History Review*, 2nd series, vol. 38, pp. 95–100.

Rowntree, B.S. (1951) *Poverty and the Welfare State*, Longman.

Sayers, R.S. (1956) *Financial Policy 1939–45*, HMSO.

Thane, P. (1982) *The Foundations of the Welfare State*, Longman.

Titmuss, R. (1950) *Problems of Social Policy*, HMSO.

Van Dormael, A. (1978) *Bretton Woods: Birth of a Monetary System*, Macmillan.

Vernon, B. (1982) *Ellen Wilkinson*, Croom Helm.

Watkin, B. (1978) *The National Health Service: the First Phase, 1948–74, and After*, George Allen and Unwin.

Williams, P. (1979) *Hugh Gaitskell, A Political Biography*, Jonathan Cape.

Wilson, T. (1952) 'Manpower', in G.D.N. Worswick and P. Ady (eds.), *The British Economy 1945–50*, Oxford University Press.

Worswick, G.D.N. (1952a) 'Direct controls', in G.D.N. Worswick and P. Ady (eds.), *The British Economy 1945–50*, Oxford University Press.

Worswick, G.D.N. (1952b) 'Personal income policy', in G.D.N. Worswick and P. Ady (eds.), *The British Economy 1945–50*, Oxford University Press.

7

The Managed Economy and the Welfare State, 1951–73

In retrospect, at least, the period 1951–73 seems to have been a golden age. Only in 1971 and 1972 did the average annual rate of unemployment in Britain rise above 3 per cent, and the annual average rate of increase in retail prices between 1950 and 1973 was 4.6 per cent (compared with 14.2 per cent in 1973–82). If Britain's gross domestic product per person employed grew more slowly than in comparable countries – at 2.2 per cent a year in 1950–73 compared with 4.9 per cent in West Germany and 4.6 per cent in France – the increase was still sufficient to allow a faster growth in public expenditure and private consumption than was to be the case after 1973. Down to 1973 Britain was enjoying the benefits of a long boom which affected the whole of the advanced, capitalist world. The reasons for the length of the boom were partly the result of policies and partly the result of circumstances. In contrast to beggar-thy-neighbour commercial policies after the 1929–31 crisis, international co-operation reduced barriers to trade. Between 1948 and 1974 world trade in manufactures increased more rapidly than manufacturing output (at 8.9 per cent a year compared with 5.45 per cent). Industrial trends in the interwar years and during the Second World War itself had reduced Britain's dependence upon a narrow range of staple products, giving it an industrial structure which seemed to be well adapted to liberalised trade. Governments in most countries stimulated demand, either by full-employment policies or by promoting economic growth. There was a backlog of investment opportunities after a period of depression and war in which European economies had fallen behind the best practice of American industry, and a flow of private American investment facilitated the transfer of technology. Inflationary tendencies were checked by the monetary discipline imposed by the Bretton Woods system of stable exchange rates, and world prices of most key commodities were remarkably stable from after the Korean War boom until 1972–73. Britain itself enjoyed an improvement in its terms of trade – i.e. the ratio between the price of its exports and the price of its imports – from about 75 per cent of the prewar level in 1951 to about 100 per cent in 1962–73. This enabled it to consume more of its own output at full employment, compared with 1945–51 (Maddison 1982, chs. 5 and 6; Wright 1979).

The long boom thus created conditions which were favourable to employment policy and an expansion in social services. All British governments[1] down to the mid-1970s were committed to the maintenance of full employment, the Conservatives having made this the party's 'first aim' in the general election of 1950, in contrast to more cautious promises in 1945. There was a widespread belief that Keynesian demand management made the fulfilment of such a pledge possible. Both the major parties also committed themselves to large-scale public expenditure on housing, health services and education, which, like full employment, were perceived as vote-winners. However, full employment made the post-Beveridge system of insurance against interruption of earnings seem a lower political priority.

Macroeconomic Policy: (1) Demand Management

Initially the objectives of the managed economy were threefold: to ensure full employment with reasonable stability of prices and balance of payments equilibrium. Later, as governments were

1. Labour under Attlee (1945–51); the Conservatives under Churchill (1951–55), Sir Anthony Eden (1955–57); Harold Macmillan (1957–63) and Sir Alec Douglas Home (1963–64); Labour under Harold Wilson (1964–70); and the Conservatives under Edward Heath (1970–74).

made aware of Britain's relatively poor economic performance when viewed against comparable countries, achievement of a higher growth rate was added as a fourth objective. These objectives were not always easily reconciled. At full employment, prices and wages tended to rise in a spiral. If prices rose more rapidly than in other countries, then, given a fixed exchange rate, imports would be sucked in and exports would tend to be priced out of foreign markets. The consequent worsening of the trade balance would give rise to fears about the future of the exchange rate, and speculation against sterling would cause a balance of payments crisis. The dynamic objective of a higher growth rate was apt to conflict with stability of prices and the balance of payments, since the more the economy was pushed to the limits of its productive capacity the more prices (and wages) would tend to rise. Governments did develop microeconomic policies aimed at removing bottlenecks to higher output (see below), but demand management remained the main short-term means of achieving the four economic objectives of full employment, stable prices, balance of payments equilibrium and economic growth. In practice, steps would be taken to reflate or deflate according to whether employment and growth, or prices and the balance of payments, were the most immediate concern, but employment policy tended to predominate in the long run (Hopkin 1981).

As we have seen in the previous chapter, wartime controls over the economy had been much reduced and relaxed by the end of the 1940s, and the single most important element in counter-inflation policy by 1950 was the chancellor's budget surplus. Gaitskell's budget in 1951 was more obviously Keynesian than those of Dalton and Cripps in its analysis of the shortfall in savings which would have to be made good by the Government (Dow 1964, pp. 58–9). Perhaps the main advantage of demand management was that it allowed the Government to appear to be in control of the economy even after the range of physical controls had been reduced. Be that as it may, it is not at all clear that the policies which were adopted from 1951 were 'Keynesian' in every respect.

The term 'Keynesian' itself is capable of different meanings and, since Keynes had died in 1946, no-one can say whether he would have agreed with subsequent interpretations of his ideas. Self-styled Keynesian economists tended to stress Keynes's logic in the *General Theory*, which aimed at showing that unemployment could result from a persistent general deficiency of demand. In consequence, they urged that governments should be ready to raise demand by running budget deficits. As we have seen, however, Keynes's concepts of national income accounting had been used in the 1940s to calculate the budget *surplus* necessary to reduce demand to prevent inflation. While these two aspects of macroeconomic policy were logically consistent, there was ample room for disagreement about the balance to be struck between high employment and stable prices. Typically, Keynesian economists were willing to risk price rises of the order of 2 or 3 per cent in order to remove any possibility of a deficiency of demand. In contrast, Sir Leslie Rowan, one of the leading Treasury officials dealing with economic policy from 1947 to 1958, warned that the protracted erosion of the value of money was the greatest single danger, in the long run, to employment. In his view, rising prices made British goods less competitive, while devaluation of a major reserve currency would disrupt world trade. He warned that the erosion of the value of savings would reduce investment, and thereby economic growth (Rowan 1960, pp. 22–5). Such ideas could have come from the era of pre-Keynesian economics, but then Keynes had said that the classical economists had been right in believing that savings were necessary for investment when the economy was at full employment. At all events, the main significance of Keynesian national income accounting in the 1950s and sixties, as in the 1940s, seems to have been that it was used by the Treasury to justify budget surpluses, whereas before the war the chancellor had merely sought to balance his budget.

Keynesian economists believed that variations in the level of government expenditure and, much more so, variations in the levels of taxation, could be used to influence the aggregate level of effective demand. While their national income analytical framework owed much to Keynes, this balance between fiscal instruments was not what he had recommended. Keynes had stressed the use of public investment to offset variations in private investment, and he had believed that private consumption would not be much influenced by taxation, since he thought that people had established standards of life. Stress on variations in investment meant that Keynes could not have advocated 'fine-tuning' of the economy, in the manner attempted from the 1950s, since investment in such things as power stations or railway electrification is 'lumpy'. Whereas most Keynesian economists of the 1950s and sixties regarded 2 per cent as the maximum permissible level of unemployment, the figure mentioned by Keynes in the 1940s had been 5 per cent (Wilson 1982, pp. 53–60).

Keynesian willingness to use fiscal policy was often associated with a tendency to deny the effectiveness of monetary policy. Low interest rates were usually regarded by Keynesians as a merely permissive influence on investment, while high interest rates were usually regarded as inadequate to restrain investment when expected profits were high. There was, however, another school of thought in the 1950s, represented most importantly by Lionel Robbins, who had been head of the Economic Section of the Cabinet Office until shortly after the end of the war. Robbins argued that balance of payments equilibrium should be regarded as the sole test of financial policy and that the country could adapt itself quickly to external circumstances, provided that monetary policy were restored to its rightful place in economic management. In Robbins's opinion, fiscal policy was 'clumsy and inadequate'. As after 1919, the Bank of England could be expected to support an emphasis on monetary policy, since this would imply a shift in institutional influence from the Treasury to Threadneedle Street (Dow 1964, pp. 67–70).

In practice, chancellors from Butler (1951–55) onwards seem to have been willing to draw upon both schools of thought. Fiscal policy, mainly variations in taxation, was generally the chief means of managing demand. However, from October 1951, Bank Rate was raised whenever it was felt necessary to restrict the supply of credit to the private sector, most commonly when there was a balance of payments problem. In 1955, though, a tightening of monetary policy was used to justify a reduction in taxes. Other credit restrictions, such as variations in hire-purchase regulations, were also used to restrict demand. Indeed, in 1959 the Radcliffe Committee on the Working of the Monetary System was sceptical about the short-run impact on aggregate demand of changes in interest rates, and regarded hire-purchase regulation as more important for that purpose (Cmnd. 827, paras. 397–472). This was probably so in the 1950s, given that most companies had had large liquid balances since the war. The first signs of an emphasis upon the control of the money supply can perhaps be seen in a letter of intent to the International Monetary Fund (IMF) in 1967, whereby the Government undertook to restrict the money supply in 1968 to that of 1967. A similar undertaking about domestic credit expansion was made in 1969/70. However, these letters of intent were connected with devaluation in 1967 and the subsequent defence of sterling, and may well have represented the ideas of the IMF's staff rather than those of the Treasury or the Bank of England.

It is difficult to know what influence economists had on policy. There were never more than a couple of dozen at any one time in Whitehall from 1945 to 1964 and, after the Economic Section had been transferred from the Cabinet Office to the Treasury in 1953, the Chancellor of the Exchequer was the main channel through which their advice reached the Cabinet. It was only after 1964, when Labour returned to power committed to economic planning, that ministers showed any enthusiasm for the recruitment of economists. By 1966 there were 70 or 80 economists serving in various departments, including the Department of Economic Affairs, which had been set up in 1964 under the Deputy Prime Minister, George Brown. The numbers of economists rose rapidly thereafter, to 120 in 1967 and 262 in 1973 (Chester 1982, pp. 137–76). The recruitment of economists might have been expected to have improved economic management through better forecasting of the components of national income and expenditure and through improved understanding of how the various components interacted. Ignorance of the future could never be dispelled entirely, however, and there was always a lag between the collection of data and the taking of decisions, with further lags before decisions were implemented and before their effects worked their way through the economic system. Managerial decisions must always cope with uncertainty, but 'fine-tuning', which aimed at less than 2 per cent unemployment, left little room for manoeuvre. It did not take much of an increase in demand to outstrip domestic productive capacity, and thus to raise prices and to threaten the balance of payments.

Given the lags in data collection, it is not surprising that the government may sometimes have reflated when unemployment was about to fall, or deflated when unemployment was about to rise. Greater flexibility in fiscal policy was required than that allowed by annual budgets. From time to time additional budgets had to be introduced in the autumn, and from 1961 the Treasury was empowered to vary purchase tax rates by up to 10 per cent between budgets. There was much criticism at the time of the adverse effect on business expectations of 'stop-go' policies, which could raise tax or interest rates soon after a company had responded to 'go' signals by committing itself to some long-term investment. It was also widely suspected that the 'go' signals of tax cuts in 1955, 1959 and 1963 were not unconnected with impending general elections. However, compared with the post-1973 period, uncertainty was not a major problem for businessmen. What the shortcomings of 'stop-go' did suggest was that it was beyond the practical limits of government to ensure perfect economic stability. While there were only four months between 1948 and 1968 when the rate of unemployment reached 3 per cent, fluctuations in the rate of growth of GDP were very much greater, from 0 per cent in a recession to 5 per cent in a boom (Artis 1972; Cairncross 1971, pp. 26–45, 122–58; Dow 1964, chs. 5, 7–8, 15; Matthews 1971; Worswick 1971; Wright 1979, pp. 151–4).

Any improvements in the techniques of domestic demand management were likely to be more than offset by the fact that, over the period, the British economy was becoming increasingly open to external influences. The real burden of sterling debts incurred during the war declined as the terms of trade improved and as the value of sterling fell through inflation or devaluation. On the other hand, balance of payments problems persisted, with crises forcing governments to deflate in 1951, 1955, 1957, 1961, 1966–67 and 1968. Sterling was made fully convertible in 1958 and sterling's role as an international reserve currency encouraged defence of the existing exchange rate with the dollar by a steady piling up of liabilities to foreign governments, central banks and international organisations (Strange 1971).

Macroeconomic Policy: (2) Going for Growth

By the 1960s the apparent success of French indicative planning in promoting growth in a capitalist economy led to renewed interest in Whitehall in economic planning. Whereas planning had hitherto been associated with the Labour Party, the initiative which led to the creation of the National Economic Development Council (NEDC) in 1961 came from members of the Federation of British Industries and received strong support from the Conservative Prime Minister, Harold Macmillan. It was hoped that the NEDC, by bringing representatives of employers' organisations and the TUC together with ministers, would be able to identify obstacles to investment and improved productivity. The Government hoped to persuade employers and trade unionists to co-operate in removing these obstacles, while the promise of economic growth was held out as a reward. The Labour Government took the process further in 1964 by setting up a Department of Economic Affairs which incorporated the planning team which had been attached to the NEDC. The NEDC itself continued as a forum for discussion, with 'little Neddies' for each industry having the same function.

The planning process was bedevilled by four problems. Firstly, there were the inherent difficulties of determining in detail the changes which were required in a complex economy, given that technology and markets themselves were always changing. Secondly, the refusal of the unions to accept a separate National Incomes Commission meant that planning became linked with the question of wages as well as productivity, and the TUC representatives pressed for high growth targets which would justify proportionate wage demands. Thirdly, there proved to be insufficient slack in the economy to allow these targets to be met without balance of payments problems. Fourthly, while the Government's macroeconomic policy could raise demand, the Government could not act directly on the critical steps necessary in industry to improve productivity, while employers' organisations and the TUC themselves could only advise their members. All previous experience of relations between the Government and the TUC suggested that the influence of the national union leadership on what happened on the shop floor would be limited. Moreover, it was by no means certain that the best way to encourage enterprise among businessmen was to reduce risk; a planned expansion of demand would raise profits even if there were no radical changes in industry.

As it happened, the Conservative Chancellor in 1964, Reginald Maudling, decided to 'go for growth' on the basis of an NEDC plan for a rate of growth in national output of 4 per cent a year over the period 1961–66. He hoped that reflation would encourage sufficient investment and improvements in productivity to enable the initial balance of payments problem to be overcome. In 1965, in the middle of the 'Maudling boom', the Department of Economic Affairs published a National Plan for a 25 per cent increase in GDP between 1964 and 1970. In July 1966, however, steps were taken to defend the existing exchange rate of sterling, and the deflationary package involved meant that the National Plan was effectively abandoned. The actual growth in GDP between 1964 and 1970 was not 25 per cent but 14 per cent (Opie 1972; Wright 1979, pp. 155–9).

Failure to achieve planned growth targets led some economic commentators to advocate devaluation as a means of escape from external constraints to growth. There were, however, problems with this suggestion. Firstly, it was not clear where, in a fully employed economy, spare capacity would be found to allow an expansion of exports if sterling were devalued. Without such spare capacity it would be easier, and just as profitable, for exporters to raise their sterling prices rather than to attempt to increase output, and if they chose the former course, the competitive advantage from devaluation would soon be eroded. Spare capacity could be created, and production diverted from home to export markets, if devaluation were accompanied by deflationary measures, but it was these very measures which advocates of devaluation tended to be anxious to avoid. A second problem was that devaluation could only have a long-term effect if British workers did not react to higher import costs by pushing up wages, but there is ample evidence of such 'real-wage resistance' on the part of the trade unions, except in the very short run (see pages 175–82). A third problem was that in so far as British exports were adversely affected by non-price factors, such as poor design or unreliable and slow deliveries, devaluation might simply allow industry to put off making the radical changes necessary to remove these characteristics.

However, it does not seem to have been any of these considerations which led the Labour Government to try to avoid devaluation. The Chancellor, James Callaghan, argued that it would be morally wrong to devalue a currency in which other countries held their reserves. The Prime Minister, Harold Wilson, seems to have felt that it would be damaging politically if, following the devaluations of 1931 and 1949, it came to be felt in financial circles that the advent of a Labour government automatically signalled a fall in the value of sterling. On the other hand, as in 1931, Labour ministers were reluctant to curb the growth of public expenditure which, in money terms, rose by 50 per cent between 1964 and 1968, nearly twice as fast as GDP (also in money terms). The pressure of demand on the economy by the first half of 1966 was indicated by the fact that unemployment was lower than it had been for ten years. It is hardly surprising that foreigners anticipated a devaluation and moved their funds out of sterling where possible. Britain's gold and foreign exchange reserves, about £1,000 million, were inadequate for a prolonged defence of the exchange rate, being only a quarter of liquid external liabilities. Credits of £3,000 million from foreign central banks and £1,500 million from the IMF bought time, as did a tightening in exchange control and also the imposition of a temporary import surcharge of 15 per cent by value on imports, coupled with a rebate on exports. These last steps were a clear breach of rules which Britain had accepted as a member of the General Agreement on Tariffs and Trade (GATT). Domestically, steps were taken to reduce demand, including an incomes policy in 1965 and the virtual sacrifice of the National Plan in 1966. Ministers were unwilling, however, to press deflation to the point where unemployment rose, and in November 1967 the Government was forced into a reluctant devaluation from $2.80 to $2.40 (Cairncross and Eichengreen 1983, ch. 5).

Even then there was some doubt in foreign exchange markets whether the new rate could be held, and a standby credit was required from the IMF to combat speculation. Since the IMF required a letter of intent regarding cuts in public expenditure and a halt in expansion of the money supply, it cannot be said that devaluation brought much relief for domestic economic policy. There was the usual 'J curve' in the balance of trade, as the impact of higher import prices was felt more quickly than the effects of devaluation on the volume of exports or imports, and speculative pressure on sterling lasted well into 1969. By 1970 there was a large current account surplus in the balance of payments, but the political beneficiaries were not Labour, who had sacrificed so many expenditure plans, but the Conservatives, who won the 1970 general election.

The Conservatives came to power under Edward Heath intent on reducing public expenditure and on restoring the discipline of the market. Faced with rising unemployment, however, they quickly did a 'U-turn'. The Chancellor of the Exchequer, Anthony Barber, had favoured some expansion in his budget of March 1971, when he said that he was aiming at a growth rate in GDP of 3 per cent a year. Four months later, when it was discovered by Treasury economists that GDP was one per cent below the level previously assumed, he announced that he was aiming at 4–4½ per cent growth. Unemployment had risen from 2.6 per cent to 3.5 per cent (800,000 people) in the eight months to July 1971, and Barber's response was to reduce taxes and to abolish hire-purchase controls. In the winter of 1971–72 unemployment neared the one million mark, then regard-

Table 7.1 The Public Sector Borrowing Requirement, 1965–73 (£m.)

1965	*1966*	*1967*	*1968*	*1969*	*1970*	*1971*	*1972*	*1973*
1,205	961	1,863	1,279	−466	−17	1,373	2,040	4,181
	As percentage of GDP:							
3.86	2.90	5.33	3.41	−1.18	−0.04	2.80	3.71	6.59

Source: Annual Abstract of Statistics (1976) HMSO, Tables 344 and 370.

ed as politically unacceptable. Although there had not been time for the effects of his July measures to work through the economy, Barber reflated again in his budget of March 1972, aiming at 5 per cent growth and a reduction in unemployment to half a million. The first objective was roughly achieved down to mid-1973, and the second objective by the end of 1973, but only at the cost of a rapid increase in public sector borrowing (see Table 7.1).

The main inflationary element in the 'Barber boom', however, seems to have come from private sector borrowing. The control of credit was remarkably relaxed from 1971, and private borrowing was greatly stimulated by a concession in the March 1972 budget which made almost all interest payments tax deductible. Between October 1971 and December 1973 bank advances to UK residents rose 2½ times. Barber apparently believed that somehow increased credit would stimulate industrial investment and sustained growth, but much of the new credit went into financing a spectacular property boom. The Government's belief that it could make a 'dash for growth' seems to have gone hand in hand with a belief that the external constraint to growth could be removed by allowing sterling to float, a step announced in June 1972. Sterling sank rather than floated and a 32 per cent rise in import prices between the third quarter of 1972 and the third quarter of 1973 was added to domestic inflationary pressures. Thus, even before the oil crisis of October 1973, Barber's financial policies had created conditions for double-figure inflation (Blackaby 1978, pp. 58–67; Reid 1982, pp. 58–85; Stewart 1977, pp. 130–73).

It can be argued that the Barber boom was grossly mismanaged and that earlier, more moderate, exercises in demand management had been successful in maintaining full employment without excessive price rises. It should be noted, however, that for much of the period in question fiscal policy seems to have been used to control inflation rather than to raise employment. Matthews (1968) pointed out that since the war, governments had run current account surpluses averaging 3 per cent of national income; budget surpluses had been varied to manage demand but the net effect had been deflationary. As late as 1969 and 1970 the public sector's debts were being reduced (see Table 7.1). Maddison (1982, pp. 130–1) estimated the annual average impact of the first-round multiplier

Sources: Department of Labour and Productivity (1971), Tables 85, 90, 91 and 93; Department of Employment (1975), Tables 44 and 48.

Figure 7.1 Prices and Wages (Percentage Increases over Previous Year)

resulting from budgetary changes over the period 1965–73 to have been +0.52 per cent of GDP. On balance it may be said that macroeconomic policy helped to stretch out the boom, mainly by preventing it getting out of hand before 1972/73, but with some net stimulus to demand in the latter part of the boom.

It may also be noted that unemployment was on a rising trend in spite of the expansionary impact of budget changes from the mid-1960s. The peak of unemployment of 400,000 in 1952 was succeeded by one of 500,000 in 1958, another of 600,000 in 1963 and another of 900,000 in 1972. As a percentage of the labour force, unemployment averaged 1.7 in 1952–64, but 2.6 in 1965–73. Even so, the main problem was a decline of employment in particular industries, leading to unemployment in areas where these industries had been concentrated. This led to a renewal of regional policy (see below), but it could be argued that macroeconomic policy, by ensuring high demand, encouraged firms to move to areas where there was surplus labour. The real question mark over macroeconomic policy relates to the stability of prices and incomes. By recent standards there was reasonable stability, especially in 1953–67, when the increase in retail prices was never more than 5 per cent a year, and averaged much less. Even so, it was in that period that the annual wage round, something unheard of before 1939, became firmly established. By the early 1970s the retail price index could rise by 9 per cent in a year, and average hourly wage earnings were rising by annual rates of up to 15 per cent (see Figure 7.1). The next section considers to what extent the upward spiral of prices and wages was a consequence of excess demand.

The State and the Trade Unions

The danger that full employment could lead to a chronic spiral of rising wages and prices had been foreseen during wartime debates on employment policy. Full employment, after all, created a seller's market for labour. Inflation was unjust to people on fixed incomes, such as pensioners, but there was also a danger that inflation could undermine economic progress. A White Paper in 1956 on *The Economic Implications of Full Employment* (Cmd. 9725) reminded workers that they could price British goods out of world markets if wages rose faster than productivity, and also pointed out that at full employment a rise in consumption could reduce the savings and investment necessary for future growth of national output. The White Paper claimed that experience of the previous ten years showed that the fuller employment was, the more liable prices were to rise. Nevertheless, the authors of the White Paper looked to increased productivity and to self-restraint by workers in claiming wage increases, rather than to more unemployment, to remedy the situation.

Looking at the 1951–73 period, it would seem that restraint in making wage demands depended upon a number of factors. What follows is a brief summary of these factors and of governments' responses to them. The first factor was employers' willingness to resist wage demands. This in turn depended upon (a) the strength of employers' organisations relative to that of trade unions; (b) employers' ability to raise prices; and (c) changes in the means of production. Brown (1983) argued that British employers lacked a tradition of cohesion and mutual support and that the strength of the working man's vote had ensured that legislation tended to favour trade unions in the conduct of industrial disputes. As for point (b), most firms had no difficulty in raising prices. Governments' commitment to full employment seemed to ensure that there would be no lack of domestic demand and, since trade unions negotiated wage rates nationally, there was little risk of losing sales to domestic competitors by acceding to wage demands. There was, however, a risk where foreign competition was concerned. Turning to point (c), firms could cut labour costs by replacing men with machines, but the more capital-intensive the means of production, the greater the cost of an industrial dispute in terms of capital kept idle, and the lower the cost, proportionate to the price of the final product, of granting wage demands. This last point alone could go far to explain why wages continued to rise even after total manufacturing employment began to fall after 1966 (from 9,163,000 jobs in June that year to 7,828,000 in June 1973).

Nevertheless, it is reasonable to believe that a second factor in determining the degree of wage restraint was workers' fear of unemployment. This was never wholly absent, even during the period of full employment – witness the preservation by trade unionists of restrictive practices which had been designed to protect jobs. Even so, fears of unemployment were presumably a less important factor in industrial bargaining than ever before. Some workers might wonder whether they would price themselves out of jobs, but this would happen only if wage demands could bankrupt their employers, something which could be avoided if the state could be persuaded to step in with subsidies, as happened in the case of some nationalised industries and, from the 1960s, in the case of some private firms as well.

Inflationary expectations were a third factor in determining the degree of wage restraint. In the 1940s it had been possible to modify inflationary expectations by subsidising key elements in the retail price index, particularly food and rent. However, such a policy was no longer practicable once workers' actual expenditure encompassed an increasing range of consumer goods, such as television sets and washing machines. By the 1950s and 1960s workers were aware that prices rose each year, and wage demands were made in relation to the erosion of real wages in the past year, the anticipated level of inflation in the coming year and, not least, changes in accustomed differentials between groups of workers.

This point leads to a fourth factor determining the degree of wage restraint: the acceptance, or rejection, by workers of the existing wage structure. Very full information was available from official and other sources of relative wage rates, and defence of existing differentials was regarded as legitimate grounds for a pay increase, regardless of the level of a firm's profits. Moreover, since different groups of workers negotiated their wage claims at different times of the year, an introduction of general wage restraint at a given point in time was bound to leave some workers feeling aggrieved about an erosion of differentials. On the other hand, a powerful group of workers might reject wage restraint precisely because they did not accept the existing distribution of income and wished to improve their relative standing in the wages 'league'. The militancy of the miners in the 1970s, as in the 1940s, was the leading example of this.

A fifth factor in wage restraint was the ability of trade unions' national leaders to control their own members. This had been much reduced by the re-emergence of a powerful shop-stewards movement during the Second World War. Trade-union leaders might negotiate national wage rates, but much of the progressive raising of unit labour costs was a result of detailed bargaining on the shop floor. For example, restrictive practices might be applied to 'make overtime'. There was a widening margin between formally negotiated wage rates and the actual cost of labour, a phenomenon known as wage drift. From the late 1950s an increasing number of strikes were begun without prior authorisation of national union officials and by 1964–66 95 per cent of all stoppages were 'unofficial' in this sense (Brown 1983, pp. 143–5). Even if trade unions' national leaders could be convinced by economic arguments that wage restraint was in the national interest, there seemed to be no-one capable of persuading workers on the shop floor that circumstances warranted sacrifice of their individual interests.

Finally, pay negotiations in the postwar period came increasingly to be conducted in terms of 'take-home' pay. Income-tax thresholds were not adjusted for inflation, so that over time, workers found income tax becoming a new or increased burden, and national insurance contributions were also raised from time to time (see page 201). The increased tax burden thus gave rise to wage claims as workers sought to maintain their real disposable incomes.

In these circumstances, it was not at all clear what governments could do to prevent an inflationary spiral of wages and prices. All parties were committed to full employment, and once unemployment had been as low as 1.5 per cent in 1953–57, it was difficult to argue that anything more represented full employment. In 1956 the Conservative Government arranged a 'price freeze' with the nationalised industries and the leading employers' organisations, but the TUC rejected wage restraint. A government-appointed Council on Prices, Productivity and Incomes reported four times between 1958 and 1961 with a view to educating public opinion, but the Council was virtually boycotted by the TUC. In July 1961 the Chancellor of the Exchequer, Selwyn Lloyd, announced an eight-month pause in pay increases in the public sector, and asked private industry to conform. Public-sector wage increases were postponed – with the exception of an award to the power workers, who threatened to strike – and there were some postponements in the private sector as well. Towards the end of the pause a White Paper on *National Incomes Policy: The Next Step* suggested that future pay increases should be linked to productivity agreements, and offered a guideline of 2 to 2.5 per cent. This guideline was ignored by the unions, as was the establishment of a National Incomes Commission later in 1962. In 1963 the NEDC, which included representatives of the TUC, issued a 'guiding light' of 3 to 3.5 per cent for pay increases, on the optimistic assumption that there would be 4 per cent growth in GDP in the next twelve months. The 'guiding light' suffered from the disadvantage that while it may have encouraged wage claims by weak unions, it did nothing to deter higher claims by strong unions (Clegg 1978, pp. 407–8, 413–7; Knowles 1963).

It is difficult to assess the effects of Conservative prices and incomes policy. Figure 7.1 (page 175) shows that the rate of increase in hourly wage earnings did fall off after the prices freeze of 1956. The freeze was not the only influence on inflationary expectations, however, since import costs had fallen sharply four years earlier, after the Korean War boom, and this had helped to moderate the rise in retail prices. Nevertheless, international comparisons do suggest that prices and incomes policy had some success. Whereas labour costs per unit of output had been rising faster in Britain than in other major industrial countries in the mid-1950s, this was no longer so between 1959 and 1964, when the United States alone among such countries showed a slower rate of increase (Cairncross and Eichengreen 1983, p. 164).

The Labour governments of 1964–70 could expect to enjoy better relations with the TUC than their predecessors, but these years saw a rise in shop-floor militancy. The annual number of industrial stoppages increased by almost a third while a Royal Commission on Trade Unions and Employers' Associations (the Donovan Commission) sat from 1965 to 1968. In 1969 a White Paper, *In Place of Strife* (Cmnd. 3888), proposed to improve industrial relations by empowering the Government to impose a conciliation pause of 28 days in industrial disputes, while an Industrial Board, with powers to fine strikers, was to be set up. This last measure in particular was too much for trade-union opinion and the Prime Minister was compelled to drop the proposals (Brown 1983, pp. 173–9). This was not a promising background for a wages policy. At first Labour relied mainly on voluntary vetting of wage claims by the General Council of the TUC, but in July 1966 the Government enacted a six-month freeze on wages, salaries, dividends and prices, to be followed by six months of 'severe restraint' with a 'nil norm' for increases. By law, a month's notice had to be given before any increase was granted, during which time the Government might refer the case to the National Board for Prices and Incomes. The Board would decide whether a claim could be justified on the basis of a productivity agreement, and clearly a lax attitude to productivity agreements, which might, or might not, be kept, was one way of avoiding conflict with powerful trade unions. Nevertheless, wage increases were certainly postponed; the index of weekly wage rates did not rise at all from July to December 1966 and it rose by only 2 per cent from July 1966 to June 1967. Thereafter, however, workers seem to have tried to make up lost ground. The TUC's voluntary vetting of claims continued, as did referrals to the National Board for Prices and Incomes, but these were essentially delaying tactics and productivity agreements became increasingly spurious. By 1970 wage settlements well into double figures had become the norm, although the cost of food imports rose by only about 3 per cent as a result of the 1967 devaluation (Blackaby 1978, pp. 366–78, 390–401; Cairncross and Eichengreen 1983, pp. 206–8).

The number of strikes in 1970 was nearly double the number in 1968. The response of the incoming Conservative Government was to introduce the Industrial Relations Act of 1971, which was drafted with minimal consultation with the TUC and the Confederation of British Industries. The Act made written agreements between employers and employees legally enforceable unless the agreement included a clause to the contrary. In practice employers seem to have had no wish to become involved in legal actions and an escape clause was invariably included in written agreements. Unions were required to register their rules so that people responsible for calling strikes could be clearly identified, but most unions refused to register. Finally, the Industrial Court was empowered to impose severe penalties for breach of legally enforceable agreements or for inducing other people to break them. 'Secondary picketing' induced some employers to go to the Industrial Court, but when five London dockers were jailed, the TUC threatened a one-day general strike, and the Government secured the men's release by applying to the Court through a hitherto little-known officer, the Official Solicitor (Brown 1983, pp. 185–93).

In contrast to this unsuccessful attempt to improve industrial relations by law, the Conservatives at first tried to avoid intervention in wage settlements, relying instead on the prospect of bankruptcy to stiffen employers' resistance. This was no policy at all, so far as local authority workers, coal miners and power workers were concerned, and all these groups won wage settlements of 12 per cent or more in 1970–71. Early in 1972 a miners' strike, which was carried out with an unprecedented amount of secondary picketing, led to pay rises of 17 and 20 per cent. The average annual increase in weekly earnings in 1969–72 was over 10 per cent and rising, and this trend cannot be explained in terms of rising import prices since these were comparatively stable before the depreciation of sterling in the second half of 1972. Some trade unionists undoubtedly disliked the Conservative Government, but the surge in pay claims had begun under Labour. Moreover, when the Conservatives finally introduced an incomes policy it was initially observed, at least in the postponement of wage claims. Under 'Stage 1', a standstill on pay, dividends, rents and most prices from November 1972 to March 1973, average earnings rose by less than one per cent (Blackaby 1978, pp. 52–62, 378–9, 390).

Prolonged creeping inflation due to excess demand could be expected to raise wage claims, but the behaviour of the miners and other groups of workers in 1970–72 went far beyond real wage resistance or rational expectations of inflation based upon past experience. It is not certain, however, that trade unionists showed any less restraint than speculators on the stock exchange or in the property market in the same years. The explanation for the collapse of wage restraint in the early 1970s may have less to do with any relationship between unemployment and prices than with the attitudes engendered by a long boom. By the late 1960s many economists believed that something called self-sustained growth could go on for ever. A belief that rising prosperity will never end is characteristic of the final stages of a boom. So is lack of self-restraint. The ethos of a consumer society, with its endless supply of new, heavily-advertised goods, certainly did not encourage restraint on the part of trade unionists or anyone else.

Problems of Public Expenditure

Even if it had been decided to lower the level of demand in the economy in the 1950s and 1960s to a level consistent with stable prices (supposing this level to be known), governments would have faced formidable problems in controlling public expenditure. The increasing size of the administrative machine in the twentieth century inevitably reduced the Treasury's ability to control expenditure in detail. What was not inevitable was the reduction in the 1950s and 1960s of the power of the chancellor to set limits to the totals of public expenditure. One incident which undermined the Treasury was Macmillan's refusal to support his Chancellor of the Exchequer, Peter Thorneycroft, in 1957 when the latter demanded that central government expenditure for 1958/59 be held at the level of 1957/58. Only £50 million, or about 0.25 per cent of GDP, was at issue, but the principle of holding the remorseless rise in public expenditure when prices were rising was important enough for Thorneycroft to resign.

The growth of public expenditure as a proportion of GDP also seems to have been promoted unintentionally by the introduction of the Public Expenditure Survey Committee (PESC) system. Under this system, which was recommended in the Plowden Report (Cmnd. 1432) of 1961, a Treasury committee made an annual survey of projected government expenditure over the next five years, in constant prices. The idea was to hold public expenditure to a fixed proportion of GDP, but future growth of GDP was assumed to be what NEDC forecasts or George Brown's National Plan said it would be, and forecasts of growth erred on the optimistic side. This, plus the usual reluctance of ministers to cut expenditure plans, helps to explain why public expenditure rose from about a third of GDP in 1961/62 to 40.2 per cent in 1967/68. A strong Chancellor, Roy Jenkins, who was determined to correct the balance of payments, reduced the proportion thereafter, to 37.7 in 1969/70, but there was a sharp rise under Barber from 37.8 per cent in 1971/72 to 40.4 per cent in 1973/74 (Pliatzky 1984).

One justification for the PESC system was the need to give the greatest stability to the planning and execution of public sector programmes. It was obviously helpful to nationalised industries or to universities to know that there would be no sharp reduction in their finance over a five-year period, but this would mean that any cuts in aggregate demand to manage fluctuations in the trade cycle would be concentrated on the private sector. This was, of course, the opposite of what Keynes had recommended, since he had wanted public capital expenditure to be used in a counter-cyclical fashion. Public expenditure programmes which had passed PESC were certainly hard to cut, and this imparted an upward bias to public expenditure as a proportion of GDP, given that growth of GDP was less than expected. However, those responsible for the short-term management of the economy never accepted that PESC gave complete immunity, and so the frustrations of 'stop-go' continued to be felt by managers in the public sector as well as in the private sector (Clarke 1978, pp. xiii–xiv, 31–2).

One might have expected that Labour's nationalisation programme after the war would have increased central government's power to manage the level of demand in the economy. It is true that the Conservatives returned the steel industry to private ownership in 1953, but the same Act set up an Iron and Steel Board with powers to regulate new investment, and Labour renationalised steel in 1967. Investment in new steel mills, not to mention power stations or railway electrification, tends to be 'lumpy', however, in that such projects are not easily cut back once they have been begun. Such projects must be completed if there is to be a return on capital. Moreover, it was difficult for nationalised undertakings to carry out their statutory obligation to cover costs, including compensation to previous owners. When nationalised undertakings made a loss, their workers and customers were in effect subsidised, and aggregate demand was increased. When nationalised undertakings made profits, as the electricity and gas industries usually did, governments tended to ask them to hold prices. Such action helped to hold down the retail price index but did nothing to hold down aggregate demand. On balance, the nationalised industries would seem to have imparted an upward bias to aggregate demand.

The coal industry's investment programme of the 1940s and fifties did produce a small surplus on current account by the 1960s. However, whereas there had been a persistent shortage of coal for most of the 1940s and fifties, increased competition from oil in the 1960s meant that the coal industry now had surplus capacity. There were large current account deficits in 1966 and 1969, and again after the large wage increases granted to the miners in the early 1970s. The railways likewise required large-scale investment on nationalisation. Most railway companies had failed to make profits between the wars, owing to competition from road transport, but the temporary eclipse of private road transport during and after the war made it possible for railways to show a surplus on current account from 1951 to 1953. Thereafter revived competition from road vehicles (itself promoted by the Conservatives' denationalisation of road haulage) made the existing rail network unprofitable. Dr. Beeching, Chairman of the Railways Board, proposed in 1963 to reduce services and to close a large number of lines and stations. However, political pressures, especially from marginal constituencies, prevented his proposals being carried out in full, and most of the gross savings achieved were absorbed by higher wages and improved working conditions for employees. The record of the nationalised steel industry was also one of financial failure, largely because of government interference in prices. It is difficult to believe that the nation as a whole got value for money from its nationalised industries, even if particular communities were protected from the social effects of closures (Kelf-Cohen 1973).

Some private-sector firms, and therefore some communities, were also subsidised through Treasury grants and loans available under various Acts relating to the distribution of industry. In theory regional policy might improve national efficiency by preventing under-utilisation of resources in some areas, including social capital, and by reducing congestion in other areas. The Barlow Report of 1940 had identified congestion in the London area as as much an economic and social problem as unemployment in the North and West of the country and had called for fundamental research into regional problems. However, there seems to have been a lack of interest in Whitehall and the research had not been undertaken by the end of the 1950s. The factors which led to a revival of interest in regional policy were: firstly, unemployment in coal mining, shipbuilding and steel, following the end of the postwar boom in these industries; and secondly, the related pronounced anti-government swing in Scotland and Northern England in the general elections of 1959 and 1964. Under the Distribution of Industry Act of 1958 and the Employment Act of 1960, the criterion for regional financial assistance was the level of unemployment. Little attention was paid to the growth potential of development districts and it was not until 1963 that attempts were made, by the NEDC, to relate regional policy to the goal of a higher growth rate in GDP (McCrone 1969, chs. 1, 2 and 4).

The Employment Act of 1960 empowered the Board of Trade to withdraw as well as to apply development status to any district, and in practice the Board used an unemployment level of 4.5 per cent as a rule of thumb. As a result, firms would sometimes find that a district was descheduled after plans had been made to invest there. The Industrial Development Act of 1966 abolished the development districts and designated 40 per cent of the country as development areas, but a year later there was a further change, with some particularly depressed districts being given special development status, which qualified them for more generous financial assistance. Then, in 1970, the coverage of regional assistance was extended to what were called intermediate areas, which were again designated according to the level of unemployment, and these areas were further extended in 1972. It was not until 1963 that negative controls were seriously applied to investment in areas which already had an abundance of jobs and where there was or might be congestion. From that year it was more common for the Board of Trade to refuse industrial development certificates and in 1964 office development controls were brought in for the London area. However, firms which had been refused permission to develop in the London area might not move very far, and Bristol, which was not in a development area, was a major example of a town benefiting from these new restrictions. The reduction of regional unemployment relied mainly on the level of industrial investment incentives, and from 1963 these were not ungenerous since they included a 10 per cent grant for machinery and a 25 per cent grant for buildings. Then in 1967 a regional employment premium was introduced to subsidise wages by 5 to 7 per cent. The Heath Government replaced investment grants with tax allowances and relaxed negative controls in prosperous areas, but its declared intention to abolish the regional employment premium was rescinded when unemployment rose in 1972 (Hardie 1972; McCallum 1979; McCrone 1969, ch. 5).

It is hardly surprising, given all the changes listed in the previous paragraph, that a major criticism of regional policy was its inconsistency. Investment in development areas may well have been delayed or withheld as a result of uncertainty felt by businessmen about the future scope and level of regional assistance. Be that as it may, inter-regional differences in unemployment rates persisted. It is difficult to assess the impact of regional policy, since one does not know what would have happened if it had not been applied. Employment trends in the 1960s and 1970s can only be compared with hypothetical trends based on the period when regional policy was not applied in the 1950s. However, there was a decline in manufacturing employment in the country as a whole after 1966 and it is by no means clear that earlier trends form a satisfactory basis for analysis. Estimates of the number of jobs created by regional policy should, therefore, be treated with some reserve, but the best available suggest that 294,000 manufacturing jobs were created directly in the main development and special development areas, including Northern Ireland, over the period 1960–76, with a further 38,000 manufacturing jobs being created directly in the intermediate areas in 1970–76. If one assumes a regional employment multiplier of 1.4, the cumulative effect of policy on regional employment would have been 480,000 jobs (Department of Trade and Industry 1984; Moore and Rhodes 1973 and 1976).

Whether the creation of something like half a million jobs justified expenditure on regional policy is a matter for debate. The annual cost in terms of subsidies and tax concessions certainly rose very rapidly under Labour, from £30.3 million in 1964/65 to £301.5 million in 1969/70 (Hardie 1972, p. 225). It was possible to claim, however, that regional policy, by raising employment, increased output and taxable capacity so that there was little or no net burden to the Exchequer. Moreover, the questions of subsidies and industrial efficiency have to be considered in a wider context than regional policy, the effects of which were very probably offset by other forms of public expenditure outside the development areas. The Labour governments of 1964–70 intended to modernise the economy by changing its structure and by developing industries based on advanced technology. There was a threefold attempt to promote structure change from 1966: firstly, cash grants replaced tax allowances for investment, and grants were concentrated on manufacturing and extractive industries; secondly, selective employment tax was used to shift some of the tax burden from manufacturing to services, and to encourage a transfer of labour from the latter to the former; and thirdly, the Industrial Reorganisation Corporation was set up with powers to buy securities or to guarantee loans. Then in 1968 the Industrial Expansion Act gave the Government powers to use loans, grants and guarantees, and to underwrite losses and the subscription of share capital, where a scheme would benefit industrial efficiency or capacity or technological improvement. Despite the emphasis on advanced technology, however, large subsidies went into the distinctly antiquated shipbuilding industry while it was being rationalised after 1967 (Graham 1972). Even advanced technology was not always profitable. The development and production of Concorde, a prestige supersonic airliner with no prospect of commercial success for its manufacturers, absorbed large subsidies. By 1970/71 Concorde accounted for 56 per cent of government support for the aerospace industry, and subsidies for the aerospace industry were equivalent to 71 per cent of subsidies dispensed through regional policy (Burton 1979, p. 6).

The Conservatives came to power in 1970 determined to reduce state intervention and to avoid subsidising what they called 'lame ducks'. The Industrial Reorganisation Corporation was dissolved and expenditure under the Industrial Expansion Act was reduced. However, when Rolls Royce, the major supplier of aero-engines for the Royal Air Force, faced bankruptcy in 1971 on account of a fixed-price contract for an American airliner, the Government nationalised the firm. Later in the year Upper Clyde Shipbuilders, a product of Labour's rationalisation of the shipbuilding industry, was on the brink of financial disaster, and the Government proposed to close two of the four yards. The workers responded by taking over the Clydebank yard and eventually all four yards were saved in 1972, although with some loss of jobs. As unemployment rose, the Government brought in the Industry Act of 1972 to provide tax incentives for investment as well as grants for capital expenditure in assisted areas and elsewhere. Subsidies to industry, like subsidies to agriculture since the 1930s, seemed to have become a permanent feature of British political economy.

Another area of public finance over which central government appeared to have little control was local authority expenditure. Local authorities' share of total domestic civil public expenditure rose from 35.2 per cent in 1950 to 40.0 per cent in 1968, and local authorities were responsible for 64 per cent of the total increase in

Table 7.2 Composition of Public Authorities' Current Expenditure as Percentages of GDP

	1948	*1953*	*1964*	*1975*
Defence	7.04	8.64	5.96	4.92
National Health Service	1.97	2.84	3.16	4.59
Education	2.13	2.14	2.82	4.79
Other	5.88	4.64	4.80	7.87
Total	17.02	18.26	16.74	22.17

Source: Wright (1979), p. 166

employment between 1958 and 1968 (Holmans 1970). This rise stemmed partly from national policies on education and housing, but much of the increase was a result of the natural desire of many local authorities to create civic amenities of a high standard. Growing expenditure on education, housing and other social services was partly the inevitable result of demographic change, since there were more children and elderly people in relation to adults of working age, and since there was an increase in the number of households.

During the 1950s and 1960s it was possible to increase expenditure on social services by more than the increase in GDP, without raising taxation, because defence expenditure was falling as a proportion of GDP (see Table 7.2). This substitution of butter for guns could not go on indefinitely, however, and by the 1970s there was little prospect of increasing social service expenditure by more than the growth in GDP except by reducing personal consumption of other goods and services, either through taxation or inflation.

Health, Housing and Education

The fact that there was a very elastic, if not unlimited, demand for free medical services, and an increasing supply of new medical services as a result of technological progress, has already been remarked upon (see page 156). After a period of financial restraint in 1951–55, during which the Government gave the construction of houses and schools priority over the construction of hospitals, there was a major expansion in expenditure by the NHS. Allowing for changes in prices, it has been estimated that by 1960 capital expenditure, largely on new hospitals, was running at a level more than 80 per cent greater than in 1949, while current expenditure, including medicines and salaries, was 30 per cent greater than in 1949. The major expansion in NHS expenditure, however, came with hospital building programmes in the 1960s and seventies, and by 1974 capital expenditure was nearly seven times the level of 1949, while current expenditure was over 90 per cent greater than in 1949 (again taking account of price changes). Even so, the hospitals' waiting lists, which had been reduced from nearly 500,000 in 1949 to about 465,000 in 1960, had risen to about 550,000 by 1974. There were particularly acute shortages of accommodation in geriatric and mental hospitals, partly as a result of a failure to anticipate demand arising from the increasing numbers of elderly people, but also because of the greater prestige of clinical medicine (Abel-Smith 1978, chs. 2–3).

The organisation of the NHS itself did not encourage either an economic or a fair distribution of resources. Prior to 1948 hospital administration had been constrained financially by the limits of private generosity, in the case of voluntary hospitals, or by the political unpopularity of raising rate revenue, in the case of local authority hospitals. After 1948 revenue came from central government, and the people overseeing hospital expenditure no longer had to worry about how to raise the money. Consultants and others naturally wanted the best standards for hospital patients, and hospital administrators found it hard to refuse them. In the case of general practitioner, pharmaceutical, ophthalmic and dental services, the only ways in which demand could be limited were to urge economy on independently-minded professionals, who were naturally more conscious of their patients' needs than those of the Exchequer, or to adopt the politically unpopular step of raising charges for prescriptions. From 1948 until 1974 hospital services, general practitioner services and local authority health services were administered separately, with no single authority capable of balancing needs and priorities on a national scale. The Department of Health (after 1968 the Department of Health and Social Security) and the Scottish Office were responsible for central budgeting, but ministers and officials lacked the information to reallocate resources between services and regions (Klein 1983, ch. 2; Watkin 1978, chs. 2 and 9).

As a result of this ignorance, finance was allocated to regional hospital boards broadly in proportion to previous expenditure, and this tended to perpetuate pre-1948 inequalities. Special account was taken of the needs of teaching hospitals, so that regions with a number of such hospitals tended to receive a disproportionate amount of money. In 1971/72 revenue expenditure per head in the South Western Metropolitan Region was £141, compared with only £77 in the Sheffield Region. Moreover, although there were restrictions on the establishment of new practices in areas designated as over-doctored, and although there were financial inducements to set up practices in less popular areas, there had been no dramatic shift in the distribution of general practitioner services by 1973 (Berthoud *et al.* 1981, pp. 204–6; Klein 1983, chs. 2–3).

Paradoxically, even as resources devoted to the NHS increased as a proportion of GDP in the 1960s, the standards of service were increasingly seen as inadequate. New forms of treatment could not be introduced in every hospital at once, and hospitals lacking the new technology were seen as second rate. A general rise in living standards made existing hospital accommodation, much of it dating from the nineteenth century, seem cramped and drab, as indeed in many cases it was. An ambitious hospital plan for England and Wales was published in 1962 by the Minister of Health, Enoch Powell, but there was often a ten-year delay between sanctioning construction and completion, and in any case rising costs forced his Labour successor to trim the plan in 1966. Despite its deficiencies, however, the NHS remained a popular service and received an increasing share of national resources.

There was a huge unsatisfied demand for housing after the war. The Conservatives committed themselves at their annual conference in 1950 to build 300,000 houses a year, and this target was broadly met in the years 1953 to 1955 inclusive. The political imperative was such that not even a balance of payments crisis in 1951–52 brought about a cut in the programme, such as had happened in 1947. The higher level of completions than under Labour also reflected a deliberate reduction in standards for local authority houses, together with an encouragement of private investment. Private building was given a big boost by the abolition in 1953 of Labour's development charges, for developers could benefit thereafter from the value realised when planning permission was given to use farmland for housing. The Conservatives vigorously promoted housing for owner-occupation, and then encouraged local authorities to restrict their activities to slum clearance, overcrowding and provision for the elderly. Exchequer subsidies ceased to be available for construction for general needs from the end of 1956. It was argued that reliance on private enterprise would reduce the cost to the Exchequer of housing subsidies, but this argument conveniently overlooked the loss of revenue to the Exchequer through tax relief on mortgage interest (McKay and Cox 1979, pp. 122–30; Merrett 1979, pp. 246–54).

Table 7.3 shows the rise of private housing and the decline of local authority housing under the Conservatives. As part of their dash for growth in 1963, the Conservatives raised their housing target to 400,000 completions a year. Recognising that their Rent Act of

Table 7.3 The Political Parties' Housing Records (000s)[a]

Annual averages	*Private completions*	*Local authority completions*	*Total completions*	*Demolition*
Labour				
1947–51	29.9	156.0	185.9	
Conservatives				7.8[b]
1952–54	62.6	213.3	275.9	
1955–64	155.6	132.9	288.5	50.9
Labour				
1965–70	198.9	164.1	362.0	81.0
Conservatives				
1971–74	178.9	107.5	286.4	74.5

Source: Merrett (1979), pp. 120, 239, 247, 256, 261.
Notes: (a) Permanent dwellings only. Figures for Great Britain.
(b) Average for England and Wales 1945–54.

1957, which had decontrolled houses on vacation by sitting tenants, had not revived private building for rent, the Conservatives saw that more local authority building for rent was necessary. Some 151,000 local authority houses were begun in 1963, compared with 124,000 the previous year. This was the beginning of a bipartisan policy on housing, for too many Labour voters were, or aspired to be, owner-occupiers for there to be any reversion after 1964 to the priority given to local authority building in the late 1940s. A five-year housing programme announced in 1965 set a target of 500,000 housing units a year, divided equally between the private and public sectors. This represented a huge capital outlay and the plan soon foundered on the fact that growth in GDP was not what the Department of Economic Affairs had forecast. The Government's decision to defend sterling before and after the 1967 devaluation required a cut in public expenditure programmes, and local authority starts fell from 191,985 houses in 1967 to 149,394 in 1969. There was a further pause for thought when a tower block at Ronan Point collapsed in

1968, leading to a reappraisal of high-rise buildings (Merrett 1979, pp. 253–9).

It is easy in retrospect to criticise the policy of building flats in very high towers or slabs. These were constructed with remarkable speed from the late 1950s. There were design problems, like the Glasgow tower blocks which had lifts which were too small for stretchers or coffins, and building standards were often low. At the time, however, the pressing need seemed to be to press on with slum clearance, which had been virtually suspended since 1939. It was estimated in 1954 that 43 per cent of houses in Liverpool and 32 per cent of houses in Manchester were unfit for human habitation, and the slum problems of some other cities were no less serious. Over the next 20 years over a million houses were demolished in Great Britain, but there were still 860,000 dwellings which were registered as unfit in 1974. Of these, 18.6 per cent were in Scotland, although Scotland had only 9.6 per cent of the population. Two generations of rent controls had left private landlords with little incentive, and often not enough income, to maintain their properties, and in the 1950s and sixties demolition seemed to be the only answer to inner city decay. By the early 1970s, however, there was increasing public clamour to replace slum clearance with improvement programmes for the existing housing stock. Much was done with subsidies under the 1969 Housing Act, although the process often led to 'gentrification' of inner city areas and to the displacement of the original inhabitants (Cullingworth 1979, ch. 5).

The decline in local authority housing starts after 1967 continued under the Heath Government, from 114,650 in 1971 to 87,290 in 1973, although these same years saw a property boom in the private sector. The Government's chief concern was to economise by reforming housing subsidies, 90 per cent of which were used to support rents irrespective of need. Under the Housing Finance Act of 1972 local authority rents were to be raised in stages to an economic level, with rebates for tenants who could not afford such rents. The Government was also happy to agree with the arguments of the housing improvement lobby, since this encouraged home ownership and cost the Exchequer less than slum clearance (McKay and Cox 1979, pp. 138–44).

Education was another area of social policy where heavy capital outlays were inescapable in the 1950s, sixties and early seventies. A higher school leaving age was one factor. The additional 14–15 year olds from 1947 had been accommodated by using temporary hutments, which had to be replaced, and in 1964 the further raising of the leaving age to 16 years was announced, and yet more classrooms were required. The original target date for the new leaving age was 1970/71, but, as with so many of Labour's plans in the 1960s, economic constraints required a reappraisal and the date had to be moved to 1972/73. Demographic change was another factor behind the school building programme. The birth-rate, which had been declining since the nineteenth century, began to rise again after 1941, from 579,000 live births in England and Wales that year to 881,000 live births in 1947, the peak of the post-war 'baby boom'. By 1955 the number of live births (668,000) was almost back to the level of 1942, but thereafter there was an unexpected peacetime 'baby boom', with 876,000 live births in the peak year of 1964. In 1951 there had been 5,738,000 pupils in maintained schools in England and Wales; by 1973 the figure was 8,512,000, an increase of 48 per cent. Moreover, as general living standards rose, higher standards of school accommodation were expected and older properties had to be renovated. This was no small task, as in 1962 a third of pupils in England and Wales were in schools where the main building was over 60 years old (Gosden 1983, pp. 1–21).

There had been a political consensus since 1944 in favour of investment in education, if only on account of a widespread belief that an investment in 'human capital' was good for national efficiency and economic growth. The consensus on education broke down in the 1960s, however, over the question of selectivity in secondary education. As early as 1958 the Conservative Government was prepared to admit the case for comprehensive schools in sparsely-populated country districts or on new housing estates, where there were no grammar schools, but the Conservatives were opposed to the closure or conversion of well-established grammar schools in order to give comprehensives a monopoly in any area. In 1965 the Labour Secretary of State for Education, Anthony Crosland, issued Circular 10/65, which requested local education authorities to submit plans for comprehensive education, and it was made clear that a complete reorganisation of secondary education over the next few years was intended. A bill was introduced in Parliament in 1970 to give statutory force to the request in Circular 10/65, but the bill was lost when a general election was called, and the Conservatives' victory in that election led to Circular 10/65 being withdrawn. The new Secretary of State, Margaret Thatcher, gave local education authorities freedom to decide whether or not to go ahead with plans for comprehensive schools. Rather to her surprise, one imagines, even many Conservative-controlled authorities preferred to continue with comprehensive plans rather than face the prospect of an upheaval every time there was a change of power in Parliament (Gosden 1983, pp. 28–42).

The merits or demerits of comprehensive or selective systems of education are beyond the scope of this book. There does seem to have been a failure on the part of secondary modern schools to gain parity of esteem, and there was consequently support for comprehensives among those middle-income parents who valued social prestige but who could not afford to pay for private education for children who failed to win a place at grammar school. Much was made of the wider mix of social classes in comprehensives, but since many middle-class parents were willing to pay premium prices for houses in the catchment areas of 'good' comprehensives (usually ex-grammar schools), it is not clear that comprehensives really did very much to bring the social classes together. Be that as it may, if the comprehensive system were to lead to a levelling up of schools to the standards of the best grammar schools, rather than a levelling down to the standards of secondary moderns, then there would have to be additional investment in buildings and teacher training. Since there already was a shortage of classrooms in the 1960s and early 1970s, and since not all secondary modern teachers were trained to the same standards as grammar school teachers, it was clear that the levelling up process would take time.

Further pressure for investment in education came from increasing demand for entry to university. The war had shown the value of university-trained people to the community and there was a consensus on the need for greater equality of opportunity in higher education. In 1952–53 there were 81,000 full-time university students – 60 per cent more than in 1938–39 – and by 1962–63 the figure was 119,000. In 1962 the Conservative Party Conference called on the Government to 'invest in the future by a rapid and massive development of university and higher technological education', and in the following year the Government accepted the principle laid down in the Robbins Report that higher education should be available 'for all those who are qualified by ability and attainment'. The Robbins Report recommended that 197,000 places should be available by

1967–68, compared with the existing plans for 153,000 places in universities and 17,000 in colleges of advanced technology. The Robbins target was in fact surpassed by 3,000. Such a rapid expansion inevitably involved improvisation and overcrowding, and conditions were created for the outburst of student unrest in 1968–69, which did much to remove good will in Conservative circles for non-vocational higher education. Moreover demographic trends, and the increasing proportion of school-leavers meeting university entrance requirements, led the Department of Education and Science to estimate a requirement for 450,000 places by 1981 if the Robbins principle were to be maintained.[2] This implied a more rapid growth in expenditure on higher education than any likely growth in GDP, and it is not surprising that by 1972–73, by which time there were 20 per cent more full-time university students than five years earlier, resources per student were beginning to fall. A similar story could be told about expansion in further education, where the numbers of full-time and sandwich students in polytechnics and other grant-aided major establishments rose from 46,000 in 1951 to 300,000 by 1973 (Gosden 1983, chs. 5 and 6).

It can be seen, therefore, that health, housing and education policies all involved large increases in investment programmes, especially in the 1960s and early 1970s, when the economy was at full employment and when there was considerable pressure for an increase in personal consumption as well. Keynes had thought of public investment as a means to counter a deficiency of demand, but in the long boom down to 1973 there was competition for scarce resources between public expenditure on what were largely social necessities, and private expenditure on goods which an earlier generation would have classed as luxuries. It was natural that working-class people should aspire to own a car, a refrigerator, a television or a washing machine, and the fact that the state provided free or subsidised services for health, education and housing released private spending power for the purchase of consumer durables. The development of a mass consumer society also had implications, as we shall see, for policies designed to prevent poverty.

2. In the event there were only 308,000 places for full-time students at university in 1981–82.

Table 7.4 Poverty Lines and Value of State Benefits at Constant Prices for Families of Two Adults and Three Children (Excluding Rent)

	Index (1948 = 100)	*As percentage of average male manual earnings*
Rowntree 1936	118.5	67.0
Beveridge 1942	111.8	62.8
National assistance:		
1948	100.0	48.6
1953	113.1	52.6
1963	148.3	51.8
Supplementary benefits (long-term rates):		
1971	184.2	51.6
1973	199.5	49.4

Source: Fiegehen *et al.* (1977), p. 131.

Poverty in the Consumer Society

As noted in Chapter 6, poverty, as that term had been understood in the 1930s, had been greatly reduced by 1951, thanks to full employment and to the welfare state. There were, and continued to be, individuals and families who lacked food or shelter necessary to maintain physical efficiency, but these were usually cases where people had not applied for national assistance – either on account of pride or inability to understand official forms – or because benefits were used for drink or gambling or other forms of 'unnecessary' expenditure. National assistance benefits, and subsequently supplementary benefits, assumed a very frugal mode of life. Moreover, the aged frequently needed more than monetary assistance as their faculties declined. All these people were in poverty, but their cases seemed to call for more social work rather than simply higher levels of benefit, and indeed the range of social work and the numbers of social workers increased enormously between 1950 and the 1970s (Younghusband 1978).

Benefits were also increased over the period, as Table 7.4 shows. The national assistance scales had originally been below Rowntree's austere poverty line of 1936. By 1963, however, national assistance benefits were worth almost half as much again as in 1948, according to the official retail price index, and by 1973 long-term supplementary benefit rates were worth twice what the Labour Government had thought to be sufficient 25 years earlier. Indeed, by 1973 a family of two adults and three children living on full supplementary benefit had a real income not far short of that of a family whose head had had average male manual earnings in 1948.

It might be thought, therefore, that poverty had been abolished by the 1960s and 1970s, if not earlier. Table 7.5 shows that in fact there were always some people living at or below the level of the 1953/54 national assistance scale (itself approximately the level which Beveridge had recommended). Not all poor people were eligible for benefits. People in full-time employment were not eligible, even if their earnings were below what families received on national assistance, nor were people in full-time education or single people who were able to work but who were not seeking work. Moreover, not all claimants received the full level of benefit; under the 'wage-stop' rule, in force until 1975, an unemployed claimant was not allowed to receive more than 85 per cent of his previous take-home earnings. The Poor Law principle of 'less eligibility' had not expired in 1948. Even so, the number of people living at or below the Beveridge level of assistance declined steadily over the years, from 6.5 per cent of households in 1953/54 to 0.3 per cent in 1973. As the general level of earnings rose, there was less likelihood that the 'wage stop' would keep people below what had once been regarded as the poverty line. Absolute poverty, in the sense of inability to maintain physical efficiency, was a diminishing feature of British society.

Nevertheless, poverty was 'rediscovered' as a problem in the late 1950s and early 1960s. Social investigators were no longer willing to apply the poverty line of an earlier generation to a more affluent society, and a considerable literature developed about the meaning and extent of poverty (Townsend 1957, 1962; Cole and Utting 1962; Abel-Smith and Townsend 1965). The common belief that full employment and the welfare state had virtually eliminated poverty was challenged by the claim that poverty had to be defined in relation to the changing standards and resources of society. It was

Table 7.5 Proportion Living At or Below the Level of Different State Benefits

	(a) 1953/54 national assistance scale			*(b) 1971 supplementary benefits scale*		
	Households	Individuals		Households	Individuals	
	(%)	(%)	(millions)	(%)	(%)	(millions)
1953/54	6.5	4.8	2.4	22.5	21.0	10.6
1963	2.5	1.4	0.8	10.5	9.4	5.0
1967	0.9	0.9	0.5	6.0	5.5	3.0
1971	0.5	0.5	0.3	4.9	4.2	2.3
1973	0.3	0.2	0.1	3.5	2.3	1.3

Source: Fiegehen *et al.* (1977), p. 27.

argued that the concept of subsistence, upon which earlier social investigators had based their work, meant less and less in a society where people habitually consumed sweets and other foodstuffs which were expensive in relation to their nutritional value. It was also claimed that certain social functions, such as ability to give children presents, were psychological necessities. Once one substituted the concept of relative poverty for absolute poverty, the scale of the problem became very great indeed. Table 7.5 shows that some 800,000 individuals lived at or below the 1953/54, or Beveridge, standard of subsistence in 1963, but the number in poverty that year would rise to 5 million if one took as one's standard of poverty an income 25 per cent above the 1963 level of national assistance benefit (i.e. the 1971 level of supplementary benefit).

Relative poverty was the inevitable consequence of economic progress in a society where incomes were unequal. The old imperatives to make a man work – basic food and shelter – had been replaced by the desire to obtain new consumer goods, a desire carefully cultivated by mass advertising. New goods, such as television sets, created new wants, and a sense of relative deprivation on the part of those who lacked these goods. The Prime Minister could say in 1957 that 'most of our people have never had it so good', but most of them wanted more. If relative poverty were to be reduced, there would have to be a major redistribution of income through taxation and through social services. This would not affect only the rich. As already noted, down to 1972 high-wage and low-wage households in local authority housing estates normally received the same housing subsidies, and inequalities of purchasing power between neighbours were a more obvious source of feelings of relative poverty than inequalities between rich and poor.

The increase in the number of old-age pensioners might have led to a redistributive element in national insurance, had general taxation met two-thirds of the cost, as Beveridge had anticipated. In fact, by the mid-1960s the proportion was the other way round, with national insurance contributions meeting two-thirds of the cost of pensions and other national insurance benefits (pensions being by far the largest element in national insurance). During the 1950s the number of pensions and the levels of benefits had increased so that outgoings from the National Insurance Fund had grown more rapidly than income drawn from national insurance stamps. The Treasury had to make up the difference out of general taxation, and since income taxes are higher for the rich than for the poor, the effect was that an increasing part of the costs of old-age pensions was being paid by higher income groups. The Government's immediate response was to abandon any actuarial link between national insurance contributions and benefits. The Treasury's contribution to the fund – and therefore the contribution from general taxation – was fixed as a proportion of the current income of the National Insurance Fund. National insurance contributions, theoretically made to finance future benefits, were raised in line with current needs. The political problem of raising flat-rate contributions on low incomes was solved by the introduction in 1961 of a graduated pensions scheme, which levied 4 per cent of weekly earnings between £9 and £15. Since average weekly earnings for manual workers were then about £16, the effect was to minimise the cost of the scheme to higher income groups, who contributed a lower proportion of their earnings than below-average income groups. In 1962 graduated pension contributions met 19 per cent of the current cost of old-age pensions, and by 1968 the proportion was 29 per cent. Earnings-related sickness and unemployment benefits and contributions, introduced in 1966, were similarly non-redistributive, especially since in their case there was no Treasury contribution at all (Dilnot *et al.* 1984, pp. 12–18; Kincaid 1975, ch. 5).

Income tax itself became a major cause of relative poverty as inflation brought more and more people with relatively low incomes above the tax threshold. This effect might have been offset by raising tax allowances more frequently, but no government in this period chose to index tax allowances. Moreover, whereas income tax was according to progressive scales, this was not true of purchase tax, local rates or television licences, while national insurance contributions were graduated only over a range of incomes which limited their redistributive effect. Surveys by the Central Statistical Office in 1971 and 1973 showed that the proportion of income paid in taxation, defined to include all these elements, varied very little according to income, except at the higher surtax levels (Kincaid 1975, ch. 6).

It is possible to take too lugubrious a view of the achievements of the social security system. Table 7.5 shows that on the basis of a constant 1971 minimum living standard, the number of people in poverty declined from 21 per cent of the population in 1953/54 to 2.3 per cent in 1973. In relative terms, however, there was little change, with the net income of the poorest fifth percentile being about the same proportion of the median income in both years. Moreover, it was possible for the Child Poverty Action Group, by focusing on the numbers of people with incomes of up to 110 per cent of the supplementary benefit level, to argue that relative poverty had almost doubled between 1960 and 1972 (Fiegehen *et al.* 1977, ch. 8). The low paid were usually low paid because they were not well organised to make wage claims, so that it was to be expected that these people would fall behind in the race for higher living standards and, indeed, that they might have their living standards reduced by 'creeping inflation'. Full employment and the welfare state had greatly reduced the extent of poverty, compared with before 1939, but many people continued to feel poor in an affluent society.

Conclusion

Too much emphasis should not be placed upon the failures of the managed economy or the welfare state. Even so, in surveying their shortcomings one is reminded of the limits to the powers of government or of 'great men' to prevail over human nature. Keynes had written in the *General Theory* that 'the ideas of economists and political philosophers are more powerful than is commonly understood. Indeed the world is ruled by little else' (p. 383). Beveridge had seen reforms as coming through the power of abstract ideas or through pragmatic administrative adjustments (Harris 1977, p. 441). Such attitudes were akin to the Platonic ideal of government by philosopher kings, but, as Plato had discovered more than 2000 years earlier, the world is ruled by self-interest and by political expediency as well as by ideas. Both the managed economy and the welfare state were imperfect reflections of the ideas of Keynes and Beveridge respectively and, in any case, their ideas were subject to obsolescence as the nature of the economy and society changed. As the long boom continued down to 1973, less and less restraint was shown in private and public expenditure. Thrift, a Victorian virtue against which Keynes had railed as a cause of under-consumption, was not much in evidence in the 'swinging sixties'. Moreover, whereas the 1944 White Paper on *Employment Policy* had warned that action taken by government to maintain demand would be fruitless if employers and workers responded by raising prices and wages rather than by allowing output and employment to rise (Cmd. 6527, paras 49–54), there was a marked tendency to raise prices and wages by 1970–73. 'Creeping inflation' had already become 9 per cent inflation by 1971 and there was little sign of public willingness to reduce the rate of increase in personal consumption. Such attitudes boded ill for a time when external economic circumstances would be less favourable than in 1951–73.

References

Documents

Cmd. 6527 *Employment Policy*, BPP 1943–44,vol. VIII, pp. 119–50.

Cmd. 9725 *The Economic Implications of Full Employment*, BPP 1955–56, vol. XXXVI, pp. 565–77.

Cmnd. 827 (Radcliffe) *Committee on the Working of the Monetary System: Report*, BPP 1958–59, vol. XVII, pp. 389–777.

Cmnd. 1432 *Control of Public Expenditure* [report of the committee under the chairmanship of Lord Plowden], BPP 1960–61, vol. XX, pp. 713–46.

Cmnd. 3888 *In Place of Strife*, BPP 1968–69, vol. LIII, pp. 265–304.

Books and Articles

Abel-Smith, B. (1978) *National Health Service: the First Thirty Years*, HMSO.

Abel-Smith, B., and Townsend, P. (1965) *The Poor and the Poorest*, Occasional Papers on Social Administration, no. 17.

Artis, M. (1972) 'Fiscal policy for stabilization', in W. Beckerman (ed.), *The Labour Government's Economic Record*, Duckworth.

Berthoud, R., Brown, J., and Cooper, S. (1981) *Poverty and the Development of Anti-Poverty Policy in the United Kingdom*, Heinemann.

Blackaby, F. (ed.) (1978) *British Economic Policy 1960–74*, Cambridge University Press.

Brown, H. Phelps (1983) *The Origins of Trade Union Power*, Oxford University Press.

Burton, J. (1979) *The Job Support Machine*, Centre for Policy Studies.

Cairncross, A. (1971) *Essays in Economic Management*, George Allen and Unwin.

Cairncross, A and Eichengreen, B. (1983) *Sterling in Decline: The Devaluations of 1931, 1949 and 1967*, Basil Blackwell.

Chester, D.N. (1982) 'The role of economic advisers in government', in A.P. Thirlwall (ed.), *Keynes as a Policy Adviser*, Macmillan.

Clarke, R. (1978) *Public Expenditure, Management and Control: The Development of the Public Expenditure Survey Committee (PESC)* (ed. Cairncross, A.), Macmillan.

Clegg, H. (1978) *The System of Industrial Relations in Great Britain*, Basil Blackwell.

Cole, D., and Utting, J. (1962) *The Economic Circumstances of Old People*, Occasional Papers on Social Administration, no. 4.

Cullingworth, J.B. (1979) *Essays on Housing Policy*, George Allen and Unwin.

Department of Employment and Productivity (1971) *British Labour Statistics: Historical Abstract 1886–1968*, HMSO.

Department of Employment (1975) *British Labour Statistics: Year Book 1973*, HMSO.

Department of Trade and Industry (1984) *Regional Industrial Policy: Some Economic Issues*, Department of Trade and Industry.

Dilnot, A., Kay, J., and Morris, C. (1984) *The Reform of Social Security*, Oxford University Press.

Dow, J.C.R. (1964) *The Management of the British Economy 1945–1960*, Cambridge University Press.

Fiegehen, G., Lansley, P. and Smith, A. (1977) *Poverty and Progress in Britain, 1953–73*, Cambridge University Press.

Gosden, P. (1983) *The Education System since 1944*, Martin Robertson.

Graham, A. (1972) 'Industrial policy', in W. Beckerman (ed.), *The Labour Government's Economic Record: 1964–1970*, Duckworth.

Hardie, J. (1972) 'Regional policy', in W. Beckerman (ed.), *The Labour Government's Economic Record 1964–1970*, Duckworth.

Harris, J. (1977) *William Beveridge, a Biography*, Oxford University Press.

Holmans, A.E. (1970) 'The role of local authorities in the growth of public expenditure in the United Kingdom', in A. Cairncross (ed.), *The Managed Economy*, Basil Blackwell.

Hopkin, B. (1981) 'The development of demand management', in F. Cairncross (ed.), *Changing Perceptions of Economic Policy*, Methuen.

Kelf-Cohen, R. (1973) *British Nationalisation 1945–1973*, Macmillan.

Kincaid, J. (1975) *Poverty and Equality in Britain: a Study of Social Security and Taxation*, Penguin Books.

Klein, R. (1983) *The Politics of the National Health Service*, Longman.

Knowles, K.G.J.C. (1962) 'Wages and productivity', in G.D.N. Worswick and P. Ady (eds.), *The British Economy in the 1950s*, Oxford University Press.

McCallum, D. (1979) 'The development of British regional policy', in D. MacLennan and J. Parr (eds.), *Regional Policy: Past Experience and New Directions*, Martin Robertson.

McCrone, G. (1969) *Regional Policy in Britain*, George Allen and Unwin.

McKay, D., and Cox, A. (1979) *The Politics of Urban Change*, Croom Helm.

Maddison, A. (1982) *Phases of Capitalist Development*, Oxford University Press.

Matthews, R.C.O. (1968) 'Why has Britain had full employment since the war?' *Economic Journal*, vol. 78, pp. 555–69.
Matthews, R.C.O. (1971) 'The role of demand management', in A. Cairncross (ed.), *Britain's Economic Prospects Reconsidered*, George Allen and Unwin.
Merrett, S. (1979) *State Housing in Britain*, Routledge and Kegan Paul.
Moore, B., and Rhodes, J. (1973) 'Evaluating the effects of British regional economic policy', *Economic Journal*, vol. 83, pp. 87–110.
Moore, B., and Rhodes, J. (1976) 'Regional economic policy and the movement of manufacturing firms to Development Areas', *Economica*, vol. 43, pp. 17–31.
Opie, R. (1972) 'Economic planning and growth', in W. Beckerman (ed.) *The Labour Government's Economic Record: 1964–1970*, Duckworth.
Pliatzky, L. (1984) *Getting and Spending: Public Expenditure, Employment and Inflation*, Basil Blackwell.
Reid, M. (1982) *The Secondary Banking Crisis 1973–75*, Macmillan.
Rowan, T.L. (1960) *Arms and Economics: the Changing Challenge*, Cambridge University Press.
Stewart, M. (1977) *The Jekyll and Hyde Years: Politics and Economic Policy in the UK since 1964*, Dent.
Strange, S. (1971) *Sterling and British Policy*, Oxford University Press.
Townsend, P. (1957) *The Family Life of Old People: an Inquiry in East London*, Routledge and Kegan Paul.
Townsend, P. (1962) 'The meaning of poverty', *British Journal of Sociology*, vol. 13, pp. 210–27.
Watkin, B. (1978) *The National Health Service: The First Phase, 1948–1974 and After*, George Allen and Unwin.
Wilson, T. (1982) 'Policy in war and peace: the recommendations of J.M. Keynes', in A.P. Thirlwall (ed.), *Keynes as a Policy Adviser*, Macmillan.
Worswick, G.D.N. (1971) 'Fiscal Policy and stabilization in Britain', in A. Cairncross (ed.), *Britain's Economic Prospects Reconsidered*, George Allen and Unwin.
Wright, J.F. (1979) *Britain in the Age of Economic Management: An Economic History since 1939*, Oxford University Press.
Younghusband, E. (1978) *Social Work in Britain: 1950–1975*, George Allen and Unwin.

8

The Challenge of Inflation, 1973–83

The year 1973 marked the end of the 'golden age' of sustained economic growth, full employment and reasonably stable prices (Maddison 1982). In 1974 and 1975 GDP at constant factor cost fell for the first time since 1946, by 3.5 per cent, and the 1973 level of output was not exceeded until 1977. There was another fall of 4.6 per cent between 1979 and 1981, and the 1979 level of output was not reached again until 1983. The initial rise in unemployment from 2.6 per cent in 1974 to 6.2 per cent in 1977 (Table 8.1) was far worse than anything experienced since the 1930s, but the rate of inflation, which at its peak in 1975 reached 26 per cent (Table 8.2), was an even more severe shock. By 1976 the Labour Prime Minister, James Callaghan, could tell his party that the option of spending one's way out of a recession no longer existed. Inflation had taken over from unemployment as the most pressing political problem. There was a further surge in both inflation and unemployment after 1979, the former reaching a rate of 21 per cent in mid-1980 and the latter rising to 12.9 per cent by 1983. From 1979 the Conservative Government under Margaret Thatcher sought to reduce government intervention in the economy. There was no attempt at reflation even before the general election of June 1983, when the rise in the retail price index was down to 3.7 per cent compared with a year earlier.

These major changes in Britain's economic fortunes and in the priorities of economic policy were partly a result of changing world conditions. Just as Britain had benefited from an expanding international economy and stable world prices between 1951 and 1973,

Table 8.1 Unemployment in the United Kingdom (Annual Average, %)

	Old basis of calculation	*New basis of calculation*
1973	2.7	—
1974	2.6	2.6
1975	4.1	4.0
1976	5.7	5.5
1977	6.2	5.8
1978	6.1	5.7
1979	5.7	5.3
1980	7.4	6.8
1981	11.4	10.5
1982	—	12.1
1983	—	12.9

Sources: CSO (1981), Table 6.8 and CSO (1985), Table 6.6.

Note: Prior to 1982 the system of calculating unemployment was to count people who registered at job centres. The new system introduced in 1982 was to count those who claimed at unemployment benefit centres. Under this system the trend in unemployment was similar to that under the old system, but the level was lower. This was partly because the new system excluded people who registered as unemployed but who were not entitled to, or did not claim, unemployment benefit, but it was also the case that benefit offices generally found out more quickly than job centres when people found work.

Neither system of registering unemployment records those people who have given up hope of finding a job, and who have opted for early retirement or, in the case of women, who have continued to be housewives when they would have preferred to be out working. After 1977 the labour force grew more slowly than the population aged between 16 and retirement age. From this it may be deduced that by 1983, when unemployment stood officially at 2,871,000, there were a further 450,000 or so people who would have sought employment had their prospects been as good as they were in 1977.

so after 1973 it suffered from the effects of world recessions and inflation. The most obvious change in the international economy was the rise in the price of oil, increases being engineered by the

Table 8.2 Inflation

	Percentage increase in retail price index at September on a year earlier	*Index of fall in internal purchasing power of pound (annual averages)*
1973	9.3	100
1974	17.1	86
1975	26.6	69
1976	14.3	60
1977	15.6	51
1978	7.8	47
1979	16.5	42
1980	15.9	35
1981	11.4	32
1982	7.3	29
1983	5.1	28

Source: CSO (1985), Tables 18.5 and 18.7, and earlier issues.

Organisation of Petroleum Exporting Countries (OPEC) at the end of 1973 and again in 1979. In 1974 the price of petroleum was four times what it had been in 1972, and in 1980 the price was 2¼ times what it had been in 1978 (Maddison 1982, p. 141). Oil had been the souce of about half of energy consumption in Western countries in 1973, so that sudden and massive changes in price had major effects on patterns of domestic consumer demand, while capital stock which depended on cheap energy was rendered obsolete. Investment plans were delayed until adjustments to new conditions could be made, and further caution was induced by uncertainty about the future. Faced with rising prices and balance of payments problems, most Western countries tended to pursue neutral or deflationary fiscal policies from 1976, although the United States was a major exception in the 1980s.

It would be wrong, however, to suggest that increases in the price of oil in 1973–74 and in 1979 were the sole causes of what came to be called 'stagflation'. Most of the once-and-for-all gains to be obtained through trade liberalisation after the war had probably been achieved by 1973. The same was probably true of trade between the original six members of the EEC, and these countries had already achieved economies of scale and efficiency in output as a result of a wider market before Britain entered in 1973. There were no doubt long-term benefits to be had from British membership of the enlarged EEC, but the transfer of resources to sectors in which Britain had a comparative advantage was likely to give rise to structural unemployment in the short run. As for price stability, the flow of dollars from the United States, in the form of aid, overseas investment and military expenditure, which had done so much for international liquidity after the war, had become excessive by the early 1970s. This was particularly so on account of the deficit financing of American intervention in the Vietnam War. As it became plain that the United States' gold reserves were no longer adequate to maintain the value of the dollar, the dollar's convertibility into gold was ended and a 10 per cent import surcharge imposed – two measures in 1971 which had the same effect as a devaluation. At the end of 1971 the Smithsonian agreement on currency realignments seemed to have restored the Bretton Woods system of stable exchange rates, but the absence of any effective barriers against international currency speculation made it impossible to maintain the Smithsonian rates without frequent balance of payments crises, and the system finally collapsed in 1973. The rise in the price of gold after 1971 was a sure sign of a flight from paper money. The reasons for such a flight were not hard to understand. The collapse of the system of stable exchange rates relaxed a major constraint to domestic monetary expansion at a time when commodity prices were rising after 20 years of comparative stability. The prices of some key commodities were clearly due to rise. For example, the price of American wheat doubled in 1972–73. So rapid an increase in a staple product was bound to raise bread and animal fodder prices, with an immediate effect on the cost of living around the world, even before the increase in the price of oil at the end of 1973.

Given Britain's dependence on imported food and raw materials, and given the fact that Britain itself was not yet a significant oil producer, the consequences of world price trends were bound to be severe. Moreover, there was a good deal of speculation against sterling as a result of domestic credit expansion after 1971 (see below). The overall result was a sudden reversal by about 25 per cent in the terms of trade between 1972 and 1974. Britain's difficulty in adjusting to the new international environment was compounded by three factors. Firstly, the inefficiency of much of its industry compared with its rivals meant that Britain suffered disproportionately from the intensification of competition for trade in the post-1973 and post-1979 recessions. Secondly, the reluctance of British workers to accept cuts in real incomes as a result of changes in the terms of trade and in the value of money made it difficult, even with a floating exchange rate, to compensate for relative industrial inefficiency by reducing labour costs. Thirdly, the reluctance of politicians to cut growing public expenditure programmes both inhibited counter-inflation policy and threw the burden of adjustment to a reduced GDP in 1974 and 1975, and again in 1980 and 1981, on to the private sector.

Increased public expenditure would have been the appropriate Keynesian remedy had the fall in GDP been a result of a lack of domestic demand, but an expansion of domestic demand, and rising money incomes, could not compensate for the transfer of real purchasing power abroad through the rise in import prices. Moreover, British consumers showed a marked preference for many foreign rather than British products, so that the multiplier effect of increased money incomes tended to leak abroad through imports. British oil production expanded rapidly after 1976 and self-sufficiency was achieved in 1980. As a result, the balance of payments was for a short time no longer a constraint to expansion of domestic demand. However, the combination of a lack of international competitiveness on the part of the industrial sector, plus a balance of payments surplus and a high exchange rate based on production of a primary product, encouraged increased import penetration by foreign manufacturers at the beginning of the 1980s. Manufacturing employment, which had peaked at 8,976,400 (annual average) in 1966, fell from 7,705,000 in 1974 to 7,193,000 in 1979 and to 5,764,000 in 1982 (CSO 1984, p. 110).

The Fall of the Heath Government

It is not known what Thatcher, then Secretary of State for Education, or other ministers later associated with her, said in 1971–74 about Barber's fiscal and monetary policies; the relevant cabinet minutes and memoranda are not due to be opened to researchers until early next century. There can be little doubt, however, that Thatcher came to believe that the Heath Government's attempt to reflate the economy had led to economic and social chaos and ultimately to the fall of the Government itself. A monetarist critique by the economists Ball and Burns (1976) of the inflationary process in 1972–75 attributed the fact that Britain had had a higher rate of inflation than the rest of the world to inadequate control of the money supply. Between the beginning of 1972 and the beginning of 1974 the money supply relative to trend industrial production in Britain started to rise much faster than for the world as a whole. By September 1973 – that is before the major oil price rise or the industrial troubles of the winter – sterling's exchange rate had fallen 13 per cent compared with mid-1972, when sterling had been allowed to float. Most of the difference in the behaviour of inflation rates in Britain relative to the rest of the world in 1972–75 could be seen in the behaviour of the exchange rate, and the timing suggested that the exchange rate fell because of domestic monetary expansion, with wage and price-level adjustments coming in 1974 and 1975. The implication of this analysis was that a strict monetary policy might have kept Britain's inflation rate below the world rate, even at the cost of some unemployment.

Be that as it may, the Conservatives' easy money policy in 1971–73 does seem to have had effects which its authors did not expect. There was a highly unstable boom in property development companies and secondary banks, a boom which broke at the end of 1973 and which forced the Bank of England and the big clearing banks to launch a joint rescue of the secondary banks (Reid 1982). The episode was a poor advertisement both for the City as a place where rational decisions were made about the allocation of resources and for the system of credit control which had been introduced in 1971. The new system stressed competition between banks, and thus increased the willingness of banks to lend at a time when the Government's anxiety to reduce unemployment led it to allow a rapid growth in the money stock. From late 1972 there was concern among the Government's official advisers about the inflationary effects of monetary growth, but then, as now, there was some doubt as how best to measure the money stock, and it was not until July 1973 that a more restrictive monetary policy may be said to have begun (Hall 1983, pp. 5–19).

The Heath Government's main counter-inflation policy,

however, was to attempt to control prices, and more particularly incomes, by law. 'Stage I' of the statutory prices and incomes policy, introduced in November 1972, had brought about a pause, down to March, 1973, in the inflationary spiral (see page 182). The provisions for Stages II and III of the statutory prices and incomes policy can only be summarised here. Under Stage II, which ran for six months from April 1973, each employee's pay increases in a year were to be limited to £1 a week plus 4 per cent of the employer's average pay bill per employee for the previous year, with a maximum pay increase of £250 a year. Price increases were limited to those allowed by a Price Commission on the basis of cost increases. The prices and incomes policy failed to win trade-union support, but even so, only the gas workers were successful in breaching the Stage II guidelines. Stage III, which was intended to run for six months from November 1973, was designed to be more flexible. Some insurance against an unexpected rise in the cost of living was provided by making flat-rate increases of 40p per week payable for every one per cent that the retail price index rose above a threshold of 6 per cent. The basic limit for pay increases was raised to £2.25 per employee per week, or seven per cent, with a maximum limit of £350 a year. It was anticipated that flat-rate pay increases would lead to disputes over differentials between the wages of different grades of workers and an additional one per cent was allowed for settlements which reduced anomalies. There was also provision for productivity agreements and for extra money for 'unsocial hours'. Despite these elements of flexibility, which seem to have been designed specifically to allow adequate concessions to be made to the National Union of Mineworkers, Stage III led to a conflict between the Government and the miners on a scale which had not been seen since 1926.

At the beginning of November 1973 – before the oil price rise had affected retail prices – the electrical power engineers began an overtime ban in support of a claim outside Stage III. Shortly afterwards the miners rejected a 16 per cent pay offer – the maximum they could be offered under Stage III – and they too resorted to an overtime ban. The Government declared a state of emergency; lighting and heating were restricted from mid-November, and a three-day week was introduced in industry from 1st January 1974. A special conference of trade-union presidents and general secretaries in January endorsed a TUC motion which indicated that if the

Government made a settlement of the miners' claim possible, other unions would not use that settlement as a basis for their own negotiations. The Government's Pay Board, which was monitoring the incomes policy, prepared reports in January and February on pay relativities – reports which could have been used to allow the miners to be made a special case. Thus a way out of the conflict between the Government and the miners seemed to be possible, but the National Union of Mineworkers, well aware that the oil crisis since November had strengthened its hand, called a strike early in February. Heath's response was to call an election to take place on 28 February and to appeal to the miners to postpone the strike until the electorate had given its verdict on the Government's policies. The miners rejected this appeal, even though their existing pay agreement was due to last until 1st March. The attempt to subordinate free collective bargaining to the political process had failed (Blackaby 1978, pp. 70–6, 378–401; Wigham 1982, pp. 173–80).

Neither the Conservatives nor Labour did well in the election. The rise of third parties, notably in Northern Ireland, Scotland and Wales, where discontent over regional unemployment could focus on a sense of separate identity, meant that neither of the main parties won a majority in Parliament. Nevertheless Labour was the biggest party and Wilson was Prime Minister again. For the Conservatives, the struggle over Stage III was a searing experience. It is not surprising that the experiment of a statutory prices and incomes policy has not (yet) been repeated or that, when returned to power in 1979, the Conservatives preferred to revert to their original policy in 1970 of relying on the discipline of the market.

From 'Social Contract' to 'Winter of Discontent'

A second general election in 1974 gave Labour a majority of three over all the other parties in the House of Commons (a slender margin which was to disappear by April 1976, following defections and by-election defeats). Labour's electoral success, such as it was, seems to have owed something to a widespread belief that a Labour government could reduce inflation and industrial unrest by means of a 'social contract' with the trade unions. The social contract had its origins early in 1973 in an agreement between the TUC and the Labour Party covering prices, food subsidies, rents, taxes and pensions. It was argued that steps to mitigate the effects of inflation, together with a repeal of the Industrial Relations Act, would create the right conditions for money incomes to grow in line with output. In the three months before the election in October 1974 the Government held back prices temporarily by price controls, by subsidies to nationalised industries, by a reduction in value added tax and by food subsidies. In these ways the rise in the retail price index in the third quarter of 1974 was kept down to an annual rate of 8 per cent, although the rate for the 12 months to June 1975 turned out to be almost 26 per cent. Labour also swiftly ended the miners' strike, by granting the miners' demands, and repealed both the Industrial Relations Act and the statutory incomes policy. On the other hand, the Stage III 'threshold' provisions of the latter were retained, and there was a series of monthly wage increases after the retail price index rose 6 per cent above the level of October 1973.

The General Council of the TUC, for its part, recommended in June 1974 that union negotiators should limit claims to what was needed to keep take-home pay level with the cost of living, and the TUC annual conference endorsed this recommendation at its annual conference in September. Average industrial earnings rose 25.9 per cent in the 12 months to September 1975, marginally less than the 26.6 per cent rise in the retail price index. The fact that Britain's inflation record was worse than that of most of its international competitors worried responsible trade-union leaders and in July 1975 the TUC accepted the need for an incomes policy, albeit a voluntary one. Under Stage 1 pay increases were limited to 6 per cent a week, up to a maximum of £12; under Stage 2, agreed in July 1976, the limits were 5 per cent and £4. As Table 8.3 shows, average earnings in industry rose much faster than the voluntary incomes policy allowed for, but even so the rate of increase in average earnings in 1976–77 was only half the rate of increase in prices.

The main reason for the fall in real incomes in 1977 was the surge in import prices following sterling's decline from $2.04 in the last quarter of 1975 to $1.65 in the last quarter of 1976. The decline in the exchange rate reflected a collapse in foreign confidence in sterling, confidence having been undermined by a belief that public expenditure in Britain was out of control (see below, pages 218–9). In these circumstances no formal agreement on Stage 3 of the voluntary incomes policy was possible, but the Government set a target of 10 per cent for pay increases in the year from July 1977. The 10 per

Table 8.3 Prices and Incomes under the 'Social Contract': Percentage Increases Compared with July of Previous Year

	Retail price index	*Average earnings in manufacturing industry*	*Average earnings (all employees)*
1975	26.3	26.4	27.6
1976	12.9	15.3	13.9
1977	17.6	8.7	8.5
1978	7.8	16.3	14.2
1979	15.6	16.5	16.5

Sources: CSO (1981), Table 6.22; CSO (1984), Table 18.7; Department of Employment (1978), Table 42.

cent limit was largely imposed on public-sector employees, and sanctions were imposed on firms in the private sector which exceeded the limit, the sanctions taking the form of withholding government assistance or contracts. Even so, average earnings rose by almost twice as much as prices, with workers in manufacturing industry doing distinctly better than the average for all employees. Clearly workers were determined to make up their loss in real income in the previous year. In 1978 the Government and the TUC were unable to agree on a ceiling for wage settlements and the figure of 5 per cent adopted by the Government proved to be too low to gain popular consent. Public sector employees in particular put in claims for higher increases than 5 per cent in order to restore their pre-Stage 3 position relative to private-sector workers. A 'day of action' by over a million local authority workers in January 1979 was the biggest one-day stoppage since the General Strike of 1926. Labour's reputation as the party which enjoyed a special relationship with the trade unions was severely damaged in a 'winter of discontent' marked by health service stoppages and by violent picketing in other disputes (Wigham 1982, ch. 10).

It was ironic that the social contract should be undermined by foreigners' fears that increased public expenditure would bring about a fall in the value of sterling. The increase in public expenditure in 1974–76 had been in no small part due to efforts to improve what was called the 'social wage'. The social wage was an expression used at the time in connection with welfare benefits and with subsidies which held down the cost to consumers of food or public services. It was hoped by many in the Labour Party that an improved social wage would both provide adequate income support for the poor and reinforce the social contract with the trade unions. The idea behind the latter hope was that wage earners would take the social wage into account as a supplement to their individual pay packets when claiming higher wages. In fact there is no evidence that wage earners were in general deflected from concern with their individual pay packets.

Cuts in public expenditure after 1976 were a bitter disappointment to those members of the party who believed that the social contract was concerned with improving the social wage and not just with pay restraint or repeal of the Industrial Relations Act. Local authority house completions fell 26 per cent from 151,800 in 1976 to 112,300 in 1978, although private house completions in 1978, at 152,200, were only 2 per cent below the level of 1976. Education expenditure in 1978/79 was back to the level of 1973/74, at constant prices, but there were 10 per cent more secondary pupils and 18 per cent more university students to be catered for. There was an increase in expenditure even after 1976 on health and personal social services (the latter include services for the disabled, the elderly, children and the mentally handicapped), and a Resource Allocation Working Party (RAWP) scheme began to reduce inequalities in NHS spending between regions (Klein 1983). On the other hand, much of the increase in expenditure on the NHS reflected the fact that NHS pay and costs rose more rapidly than the average for the community as a whole, while the increase in some NHS and personal social services reflected an increase in the numbers of elderly or other people needing care. All in all, it is not surprising that one Marxist critic of the welfare state has described its growth as having ended in 1976, rather than after Thatcher came to power (Gough 1979, ch. 7).

Labour did, however, exempt social security from major cuts and some efforts were made to help the poorest members of society, although inevitably these efforts fell short of satisfying the poverty lobby which had developed since the 1950s. Retirement pensions were increased faster than prices, so that the real incomes of people who were wholly dependent upon state pensions increased by 20 per cent in the five years to November 1978. On the other hand, pensioners' savings and annuities were badly hit by inflation. Non-contributory invalidity pensions were introduced in 1975, but at a level which was too low to relieve sick and disabled people from the need to apply for supplementary benefits. Long-term supplementary benefit rates themselves were increased, however, so that a married couple would receive 51.4 per cent of net average earnings in 1978 instead of 41.8 per cent in 1973. The Child Benefit Act of 1975 ended family allowances and tax allowances for children, and replaced them with a new tax-free child benefit payable for all children, including the first, with increased allowances for single-parent families. The last provision reflected changed social attitudes to marriage, and the rapid increase in the numbers of single-parent families from 570,000 in 1971 to about 750,000 in 1976. In the latter year it was estimated that only 300,000 single parents were in a position to rely upon earnings as the main source of family income (Berthaud *et al.* 1981; Bosanquet and Townsend 1980).

The biggest changes affecting the numbers of people in relative poverty, however, were inflation and rising unemployment. Supplementary benefit scales were revised annually; but inflation eroded the real value of benefits between annual adjustments. If the effects of inflation between adjustments are neglected, then the number of households living on or below the level set by supplementary benefit rates in 1975 was about 760,000. If, however, allowance is made for the fall in real incomes over the year, then the number of households living on or below the original value of supplementary benefit rates would rise to 1,570,000. Similarly, for 1976 the figures would be 910,000 and 1,670,000 respectively (Beckerman and Clark 1982, pp. 85–92). The rise in unemployment – from 595,000 in 1973 to 1,383,000 in 1978 – also greatly increased the numbers of people who found themselves dependent upon supplementary benefit and, therefore, in relative poverty. Labour's failure to solve the problem of relative poverty was thus in large measure a consequence of a failure of economic policy to solve the problems of inflation and unemployment.

The End of the 'Keynesian' Era

Labour had entered office in 1974 with what it called a 'new industrial strategy', which was in fact an extension of industrial policies pursued in the 1960s. There was to be regular consultation between government, management and trade unions in the NEDC and there were to be planning agreements between the Government and individual firms based on past performance, future demand and possible technical developments. A key role was envisaged for the National Enterprise Board, which was set up in 1975 to invest government funds in appropriate firms. Total government funding for industrial innovation (excluding the Concorde project) increased by 39 per cent at constant prices between 1973/74 and 1975/76, while general support for industry (excluding regional subsidies) increased by the same percentage. Over the same period the sums paid out in regional subsidies rose by 63 per cent, also at constant prices (Burton 1979). It was by no means clear, however, that the new industrial strategy had the desired effect on Britain's industrial performance. Subsidies were not necessarily the best way to persuade workers to meet competition by adopting new technology – or the reduced manning levels appropriate to that technology. The biggest single investment made by the National Enterprise Board was in motor vehicle manufacture by British Leyland, where overmanning, restrictive practices and industrial disputes continued to contribute to a series of losses (Pryke 1981, ch. 11).

Any benefits from the new industrial strategy, in the shape of improved international competitiveness, were likely to take time to emerge. In the meantime growing industrial subsidies and measures to improve the social wage contributed to a growth in public expenditure from 40.4 per cent of GDP in 1973/74 to about 45.5 per cent in 1974/75 and 1975/76, with the Public Sector Borrowing Requirement (PSBR) rising from 6.5 per cent of GDP in 1973 to 11.0 per cent in 1975.

Sterling had already fallen by about 14 per cent from $2.40 in 1974, but had been kept above $2.00 by the prospect of Britain becoming self-sufficient in oil by 1980. However, by the spring of 1976 it seemed to many foreigners that the British, by borrowing abroad to finance their expanding PSBR, had already mortgaged their future. By July there had already been a further depreciation of sterling against the dollar of 12 per cent. The Treasury had considered sterling to be over-valued above $2.00 from the point of view of the price competitiveness of British manufactures, and had favoured some depreciation in order to offset the effects of inflation on domestic industrial costs since 1974. Too rapid a decline in sterling, however, would raise import costs to a level which would make inflation harder to control. The Bank of England's reserves plus central bank credits were inadequate to buy all the sterling which foreigners wanted to sell at about $1.80, and only support from the IMF could prevent a free fall in the exchange rate. The Government was unwilling to apply for an IMF credit, for, as in 1967, the IMF would certainly insist on Britain taking steps to improve its balance of payments so as to be in a position to make repayment. Such steps would involve a reduction in the PSBR and, therefore, in public expenditure programmes. It seemed to some as if Labour faced another crisis like that of 1931. However, a sharp fall in the exchange rate to $1.64 in September 1976 persuaded the Government to make a formal application to the IMF, and a further fall in October to $1.56, despite a rise in minimum lending rate to a record 15 per cent, weakened resistance to cuts in public expenditure programmes. These were finally fixed by negotiations with the IMF, and after protracted debate in the Cabinet, at £1 billion for 1977/78 and £1½ billion for 1978/79 (Barnett 1982, chs. 9–10; Keegan and Pennant-Rea 1979, pp. 159–70; Pliatzky 1984, pp. 130–56).

The crisis year of 1976 also saw the introduction of publicly announced targets for monetary aggregate growth as an important element in economic policy. The July 'package' of cuts in public expenditure programmes and the increase in employers' national insurance contributions was accompanied by a statement by the Chancellor, Denis Healey, that monetary growth should amount to about 12 per cent in 1976/77. Subsequently a 'letter of intent' to the IMF stated that domestic credit expansion would be kept within the limits of £9 billion in 1976/77, £7.7 billion in 1977/78 and £6 billion in 1978/79. The new emphasis on monetary policy need not have been a result of new economic doctrines; the Treasury and the Bank of England needed a new target to guide economic policy. Prior to 1972 the commitment to maintain a more-or-less fixed exchange rate under the Bretton Woods system had acted as a brake on government loan-financed expenditure, much as the gold standard had done down to 1931. In the three years after the floating of sterling in 1972 the PSBR had trebled as a proportion of GDP. From

1976 restrictive domestic monetary policy would act as a brake on government loan-financed expenditure, for, if the money supply for a year were fixed, too much government borrowing would tend to 'crowd out' private investment. Moreover, there seems to have been a hope in official circles that the inflationary expectations of trade unionists and businessmen (and also of foreign holders of sterling) could be influenced by a clear signal as to the amount of money which would be available to finance wages and prices (Hall 1983, pp. 43–57). Be that as it may, the experience of the 'winter of discontent' in 1978–79 did not suggest that the wage-bargaining process would respond quickly or painlessly to such a signal.

The curbs on public expenditure and domestic credit expansion, and the rise in the exchange rate, all contributed to a sharp fall in the rate of inflation, which fell below 10 per cent in 1978 for the first time since 1973.

However, neither monetary policy nor control of public expenditure could have been said to have been an exact science under Healey. Domestic credit expansion was held well within the limits agreed with the IMF for 1976/77 and 1977/78, but was allowed to exceed the agreed limit slightly in 1978/79 (in the run up to the general election). It did not prove to be possible to forecast accurately the effect of policy on the demand for money and, as with 'fine-tuning' in Keynesian demand management, there was the inevitable problem of lags in collecting and analysing data (Hall 1983, pp. 51–4). As for control of public expenditure, the introduction of cash limits led to under-spending (in terms of constant prices) by central government departments and local authorities, since inflation tended to be higher than cash limits allowed for. The shortfall in public expenditure in 1977/78 was over £2 billion, or twice the amount of the cut in programmes agreed with the IMF, and in 1978/79 the shortfall was of a similar magnitude (Pliatzky 1984, pp. 154–6).

With unemployment rising to twice the level which had been regarded as full employment in the 1950s and sixties, it was inevitable that there should be concern about the difficulty experienced by many young people in finding jobs. There was a fear that if denied some experience of work, the unemployed might become unemployable. From 1975 to 1978 a Job Creation Programme provided a total of 230,000 jobs, mainly for young people who would otherwise have been unemployed. Projects under the programme had to be of value to the community and employment for any person was limited to a maximum of 52 weeks. A Special Temporary Employment Programme followed in 1978, with priority for people aged 19–24 years who had been continuously unemployed for more than six months, and for people over 25 years who had been continuously unemployed for over 12 months. In addition there were recruitment subsidies for employers taking on school leavers or young people, but an official valuation in 1978 suggested that most of the recruits would have been taken on without subsidy. Temporary employment schemes and employment subsidies marked an increasing grey area between employment and unemployment (Berthaud *et al.* 1981, pp. 108–11).

The temporary nature of these job-creation measures presumably reflected a hope that eventually there would be a rise in the demand for labour and that young people who had been given work experience would be equipped to take on permanent jobs in industry or services. It was not clear, however, where the demand for labour would come from. Even if most Labour ministers held to Keynesian doctrines of stimulating demand by loan-financed public expenditure, their room for manoeuvre was limited by the need to sustain confidence in sterling in a world which was coming increasingly to believe in monetarist doctrines (Barnett 1982, pp. 109–10, 146–7). There is no evidence that Labour ministers or the majority of their official advisers were convinced by monetarist arguments. On the other hand, many financiers and IMF officials were attracted to economic doctrines which seemed to offer price stability in an age of inflation. The Labour Government had to announce monetary targets acceptable to those from whom it wished to borrow, and for that reason had to eschew reflation. In this sense the sterling crisis of 1976 may be said to have marked the end of the 'Keynesian era' in British economic policy. As James Callaghan, Wilson's successor as prime minister, told the Labour Party Conference in September 1976:

> We used to think that you could just spend your way out of a recession and increase employment by cutting taxes and boosting government spending. I tell you in all candour, that option no longer exists, and that in so far as it ever did exist, it worked by injecting inflation into the economy. And each time that happened the average level of unemployment has risen. Higher inflation followed by higher unemployment. That is the history of the last 20 years.

Margaret Thatcher's First Term

If 1976 marked the end of the 'Keynesian' era, the election of the Conservatives under Margaret Thatcher in the general election of 1979 saw the beginning of a determined attempt to reverse the trend towards greater state intervention in the economy. The new Prime Minister's avowed goal was to alter fundamentally popular attitudes towards the respective responsibilities of government and of the individual. She spoke warmly of Victorian values, such as self-help and enterprise, and, indeed, she is perhaps unique among prime ministers in having given her name to a comprehensive set of economic and social ideas. 'Thatcherism' may mean different things to different people, but essentially it embodies related values, attitudes and beliefs which favour the free market rather than the state as the preferred means of allocating resources. 'Thatcherism' looks to a sense of responsibility and a spirit of enterprise on the part of individuals, rather than to state-directed collectivism, as the best means of making Britain more competitive in relation to other industrial countries. It will be many years before the success or otherwise of policies since 1979 can be judged in historical perspective since these policies are intended to have their full effect only in the long term.

The Thatcher Government came to power with a programme to control inflation and to reverse Britain's decline relative to other advanced economies. Firstly, there was to be firm control of the money supply. The Government hoped that by announcing targets for limited monetary growth, it could lower inflationary expectations and thereby influence wage claims. If workers insisted on high wage settlements they would, in theory, risk their jobs. (In practice, the risk to workers varied according to the degree to which they were exposed to foreign competition or the ability of the Government to resist calls for subsidies.) Secondly, enterprise was to be encouraged by tax cuts which would allow those who risked capital to enjoy a greater share of profits. Thirdly, market forces were to be allowed a greater influence in economic decisions. In practice this meant a reduced role for subsidies to industry, including those made under regional policy, and, where possible, the sale of state enterprises. Public expenditure was described as 'the heart of Britain's economic difficulties', and it was made plain that the Government intended to keep its expenditure within the limits set by its objectives on borrowing and taxation (Cmnd. 7746, p. 1).

It is important not to exaggerate the novelty of 'Thatcherism'. The Conservative election manifesto of 1979 was not unlike that of 1970, so far as a belief in the invigorating power of the market economy was concerned. The difference was that Thatcher was to make a virtue of not performing a 'U-turn' when unemployment increased from 1,175,000 to 2,299,000 between 1979 and 1981, whereas the Heath Government had reflated when unemployment had approached one million in 1971–72 (from a level of 577,000 in 1970). The Conservatives' policies after 1979 were justified with reference to the monetarist doctrines of Milton Friedman, but, as already noted, monetary targets had already been imposed on Labour governments by the IMF in 1967 and 1976. The difference after 1979 was that the Thatcher Government enthusiastically placed control of the money stock at the centre of its counter-inflation policy. There was to be no deliberate attempt to match increased demand for money, if that demand had been caused by higher prices or money incomes, or any attempt to reduce the demand for money through a prices and incomes policy. The priority given to counter-inflation policy over employment policy had begun under Callaghan; the difference under Thatcher was that Keynesian reflation was eschewed indefinitely, and not merely until such time as the balance of payments and foreign confidence in sterling had improved.

There was undoubtedly a great change in the kind of economic advice sought by the Government after 1979. Members of the 'Keynesian establishment' of the economics profession found themselves exiled from the corridors of power, reduced to protesting against the Government's policies by writing letters to the press. One such letter attracted the signatures of no less than 364 economists (Cairncross 1981, p. ix). Thatcher and the ministers closest to her, however, preferred to listen to the advice of monetarists, such as Terry Burns, Patrick Minford and Alan Walters. Indeed, the growing split in the economics profession in the 1970s made it possible for politicians to choose whichever economic advice suited them. It is possible, therefore, that monetarism was seized upon to give theoretical justification to the abandonment of policies which had proved to be politically embarrassing in 1970–74. In particular, Friedman's advice (1968) that 'real' jobs could not be created by demand management was attractive to ministers who wished to be relieved from political responsibility for rising unemployment. (By 'real' jobs, Friedman seems to have meant jobs which could be sustained in the long run by marketable output.) Friedman's belief that in the long run unemployment would fall only when wage earners' expectations adjusted to stable prices could be used to justify 'sound' money policies which were also desired to maintain the real value of savings, annuities and private-sector pensions.

Friedman's recommendation that prices and incomes policies should be avoided, on the grounds that such policies interfere with market forces which guide labour to where it is most needed, was not unwelcome to ministers who had experienced the Heath Government's confrontation with the unions. On the other hand, Friedman's advice that governments should try to reduce imperfections in the market raised the awkward problem of reducing the unions' power over the labour market. In practice, notwithstanding legislation in 1980 to limit secondary picketing and the closed shop (legislation significantly called the Employment Act), the Thatcher Government proceeded more cautiously than the Heath Government had done in industrial relations. This was no doubt partly because James Prior, a noted 'Wet', was in charge of the Department of Employment in 1979–81 (Wigham 1982, pp. 210–15), but it was also the case that rapidly rising unemployment in the 1980s cowed most trade unions more effectively than legislation could ever have done.

The Government also found it difficult in practice to follow Friedman's advice that monetary policy should be confined to aiming at a moderate and stable growth in the money stock. In the spring of 1980 a medium-term financial strategy (MTFS) was announced, with targets showing a declining rate of growth in the money stock in the years ahead (Table 8.4). The actual out-turn for sterling M3, the definition of money used in the MTFS, proved to be very high, however, and in 1982 the target range for 1982–83 had to be revised upwards, with only 'illustrative' figures being given for subsequent years. There are several definitions of what constitutes money, and in 1980/81 and 1981/82 the figures for M1, the narrow definition of money, suggested that monetary policy was tighter than was suggested by the figures for M3. A record minimum lending rate (MLR) of 17 per cent was reached in November 1979, and this was uncom-

Table 8.4 Percentage Changes in Monetary Aggregates*

	Sterling M3	*M1*	*PSL2*
1980–81			
Target in 1980 MTFS	7–11	—	—
Actual	15.5–16	11.4	13.9
1981–82			
Target in 1980 MTFS	6–10	—	—
Actual	13	7.2	11.9
1982–83			
Target in 1980 MTFS	5–9	—	—
Target as revised in 1982	8–12	8–12	8–12
Actual	11.4	11.8	11.6
1983–84			
Target in 1980 MTFS	4–8	—	—
Target as revised in 1982	7–11	7–11	7–11

Source: Wilson (1984), p. 53.

Note: *M1 is a narrow definition of the money stock, consisting of notes and coins in circulation with the public, plus sight deposits held in banks by the private sector only. Sterling M3 comprises notes and coins in circulation with the public, plus bank deposits (including certificates of deposit) held by UK residents in both the public and private sectors. PSL2, or private-sector liquidity, includes notes and coins, bank deposits, other money-market instruments and certificates of tax deposit, building society share and deposit accounts, deposits with savings banks and certain National Savings securities.

fortable for politicians who were aware that high mortgage rates hit large numbers of people who had voted for them six months earlier. Meanwhile funds, both British and foreign, were being attracted into the banking system by the high returns on deposits. This had the absurd effect of expanding the money stock on the Government's chosen definition, sterling M3. The Government hoped that it could lower interest rates by reducing public sector borrowing, thereby reducing demand for loanable funds. However, there was no constant relationship between the PSBR and the volume of bank credit, and the deflationary effect of a tighter fiscal stance was added to the deflationary effect of monetary policy (Hall 1983, chs. 7 and 8; Keegan 1984, pp. 132–63; Wilson 1984, pp. 49–60).

Another aspect of high interest rates was that in so far as they attracted foreign funds into Britain, they tended to raise the sterling exchange rate. Self-sufficiency in oil by 1980, and the consequent improvement in the balance of payments, acted in the same direction. Sterling had stood at about $2.00 early in 1979, but by the third quarter of 1980 the exchange rate reached $2.40 and it did not fall back to about $2.00 until the second quarter of 1981, by which time funds were being attracted to New York by still higher interest rates there. However, there was bound to be a lag before a higher exchange rate had an effect on prices, and the first twelve months of the Thatcher Government saw the retail price index rise by 21.9 per cent. Some of this increase could, of course, be attributed to the rise in the price of oil which in 1980 was 2¼ times what it had been in 1978. Even so, the price of oil could not explain why, according to OECD figures (1982), consumer prices in Britain were 17.9 per cent higher in 1980 than in 1979, whereas the average rise for EEC countries was 11.2 per cent. It was not until 1981 that the rate of increase in consumer prices in Britain fell to about the EEC average (11.9 per cent compared with 11.5 per cent) and the annual rate of increase in the retail price index did not fall below the level of May 1979 (10 per cent) until the spring of 1982.

The Government's domestic policies go far to explain why prices in Britain rose more rapidly in 1979–80 than in the EEC as a whole. The Conservatives came to power committed to reductions in taxation and public expenditure. However, the Government set about the first of these objectives before the second had been achieved. In June 1979 the top rate of income tax was cut from 83 per cent to 60 per cent, and the standard rate was cut from 33 per cent to 30 per cent. These changes were supposed to increase incentive to enterprise, but they could also be seen as a reward to Conservative supporters, many of whom were not in any sense entrepreneurs. Whatever the consequences for enterprise, the effect of income tax changes was to increase consumers' purchasing power and to reduce government revenue, at least in the short run. Public expenditure programmes could not be changed so quickly, so that if the PSBR were not to increase, the lost revenue would have to be clawed back in some way. This was done by raising the rate of VAT from 8 to 15 per cent. However, this move automatically added four percentage points to the rate of increase in the retail price index, and this in turn made wage restraint less likely, since trade unions used the retail price index as a guide to the appropriate level for wage claims (Keegan 1984, pp. 118–27). The Government tried to counter this by publishing a new tax and price index, designed to show how real take-home pay was increasing. However, the Government's determination to reduce the PSBR, and failure to reduce public expenditure (see below), made further major tax reductions impossible, and by 1981 the tax and price index was rising more rapidly than the retail price index. By 1982 most workers were paying a higher percentage of their earnings in income tax and national insurance contributions than in 1979, and only people who had been paying top tax rates in 1979 had benefited substantially from tax cuts.

The Conservatives also contributed to the surge of inflation in 1979–80 through their policies towards public-sector pay and prices. The Labour Government had sought to assuage public-sector pay demands in the 'winter of discontent' by setting up a commission on pay comparability under Hugh Clegg; and in their election campaign in 1979 the Conservatives had promised to abide by Clegg's findings. Indeed, the Conservatives referred new cases to the Commission before winding it up in 1980. Public-sector pay had fallen behind the private sector in 1977–78 as a result of the Labour Government's wages policy (see pages 214–5), so that the general effect of Clegg's recommendations on pay comparability with the private sector was to increase the public-sector pay bill. This, in turn, increased the cost of public services at a time when the Conservatives were removing the subsidies with which Labour had held down the price of public services, such as gas and electricity. Higher prices for these services fed through to the retail price index and thereby laid the basis for further wage demands. It was only from the latter part of 1980 that the Government made a serious attempt to hold down public-sector costs by holding down pay increases (Wigham 1982, pp. 210, 221–2).

The success of the Government's counter-inflation policies after 1980 may be attributed to the tight rein kept on the PSBR, which fell from 7.47 per cent of GDP in 1979 to 2.34 per cent in 1982. This tended to reduce aggregate demand in the economy and thereby contributed to the rise in unemployment, from an annual average of 5.3 per cent in 1979 to over 12.0 per cent by 1982. Government warnings that people could price themselves out of jobs seem to have begun to have some effect on trade-union negotiators, and the annual rate of wage increases in industry fell from 18.7 per cent in 1980 to 11.0 per cent in 1982. Even so, this was still above the rise in retail prices, and, while the annual rate of increase in the latter fell to 9.0 per cent in 1982, and as low as 3.7 per cent in the twelve months to May 1983, there was no sign that employees were in general willing to take real wage cuts so as to enable employers to take on extra workers from the ranks of the unemployed.

The Conservatives had avoided any commitment to full employment in 1979, the first government to do so since the war. Even so, their slogan, 'Labour isn't working', with pictures of 'dole queues' of actors hired to represent some of the 1.3 million unemployed in 1979, had helped to damage Labour's prospects in the election and had certainly not raised an expectation that unemployment would increase to over 3 million under the Conservatives. Much of the initial surge of unemployment could be attributed to sterling's high exchange rate in 1979–81, which made British products uncompetitive in export and domestic markets, especially as British labour costs were still rising more rapidly than in most other industrial countries. It is not surprising that employment in British manufacturing industry fell by over 15 per cent between 1979 and 1981, with a loss of 1,079,000 jobs, a trend which accounted directly for most of the increase in registered unemployment (1,200,000) in these years. From the second half of 1982 a rise in real incomes of the employed led to a revival of consumer spending, and therefore to a limited revival of manufacturing production, but increased output was achieved by higher productivity and overtime, and the downward trend in employment continued. This was in marked contrast with the recovery from depression in the 1930s, when the rate of unemployment had been halved between 1932 and 1937.

A relative decline in manufacturing's share of GDP was a natural concomitant of the great increase in oil output. Nevertheless, an absolute decline in manufacturing production, such as occurred in 1979–81, was not inevitable, since it would have been open to the Government to use fiscal policy to decrease demand for manufactures. This would have required a fall in the exchange rate to correct the balance of payments, however, and there would have been inflationary effects, both through higher import prices and through higher incomes resulting from full employment. As things were, the political priority for a solution to inflation was such that industrial production was lower in 1983 than it had been in 1979 (Atkinson and Hall 1983, ch. 4).

One of the reasons why manufacturing industry had been so badly hit in the post-1979 depression was that whereas GDP fell between 1979 and 1981, public expenditure rose, even when measured at constant prices. The increase in public expenditure was not reflationary since less and less of it was being financed by borrowing. Instead, spending power was being diverted from private individuals to the public sector, as non-North Sea taxes plus national insurance contributions increased from about 34 per cent of GDP in 1978/79 to almost 39 per cent in 1982/83 (Cmnd. 9189, p. 10). What had happened to control of public expenditure which, in 1979, had been described as the heart of Britain's economic difficulties?

Government ministers were inclined to accuse local authorities of extravagance, and total local authority expenditure did indeed increase by 40 per cent in cash terms between 1979/80 and 1982/83. On the other hand, central government expenditure increased by 48 per cent over the same period (CSO 1985, Tables 16.4 and 16.14). Whitehall did give an example of good housekeeping by pruning the civil service, from 731,000 in 1978 to 643,000 in 1983, but savings in salaries could only have a limited effect on public expenditure. Big savings could only come through changes in policy, and ministers in charge of spending departments were in general reluctant to make the kind of cuts which would have prevented public expenditure from rising by over 7 per cent at constant prices between 1979/80 and 1982/83. In contrast, public expenditure had fallen by 0.7 per cent under Labour between 1974/75 and 1978/79.

Two-thirds of central government expenditure was accounted for by three programmes: social security, the NHS and defence. The Government had inherited an undertaking to NATO to increase the defence budget by 3 per cent a year in real terms, and this raised defence expenditure as a proportion of GDP from 4.5 per cent in 1979/80 to 4.9 per cent in 1981/82, even before the cost of the Falklands War in 1982 pushed the figure over 5 per cent, the highest level since 1969. Within the social security programme, economies were made by allowing increases in cash benefits to lag behind the rate of inflation between 1979 and 1981. However, no politically acceptable reduction in the real value of benefits could offset completely the effects of the sharp increase in the numbers of claimants resulting from unemployment. As it happened, the real value of unemployment and supplementary benefits was restored as inflation fell in 1982 and 1983. It was even harder to impose cuts on the NHS, which was used by almost all of the electorate. Indeed, the Government pledged itself to keep total spending 'in line with the plans of our predecessors and so maintain a modest level of annual growth' (Cmnd. 9189, pp. 4–9; Pliatzky 1984, pp. 171–88). Given that the three programmes accounting for two-thirds of public expenditure were bound to increase, and given that there was no growth in the economy between 1979 and 1982, it is hardly surprising that there was a desperate search by ministers for economies wherever they could be found. This included steps to exercise greater central control over local government spending, although how far this would be taken in practice was uncertain even in 1985.

Changed Priorities in the Welfare State

Housing was the main target of cuts in public expenditure; indeed, the Government's expenditure plans, published in March 1980, aimed at making changes in housing policy responsible for 38 per cent of total net savings in public expenditure between 1980/81 and 1982/83 (Cmnd. 7841, p. 179). Local authority building, already reduced by Labour's public expenditure cuts, was more than halved between 1980 and 1982. The Conservatives had an electoral interest in making Britain a 'property-owning democracy', and the Housing Act of 1980 encouraged council tenants to become owner-occupiers. By 1983 some 500,000 council houses had been sold, on very favourable terms, to sitting tenants. These sales, together with the decline in local authority building, raised the proportion of owner-occupiers among householders from 54 per cent in 1978 to 60 per cent in 1983. Some justification for a smaller role for the public sector could be found in the virtual elimination since the 1940s of the worst of the housing shortage, and in the considerable improvements in the housing stock. Even so, old-fashioned squalor was still to be found and much renovation was needed (Donnison and Ungerson 1982, pp. 160–96, 248–50). Moreover, it remained to be seen whether private enterprise and a reduced public sector could meet the increased demand for housing which could be anticipated later in the 1980s, once people born in the 'baby boom' of the 1960s set up households. There seemed little prospect of reviving the privately rented sector, which had fallen from 53 per cent of all dwellings in the United Kingdom in 1950 to 13 per cent in 1978.

A second major change in social policy after 1979 was reversal of the attempts made by Labour to reduce relative poverty (see pages 216–7). To some extent this was a result of the general search for economies in public expenditure. For example, old age pensions were indexed to prices only, instead of being kept in line with the increase in prices or the increase in average earnings, whichever was the more favourable (as Labour had done). It was also the case, however, that the Government wished to widen the gap between incomes of employed and unemployed persons, to encourage the latter to seek work. Earnings-related unemployment benefit was abolished in 1981 and steps were taken to reduce the 'poverty trap' whereby low-paid workers with families would be better off living on supplementary benefit. By 1984 the 'thresholds' at which people started paying income tax had been raised by about 16 per cent more than inflation since 1978/79, and the married man's income-tax allowance was the highest in real terms since 1945. As a result nearly a million fewer people paid income tax than if thresholds had simply been indexed to prices. The Government could thus claim to be helping the low-paid, even while seeking to make the labour market more efficient.

Other attempts to make labour more 'marketable' included expenditure on training schemes to equip workers for new technologies. Like its Labour predecessor, the Government wished to provide young people with work experience, and in 1983/84 some 350,000 places were taken up in a Youth Training Scheme. In addition, under the Young Workers Scheme introduced in 1982, subsidies were paid to employers of 17 year olds, in their first year of employment, who earned £50 a week or less. Conservative employment policy sought, in short, to act on the supply of labour rather than on the demand for labour. Even the Government's opponents seemed to have lost some of their faith in the efficacy of public investment as a cure for unemployment. For example, in 1981 the TUC put forward a five-year programme for *The Reconstruction of Industry* which, even on optimistic assumptions, would have generated only 500,000 jobs by 1986, compared with the loss of about a million jobs in production industries between 1979 and 1981. The TUC's stress on reconstruction itself reflected an increased awareness that macroeconomic policies could not prevent industrial decline unless supply-side changes were made to promote efficiency and structural change (Aldcroft 1984).

The quest for economic efficiency was not in itself likely to solve the problems of the old, the sick and disabled, and single-parent families, and even the unemployed could only hope to benefit in the long run. All these people, therefore, had to look to social security for an improvement in their lot. It was generally accepted in the 1980s that the social security system, as it had evolved over the previous 40 years, was as much in need of overhaul as it had been at the time of the Beveridge Report. The range and complexity of means-tested benefits led to poor 'take-up' by many who needed them, while officials were too over-worked to prevent abuse of the system by those who were not entitled to benefits. Administrative costs were high, with much unnecessary duplication between different branches of government engaged in similar activities. Information about household incomes was collected by the Inland Revenue, the Department of Health and Social Security and (for rent rebates) by local authorities; many households were entitled to national insurance benefits, means-tested supplementary benefits, and rent rebates all at the same time (Dilnot *et al*. 1984, pp. 26–69).

More than administrative reform is needed, however, if the gap between the incomes of the poorest members of society and the national average is to be reduced. The fundamental stumbling block is an unwillingness on the part of taxpayers to vote for the kind of transfer of incomes which would confer significant increases in social security benefits. Survey evidence put forward by Mack and Lansley (1985) has suggested that 74 per cent of the electorate would be prepared to pay an extra penny in the pound in income tax to help the poorest members of society. However, only 34 per cent would definitely be prepared to pay an extra 5p in the pound (with another 13 per cent 'don't knows'). There is, therefore, some public support for increased measures to help the poorest members of society, but not to a degree which would interfere significantly with the personal consumption of the majority.

Conclusion

Priorities in economic and social policy have been created by experience, and, therefore, have altered from time to time, according to whether, for example, unemployment or inflation or poverty or the burden of taxation have been seen to be the most pressing political problems. At all times policy has been the product of competing and often contradictory pressures on the government of the day and there has been no simple, linear development of a 'welfare state'. The first lesson of history is that one can be certain of nothing except that the future will be different from the past. It is quite possible that unemployment and housing will shortly replace inflation and taxation as the dominant political problems, just as the latter problems came to the fore in the 1970s. Even so, it would appear that there are lags in political attitudes: the experience of inflation in 1914–20 cast a long shadow over the interwar period, just as the experience of unemployment in the interwar period cast a long shadow over the 30 years or so after the Second World War. It is quite possible that the experience of inflation in the 1970s and early 1980s will similarly have a long-term influence. Moreover, in the 1980s, as in the 1930s, the unemployed and the relatively poor, although numerous, are still a minority of the electorate and much must depend upon the attitudes of people who are enjoying secure employment and, on average, rising real incomes.

The historical record suggests that however great the growth in national income, there will not be enough to meet all the claims for better health and education services, for higher standards of housing and more generous social security. Economic growth reduces but does not eliminate the necessity of making choices, either between private expenditure and public expenditure or between different forms of public expenditure. It would seem to have been the continual struggle against claims from the spending departments which has led the Treasury to adopt economic doctrines which have favoured restraint in public expenditure. The orthodoxies of the gold standard and the 'Treasury view' on public works were used in this way. Less obviously, perhaps, 'Keynesian' demand management was accepted in the 1940s at a time when the economy was at over-full employment and when Keynes's ideas could be used to justify budget surpluses. Only historical research, presumably in the next century, will reveal the relationship between economic ideas and policy in the 1970s and eighties, but once more the new orthodoxy – monetarism – has been used to restrain public expenditure.

References

Documents

Cmnd. 7746 *The Government's Expenditure Plans 1980–81*, BPP 1979–80.
Cmnd. 7841 *The Government's Expenditure Plans 1980–81 to 1983–84*, BPP 1979–80.
Cmnd. 9189 *The Next Ten Years: Public Expenditure and Taxation into the 1990s*, BPP 1983–84.

Books and Articles

Aldcroft, D. (1984) *Full Employment: The Elusive Goal*, Harvester Press.
Atkinson, F. and Hall, S. (1983) *Oil and the British Economy*, Croom Helm.
Ball, R.J. and Burns, T. (1976) 'The inflationary mechanism in the UK economy', *American Economic Review*, vol. 66, pp. 467–84.
Barnett, J. (1982) *Inside the Treasury*, André Deutsch.
Beckerman, W. and Clark, S. (1982) *Poverty and Social Security in Britain since 1961*, Oxford University Press.
Berthoud, R., Brown, J. and Cooper, S. (1981) *Poverty and the Development of Anti-Poverty Policy in the United Kingdom*, Heinemann.
Blackaby, F. (ed.) (1978) *British Economic Policy 1960–74*, Cambridge University Press.
Bosanquet, N. and Townsend, P. (1980) *Labour and Equality: A Fabian Study of Labour in Power 1974–79*, Heinemann.
Burton, J. (1979) *The Job Support Machine: A Critique of the Subsidy Morass*, Centre for Policy Studies.
Cairncross, F. (1981) *Changing Perceptions of Economic Policy*, Methuen.
Central Statistical Office (1981, 1984, 1985) *Annual Abstract of Statistics*, HMSO.
Department of Employment (1978) *British Labour Statistics Year Book 1976*, HMSO.

Dilnot, A.W., Kay, J.A. and Morris, C.N. (1984) *The Reform of Social Security*, Oxford University Press.
Donnison, D. and Ungerson, C. (1982) *Housing Policy*, Penguin Books.
Friedman, M. (1968) 'The role of monetary policy', *American Economic Review*, vol. 58, pp. 1–17.
Gough, I. (1979) *The Political Economy of the Welfare State*, Macmillan.
Hall, M. (1983) *Monetary Policy since 1971: Conduct and Performance*, Macmillan.
Keegan, W. (1984) *Mrs Thatcher's Economic Experiment*, Allen Lane.
Keegan, W. and Pennant-Rea, R. (1979) *Who Runs the Economy? Control and Influence in British Economic Policy*, Temple Smith.
Klein, R. (1983) *The Politics of the National Health Service*, Longman.
Mack, J. and Lansley, S. (1985) *Poor Britain*, George Allen and Unwin.
Maddison, A. (1982) *Phases of Capitalist Development*, Oxford University Press.
Organisation for Economic Cooperation and Development (1982) *Main Economic Indicators*, July, p. 21.
Pliatzky, L. (1984) *Getting and Spending: Public Expenditure, Employment and Inflation*, Basil Blackwell.
Pryke, R. (1981) *The Nationalised Industries: Policies and Performance since 1968*, Martin Robertson.
Reid, M. (1982) *The Secondary Banking Crisis 1973–75*, Macmillan.
Wigham, E. (1982) *Strikes and the Government 1893–1981*, Macmillan.
Wilson, T. (1984) *Inflation, Unemployment, and the Market*, Oxford University Press.

Index